Race, Politics, and Memory

The University of Arkansas Press   *Fayetteville*   2007

CONTENTS

ACKNOWLEDGMENTS

Books are always collaborative ventures that rely on the assistance of numerous people, and this one is no exception. We would like to begin by thanking Larry Malley, Julie Watkins, Shay Hopper, Michael W. Bieker, and Thomas Lavoie at the University of Arkansas Press. Their enthusiasm for and support of this project inspired us throughout the writing and research. We would be remiss if we failed to thank Larry and Maggie Malley for their warm hospitality during our trip to Fayetteville, Arkansas, in the summer of 2006.

Anne Prichard and Tom W. Dillard at the University of Arkansas Libraries Special Collections helped us in innumerable ways throughout the process, and we are grateful for their knowledge of their fine repository. Jillian Barrett, Amanda Paige, and Tony Shephard guided us through the special collections at the University of Arkansas, Little Rock. Jeff Bridgers at the Library of Congress Prints and Photographs Division dedicated numerous hours to helping us locate and download photographs from that vast collection. His good humor and support are much appreciated. Laura Miller, the chief of interpretation at the Central High School National Historic Site, was particularly helpful as we were selecting the documents, and during the final stages she offered us her keen editorial eye. The staff at the Arkansas History Commission and Kim Coryat and Kelly Henderson at the William J. Clinton Presidential Library and Museum also deserve recognition for their assistance.

Herb Pankratz at the Dwight D. Eisenhower Library in Abilene, Kansas, identified a variety of documents that helped shape our understanding of this important moment in American history. His guidance proved invaluable. Michael Hussey at the National Archives helped locate several obscure State Department documents, and we are grateful for his efficiency and good humor.

Dr. Roy G. Brooks, superintendent of schools of the Little Rock School District, kindly agreed to an interview in the summer of 2006 and helped us locate the Little Rock School Board minutes from 1955. We are particularly grateful for his insights. Dr. R. W. Ross consented to a phone interview about his time at Central High, and we are delighted to be able to include an editorial he sent to the *Arkansas Gazette*.

There are numerous individuals who helped us secure permissions to use many of the documents included in this volume, and they include Frank Fellone (*Arkansas Gazette*), Ann Walding-Phillips (Library Link, *Omaha World-Herald*), Spirit Trickey (Central High School National Historic Site), Scott Whiteley Carter (City of Little Rock), Tom Branigar (Dwight D. Eisenhower Library), Katie Laning (press secretary for U.S. Senator Blanche L. Lincoln), Vicky Wells (University of North Carolina Press), Linda Stafford (*Birmingham News*), Ayana Haaruun (*Chicago Defender*), Whitney Krahn (Columbia University Library).

Marie Stanton took on the seemingly endless task of converting many of the documents into an electronic format. Her diligence and hard work made our job all the easier. Tony Lewis also helped with some of the last-minute additions. Zoila Torres of SoliDesign helped touch-up and format the cartoons and photographs used in this volume. Stacy Braukman once again proved to be a fine copyeditor, helping with the introduction and the items included in the appendixes.

We would also like to thank Betty Lewis, wife and mother, who spurred us on with her constant question, "When will you be finished?" We love you.

INTRODUCTION

In September 1957, President Dwight D. Eisenhower and Arkansas Governor Orval E. Faubus found themselves locked in an epic struggle over the desegregation of Central High School in Little Rock, Arkansas. The two men viewed the crisis through very different political lenses, which shaped their responses and the nation's perception of the event. Faubus, a social moderate who had a track record of conciliation, pandered to segregationist constituents to preserve his political position. Eisenhower, ambivalent about desegregation, sought to protect the power of the federal government. He worried that displays of rampant racism would tarnish the nation's reputation as a global power and undermine efforts to thwart the spread of communism. The segregationist teenagers and adults involved in the conflict argued that the presence of black children in white schools undermined state's rights, not to mention their racial privilege. The NAACP and much of the African American community saw the crisis in the context of the organization's fight for social justice. For the nine black students—Elizabeth Eckford, Ernest Green, Jefferson Thomas, Terrence Roberts, Carlotta Walls, Minnijean Brown, Gloria Ray, Thelma Mothershed, and Melba Patillo— Central High was a cauldron of racial tension. In this context, the desegregation crisis reflected the complex politics of the day. The documents collected in this volume and the supporting materials gathered in the appendixes examine how this local, southern conflict became a national and international cause.

The Prelude to the Crisis

Arkansas in the early twentieth century, like much of the South, struggled to survive economically and develop industry and infrastructure. African Americans, barely three generations removed from slavery, were economically paralyzed by a labor system that restricted them mainly to low-wage labor or sharecropping, segregated them within public transportation and other public facilities, and disenfranchised them through poll taxes and threats of violence. In 1920, African Americans made up 33 percent of Little Rock's population and 27 percent of the state's. By 1950, their overall numbers had grown, but their proportion of Little Rock's population decreased to 24 percent and 22 percent statewide.[1]

In comparison to much of the rest of the South, however, Arkansas had a moderate civil rights record. Indeed, before and after World War II, the Progressive movement, which focused on improved conditions for ordinary people in health care, education, and jobs, found strong support in Arkansas. The state also boasted liberal twentieth-century politicians such as Joseph Taylor Robinson (who was a governor, senator, and confidant of President Franklin D. Roosevelt) and moderates like J. William Fulbright (who served as a U.S. senator from 1945 to 1974). The state elected returning veteran Sidney S. McMath governor (1949 to 1953); he proved to be a progressive leader and one of Faubus's political mentors.[2] Revealing his political philosophy, McMath explained, "We are not spending all our time on white-columned verandas sipping mint juleps, and plotting to keep our people in economic slavery. In fact, there is abroad in all the south-land a vigorous progressive movement—a growing demand for the development of the human and economic resources of our region."[3] McMath's agenda, however, never included the elimination of Jim Crow.

In light of this history, Little Rock was the last city in the South that anyone expected to make the evening news over desegregation. Orval Faubus, who came to the governor's office after winning a bitter 1954 election, followed in the path of McMath, his predecessor, in whose administration he had served. Both governors worked for the poor of both races throughout the state and made appropriations for African American institutions, appointed African Americans to the Democratic State Committee, and took public, albeit unsuccessful, stands against poll taxes and lynching.[4] When *Brown II* was handed down in 1955, Faubus declared, "Our reliance must be upon the good will that exists between the races—the good will that has long made Arkansas a model for other Southern states in all matters affecting the relationship between the races."[5] In contrast to states such as Alabama and Mississippi, Arkansas, by 1957, had peacefully integrated the bus system, several smaller colleges, the state's university and medical and law schools, and a handful of public school districts in Ozark, Fayetteville, Hoxie, Fort Smith, and Van Buren.[6]

Few anticipated a conflict in Little Rock because Faubus and other state leaders supported the gradual desegregation plan. They had supported the plan developed by Virgil Blossom, the school superintendent, and were determined to show the nation that Arkansas was a model southern state in relationship to *Brown*.[7] But the pressure exerted by other southern politicians, including segregationists in Arkansas, ultimately changed Faubus's mind. Two weeks before the first black students were scheduled to enter Central High School, on August 22, 1957, Marvin Griffin (the segregationist governor of Georgia) and Roy V. Harris (founder of the segregationist Citizens' Councils of America) visited Faubus at the governor's mansion to persuade him to oppose the Blossom plan. This visit and other factors revealed to Faubus that failure to change his position jeopardized his political future.

It is intriguing to examine the dramatic shift of a man who at the beginning of the conflict was called a "race-mixing scalawag" by segregationists.[8] Growing up in poverty in a socialist household in rural Madison County, Arkansas, Faubus was taught the evils of capitalism and racism by his father, Sam.[9] In fact, Sam gave Orval the middle name "Eugene" after the socialist leader Eugene V. Debs.[10] Orval also attended Commonwealth College, a center of radical socialism in the state, and used what he learned there and at home to develop a practical, populist platform that propelled him into the governor's chair. Until well into his second term, he was a racial moderate. By 1957, Arkansas had more desegregated schools than all eleven of the southern states combined, a fact of which he was always proud.[11]

How then did Faubus come to defy the Supreme Court? Most historians argue that he abandoned the integrationist position and opportunistically shifted his allegiances to gain a second term as governor. Arkansas governors stood for election every two years and, unlike most of his peers, Faubus did not have education, professional training, or wealth to protect him if he lost the next election. He was not well educated and would not be invited to join a prestigious Little Rock law firm or university after his term. Instead, he would have likely returned to his position as the owner of a rural newspaper. That fear of failure and the resulting isolation partially explains his actions at Central High.

But there were other forces at work. Faubus found himself at the intersection of several converging and powerful forces that may have pushed him into adopting an extreme position on school segregation. Central among the forces working against him was the ambiguous

language used by the Supreme Court in *Brown II,* which gave segregationists ample room for delay.[12] The mandate to move with "all deliberate
speed" and other ambiguities suggested that resistance was permissible,
and reversal of the decision possible. Several states, including Arkansas,
soon even passed laws aimed at nullification, in which a state could negate
federal rulings with which the state disagreed.[13] Adding further pressure
on Faubus, Arkansas's U.S. representatives and senators also sought to
publicly defy the Supreme Court decision.

Another issue was the absence of leadership on the part of
Eisenhower. Eisenhower was very much a product of his times and culture, and his racial politics were far from progressive. He did sponsor a
civil rights bill in 1957 (the first since 1875) at the urging of his attorney
general, Herbert Brownell, mainly to counter criticism from Democrats.[14]
But it was weak and proved ineffectual. Raised in Abilene, Kansas,
Eisenhower had little contact with African Americans, and his record is
mixed. In high school, he chastised his fellow teammates for refusing to
play against a local football team with a black player. After graduating
from West Point, Eisenhower was posted as a young army officer to several southern military bases where he occasionally denigrated the black
soldiers with whom he served.[15] He appointed E. Frederic Morrow, an
African American lawyer, to the White House staff, but rarely asked his
advice. After the two *Brown* decisions, Eisenhower did not articulate a
clear plan for implementation. He was also reluctant to meet with African
American leaders, claiming that to do so would require him to meet with
members of the Ku Klux Klan.[16] A year after the crisis in Little Rock, he
refused to allow Daisy Bates and the Little Rock Nine to visit the White
House, fearing that he would offend his southern friends and
constituents.[17]

Historian Stephen Ambrose, who generally admired Eisenhower,
argued that the president's failure to take a firm position against segregation "did incalculable harm to the civil-rights crusade and to America's
image."[18] When he did act in the case of Central High School, it was
more to affirm the ascendancy of the federal government's power over
individual states and to dampen international criticism than to secure
the civil liberties of people who had been denied them for centuries.

From Faubus's perspective, the court had handed down a decree that
even the president of the United States privately criticized. Locally, he

found an even more complex situation. Business and political leaders throughout the state, and especially in Little Rock, did not see the *Brown* decisions in moral terms and were mostly hostile to it. If they supported it at all, it was in the context of economic growth. Segregation was not wrong, they argued; it was simply bad for business. In summary, the ambiguous Supreme Court timetable, the reluctant president, and silent or hostile state and community leaders left the responsibility for implementation of *Brown* on the shoulders of state officials. Whether these reasons motivated him or not, Faubus made a clear choice, and for him it was the right one. His actions ensured his reelection and catapulted him into the national spotlight.

The International Climate

Little Rock became a battle of historic proportions that reverberated far beyond the confines of the city, the region, and even the nation. Both the national and international implications largely explain why Eisenhower supported the nine black students seeking admission to Central High. He was not in favor of wholesale desegregation; in fact, Eisenhower considered the *Brown* decision and his appointment of Earl Warren to the Supreme Court mistakes. Eisenhower primarily took a progressive stand on race in this local context at this particular moment because he believed it was his responsibility as president to uphold federal law. Doing less would have undermined his authority and the very office of the presidency. Second, he was keenly aware that his actions in Little Rock had far-reaching foreign policy consequences. Before the Little Rock crisis, the United States had been roundly criticized for its support of white supremacy, and it was often compared to the apartheid regime in South Africa, a government that Eisenhower openly supported. Similar criticism occurred during and after the crisis.

Several racial incidents in the 1940s and early 1950s tarnished the nation's reputation as a global power at the dawn of the Cold War. United Nations delegates from Liberia, Haiti, and Ethiopia were refused hotel accommodations in New York in the fall of 1946 because they were black, drawing international condemnation. In 1953, the French and Swiss press widely criticized the acquittal of white vigilantes accused of lynching fourteen-year-old Emmett Till in Money, Mississippi. The all-white jury deliberated for a little over an hour, including a break to drink a Coca-Cola. In 1956, the University of Copenhagen offered admission to Autherine Lucy, a young black woman who was admitted to the University of Alabama but greeted by mob violence and forced to withdraw. From Tokyo to Calcutta, the international media criticized America's rampant racism.

Eisenhower and his administration feared that continued international scrutiny of the nation's racial policies would impede America's attempts to extend influence over African and Asian nations that were vulnerable to overtures from the Soviet Union and other communist states as they transitioned from colonial rule. Historian Cary Fraser argued, "Little Rock had become the Suez of the Eisenhower administration—a moment of crisis that forced a fundamental and radical reassessment of existing approaches to dealing with the world of color."[19] To put it simply, Ike was afraid that communists would use evidence of racial strife in the United States as propaganda to persuade countries that had not yet declared their political allegiance to reject the democratic ideals advanced by the United States.

The Specter of Communism

The Little Rock crisis unfolded in the midst of the Cold War, and anti-communist hysteria shaped perceptions of the event. To protect business interests and influence abroad after World War II, the United States sought to undermine communist-led revolutions in China, Indonesia, and Vietnam and supported dictators in Guatemala, Greece, and Iran who were sympathetic to the West. America sought to retain its sphere of influence, largely on moral grounds. In this context, the Eisenhower administration's sensitivity to international criticism of American racial policies makes sense.

During the Great Depression, leftist elements of society, including labor unions, artists, and intellectuals, became more influential in American politics. The Democratic Party, led by Franklin D. Roosevelt and devoted to his New Deal policies, gained widespread support. The Republicans, out of power since 1932 and dismayed by Harry S. Truman's surprising 1948 defeat of Thomas Dewey, went on the offensive and used red scare tactics. But the strategy soon crossed party lines. Fed a steady diet of anticommunist propaganda through movies, pulp fiction, newspapers, and magazines throughout the 1950s, ordinary people accepted tightening security measures, often at the price of restrictions to civil liberties. Even superheroes got into the act, as Captain America warned, "Beware, commies, spies, traitors, and foreign agents!"[20]

The most tangible symbol of the red scare was the House Committee on Un-American Activities (HUAC). HUAC became notorious for character assassinations, illegal investigations, and other repressive tactics.[21] More than six million people were investigated by various security agencies. Yet almost no cases of espionage were uncovered. Even so, liberal and moderate politicians such as Hubert Humphrey and John Kennedy soon joined the hunt for subversives. Humphrey sponsored legislation to establish detention camps where suspects could be held without trial. Harry Truman continued the search for disloyal "Reds and parlor pinks," as did Eisenhower with the Communist Control Act of 1954.[22] Joseph McCarthy, the junior senator from Wisconsin, was perhaps the most effective red-baiter, with his notorious and constantly evolving accusations against members of the State Department. By 1954, he began targeting the U.S. Army and was finally censured by the U.S. Senate.

Arkansas, like most southern states, had its share of red-baiting politicians who equated desegregation with communism. In fact, during the Little Rock crisis, rabid segregationists declared that everyone from Virgil Blossom to Orval Faubus was in the employ of communist agents. The nine black students and the NAACP were accused of being a communist front. This kind of hysteria shaped the public's perception of the debate over Central High but almost completely disappeared from the discourse in the commemorative events after the crisis had passed.

Brown v. Board of Education of Topeka

The civil rights movement did not begin with the passage of *Brown v. Board of Education of Topeka* or Rosa Parks's defiant gesture on a Montgomery bus in 1955. Throughout the nineteenth and early twentieth century, African Americans vocally criticized segregation in schools, restaurants, public parks, and sports. After World War II, average men and women were no longer content to remain silent on the issue. But the Supreme Court decision and the Little Rock crisis galvanized even the most conservative members of the African American community.

Brown overturned two nineteenth-century decisions—*Roberts v. City of Boston* (1850) and *Plessy v. Ferguson* (1896)—that had upheld the concept and practice of state-endorsed racial discrimination. *Roberts,* the ruling of a Supreme Judicial Court in Massachusetts, held "that separate common or public schools for Boston's black schoolchildren did not deny them the legal rights and did not expose them to undue logistical difficulties or degradation."[23] *Plessy,* a Supreme Court ruling that legitimized separate but equal railway accommodations, gave official imprimatur to what was already common practice in the North and the South and was, like *Roberts,* the law of the land.

Brown was the result of many years of preparation. For years, lawyers for the Legal Defense Fund at the National Association for the Advancement of Colored People (NAACP) had been presenting cases to lower courts as well as the Supreme Court. The effort was led first by Charles Hamilton Houston, dean of Howard University Law School. After Houston's death in 1935, Thurgood Marshall (who would later become the first African American Supreme Court justice in 1967) coordinated the effort. Most of the early attempts to overturn segregation failed, but a focused assault on integrating elementary and secondary schools proved a success. *Brown* was actually a collection of four cases: *Brown v. Board of Education of Topeka, Kansas; Davis v. County School Board of Prince Edward County* of Virginia; *Gebhart v. Belton* of Delaware; and *Bolling v. Sharp* of the District of Columbia. Collectively known as *Brown v. Board of Education* (or *Brown I*), they were first argued in 1952 before the U.S. Supreme Court. Under the leadership of Chief Justice Earl Warren (appointed chief justice in 1953), the court decided in favor of the NAACP on May 17, 1954, ruling that separate but equal schools were inherently unequal and unconstitutional because they violated the "equal protection of the laws" clause of the Fourteenth Amendment. Further deliberations (known as *Brown II*) in May 1955 defined the pace at which desegregation should occur, urging school districts to act "with all deliberate speed."[24] The ambiguous timetable set forth in *Brown II* set the stage for massive resistance to the decision.

The immediate reaction to *Brown* was predicable; African American newspapers hailed the decision while the white press reflected regional perspectives. Major papers in the North and West were generally supportive of the court's ruling; the southern press largely condemned the decision. A few southern papers in larger cities were cautiously optimistic, but they were in the minority. President Eisenhower, who disagreed strongly with the decision, said later that the biggest mistake of his presidency was the appointment of "that dumb son of a bitch Earl Warren."[25] His ambivalence about race relations was relatively typical, and it is reflected in much of his writing. In 1965, he declared in his memoir, *Waging Peace,* "I had accepted without qualification the right to equality before the law of all citizens of this country, whatever their race or creed."[26] Yet his actions belied his words as he sympathized with conservative southerners, key constituents in 1952 and 1956, whose main concern was to ensure that their "sweet little girls are not required to sit in school alongside some big overgrown Negroes."[27]

Opponents of *Brown* in Georgia, Mississippi, Alabama, Louisiana, and Virginia began making plans to resist the decision, and organizations such as the Citizens' Councils, led by Roy Harris, were created to combat integration. During this same period, the Ku Klux Klan experienced a growth in membership. In 1956, almost all of the southern members of Congress signed the "Southern Manifesto," a document drafted by Senator Strom Thurmond of South Carolina that called the ruling "a clear abuse of judicial power."[28] All eight members of the Arkansas delegation to Congress, including Senator Fulbright and Representatives Brooks Hays and James W. Trimble (the two most liberal members of the House delegation), signed.[29] Fulbright's decision was particularly problematic because it revealed his position on race. Even if he had not been previously allied with southern demagogues, he shared many of the same racist attitudes of the segregationists but was far more discreet and genteel in his display of them.[30] Fulbright discovered, as Faubus would in 1957, that failure to join his Arkansas colleagues would be political suicide.

The Promise of Moderation

Despite nationwide discussion and debate about the Supreme Court decision, several Arkansas districts moved almost immediately after *Brown I* to desegregate the schools. The motivating factor was usually simple economics—operating dual school systems often proved too burdensome to state and local budgets. Charleston integrated its schools in August 1954, making it the first district in the state. Two weeks later Fayetteville, the home of the University of Arkansas, followed suit under the leadership of Virgil Blossom, who would later lead the efforts in Little Rock.[31] By the fall of 1957, of the South's 2,300 school districts, 740 had begun or completed desegregation efforts.[32]

Little Rock, with the largest school system in the state, had a reputation for being a progressive city, and its status as the state capital made it a powerful symbol. Even before *Brown,* there had been discussions with the school board about black students from Paul Laurence Dunbar High School using the print shop at what was then known as Little Rock Senior High (soon to be Central High) because theirs had inadequate facilities. But then Superintendent Harry B. Little, an avowed segregationist, intervened to prevent it.[33] Shortly after the *Brown* decision, newly arrived Superintendent Virgil Blossom began developing what became known as the "Blossom Plan" to eventually integrate all of the schools of Little Rock. By 1957, peaceful implementation of the plan had begun, despite negative reactions from some African Americans, who called the plan "vague, indefinite, slow-moving and indicative of an intent to stall further on public school integration."[34]

Blossom originally proposed starting with desegregating the city's elementary schools, believing that prejudice among younger children was less entrenched. Only after receiving complaints from parents did he decide to focus on the local high schools.[35] Through 1955 and 1956, and especially after *Brown II,* the Blossom plan changed several times, further restricting black access to white schools. For example, the newly built Horace Mann High, located in the black neighborhoods, would remain all black, while the new Hall High, in the affluent white western suburbs, would remain white. Integration would occur only in the working- to lower-middle-class Central High School.[36] These changes reflect Blossom's growing caution as resistance to the plan grew in some quarters.[37] Several court cases challenged the Blossom plan, including a suit filed by the Mothers' League of Central High School (an auxiliary of the Citizens' Council) based on warnings from Faubus of impending violence. The suit resulted in an injunction against the plan issued by Chancellor Murray O. Reed of the chancery court, but federal judge Ronald Davis overruled the injunction within a matter of days.[38] The plan remained in effect.

Virgil Blossom was committed, if somewhat reluctantly, to the integration of the Little Rock schools. It was, after all, under his leadership that the schools in Fayetteville had integrated promptly after the *Brown* ruling. Harry Ashmore, the liberal editor of the *Arkansas Gazette,* an early supporter of Blossom's and a major player in the events soon to follow, called him "a natural Rotarian" with the ability to bring people together for a common purpose. Blossom was even named Little Rock Man of the Year in 1955.[39]

Yet the plan had major flaws, as John Kirk detailed:

> Importantly, the Blossom Plan ignored the class tensions within the white community surrounding school desegregation. By building a white high school for affluent whites in western Little Rock while focusing desegregation efforts on working-class and middle-class Central High School, the Blossom Plan angered those whites who would be directly affected. Since the main constituency of hard-core support for continued segregation emanated from the very people the Blossom Plan targeted, and at the same time the school board's plan distanced those in the white community who had the ability to help steer a course of acceptance and moderation, the plan appeared particularly vulnerable. The fact that only one school was to desegregate also proved an unfortunate logistical mistake since it played into the hands of the Capital Citizens Council, which, working with only limited resources, could concentrate all their efforts of agitations and disruption at one particular site.[40]

By August 1957, rumors of impending violence, increased weapons sales, and caravans of angry, violent whites traveling to Little Rock began to circulate. Though they proved false, they provided Faubus with a platform to file a petition in the county court to block the integration efforts based on his perception of "evidence of disorder and threats of disorder."[41]

The Main Event

For all its flaws and vague timetable, the Blossom Plan represented a step in the right direction. It called for integrating first the high schools and then working downwards, one grade at a time, until the task was completed.[42] With Central High as the targeted school, first eighty, then thirty-two, and finally nine African American students were selected to attend classes at Central High in the fall of 1957. The numbers declined throughout the summer because some of the students were not academically prepared or were unable to manage the stress of such an undertaking. The first day of classes was scheduled for September 3, 1957.

While the black community helped to prepare the students throughout the summer, the pressure on Faubus grew. Amis Guthridge, a lawyer from Little Rock, organized a segregationist rally at nearby Jacksonville High School, where he declared, "We are not going to have trouble with public office holders, now that they know what we want."[43] Mississippi Senator James Eastland warned, "If the Southern states are picked off one by one under the damnable doctrine of gradualism I don't know if we can hold out or not." He called Faubus one of the "weak-kneed politicians at the state capitols."[44] Eastland was not alone.

Fighting for his political life and under the pretext of preventing violence, Faubus ordered the Arkansas National Guard to Central High, claiming "there is imminent danger of tumult, riot and breach of the peace and the doing of violence to persons and property in Pulaski County, Arkansas."[45] Guardsmen were posted around the perimeter of the school, and when one of the soldiers was asked, "What are your orders?" he answered, "To keep the niggers out."[46] *Time* magazine reported that Faubus's fear of violence was the result of a political calculation rather than a genuine concern for the community: "When the dawn of integration day came, the Faubus fabric was even more tattered. His early-morning 'March of the Mothers,' at Central High found only 15 curious bystanders—and one shaggy dog. A check of 21 Little Rock stores disclosed no run whatever on knives or pistols. And the only 'caravans' converging on Little Rock were those of National Guard reinforcements called by Orval Faubus."[47]

Daisy Bates, president of the Arkansas NAACP, arranged for black and white ministers and a police car to accompany the students, but was only able to notify eight of the nine students of her plan. In the flurry of events, she forgot to inform Elizabeth Eckford, whose family did not have a telephone. So, Eckford arrived at Central High at the north end of campus alone, while the other students gathered at the south end. After being tormented and threatened by the crowd and turned away by the guardsmen, she was finally able to get onto a city bus and away from the chaotic scene, accompanied by Grace Lorch, a local resident and a member of the communist party.[48] In the struggle, Lorch admonished the crowd: "This is just a little girl. Next week you'll all be ashamed of yourselves."[49] Eckford remembered that, while Lorch may have meant well, her comments to the menacing crowd made matters worse.[50] The other eight students at the south entrance were also turned away.

The battle lasted for sixteen days, and it now had the attention of the nation and the president of the United States. Acting against the advice of Herbert Brownell, Eisenhower agreed to meet with Faubus in Newport, Rhode Island, where he was on an extended golf vacation. After a short discussion on September 14, Eisenhower reported that Faubus had agreed "to act within the matter of hours to revoke his orders to the guard to prevent reentry of the Negro children into the school."[51] Faubus had no such plans, which only became clear over the next several weeks. But the black students persisted. On September 23, the Little Rock Nine gathered at Daisy Bates's home and rode to school with a police escort. They entered Central High through a side door, and over the next several hours the angry mob outside became so inflamed that both police and school officials feared for the lives of the children. After attending several classes, the students were rushed out of the building in police cars at lunchtime.[52]

With clear evidence that local forces were unable to comply with the court order and realizing that Faubus had betrayed him, Eisenhower immediately ordered 1,100 troops from the 101st Airborne to Little Rock and nationalized the Arkansas National Guard.[53] In making the decision, he exclaimed, "Mob rule cannot be allowed to override the decisions of our courts."[54] Privately, he was enraged by Faubus's disobedience.

Two days later, on September 25, armed soldiers of one of the most honored divisions in the U.S. Army escorted the nine black students into Central High School and found little overt resistance. America watched the events unfold in Little Rock on the evening television news with wonder and dismay. The events that began on September 3 were widely documented by print and television reporters, and this coverage shaped how Americans viewed the issue. Nothing was more powerful than the images of children, both black and white, being held at the point of a bayonet. The Little Rock story was so widely reported that thousands of people wrote letters to those involved in the crisis. The editorial board at the *Tiger*, Central High's student newspaper, received a telegram from the Columbia University School of Journalism praising them for the "ideal of clear thinking under pressure."[55] Harry Ashmore, editor of the *Arkansas Gazette,* won a Pulitzer prize for his fearless editorials during the crisis, which cost his newspaper millions of dollars in lost advertising revenue.[56]

After the camera crews had left Little Rock, the nine students were left to find their own way. All were harassed by some of their classmates, including Sammie Dean Parker. They were tripped, pushed down stairs, and spat upon. In her memoir, *Warriors Don't Cry,* Melba Pattillo Bealls recalled being stabbed with a sharp-pointed stick holding a Confederate flag, being burned and punched, and having acid thrown in her face.[57] After almost a year of abuse, Minnijean Brown was finally expelled in February of 1958, unable to refrain from striking back after first being suspended for dumping a bowl of chili on the head of one of her tormenters. The white students who tried to help their new peers were quickly intimidated by threats from racist students.[58]

The 101st Airborne and later the Arkansas National Guard that replaced them were less helpful to the students once they were inside Central High because the soldiers had been ordered to intervene only when the nine students' lives were in danger.[59] Few of the teachers or administrators proved helpful either. A notable exception was Elizabeth Huckaby (the vice principal for girls). Principal Jess W. Matthews did little to protect the students from being terrorized by their peers.[60] Nevertheless, on May 27, 1958, Ernest Green became the first black student to graduate from Central High. His achievement, though, did not end the battle.

In August 1958, Orval Faubus called a special session of the state legislature, where he requested and received overwhelming support for a series of laws aimed at stopping further integration. This approach allowed him to close schools slated for desegregation and to call for an election to determine the people's preference. He received permission to withhold funds from integrated schools and transfer them to private schools or segregated public schools, to allow students to transfer to schools comprised of their own race, to allow segregated classes within a school, and to require a loyalty oath from teachers and a list of organizations in which they were members. He was also allowed to restrict the ability of certain organizations to operate and to require them to submit membership lists to the state (an action aimed mainly at the NAACP).[61]

Finally, Faubus was empowered to lease the schools to a private corporation, thus exempting them from the *Brown* decision. A vote on September 27 regarding the future of the high schools proved a lopsided victory in favor of closure. Schools remained closed for the entire year, forcing some white students to attend local segregationist academies such as the T. J. Raney High School and Baptist High School.[62] Students, both black and white, had other options: they could move out of the city or the state, they could complete instruction via their television sets in a series of classes set up by Blossom, or they could simply miss a year of their education.

Local organizations, formed in the midst of the crisis, helped shape its outcome. The Women's Emergency Committee to Open Our Schools (WEC), organized by Adolphine Fletcher Terry and Vivion Brewer, was formed on September 16, 1958. The group of about fifty women was "dedicated to the principle of free public school education, and to law and order." They claimed to stand "neither for integration nor segregation, but for education."[63] They focused on getting the shuttered public schools reopened. In spite of their efforts to resolve the matter, when a vote was held for total integration and was tallied in September, an avalanche of negative votes (129,470 to 7,561) impeded their progress and kept the schools closed.

Further hampering compromise or resolution, on November 12, 1958, five of the six school board members resigned in frustration when a federal appeals court ordered them to proceed with integration despite having no high schools to integrate. At that same meeting the board voted to buy out Superintendent Blossom's contract for $19,741.41, officially ending his tenure on November 30.[64] The new election, in December 1958, yielded a board evenly divided over the court's action, and they promptly appointed as new superintendent Terrell E. Powell, former principal of Hall High School.[65]

Most dramatically, on May 5, 1958, the segregationist members of the school board—after an ill-timed walkout by the more moderate members—attempted to fire forty-four teachers and administrators. This action prompted the formation of Stop This Outrageous Purge (STOP), which collaborated with the energized WEC in a recall of the most segregationist board members. In response, segregationists established the Committee to Retain Our Segregated Schools (CROSS). By a narrow margin, the segregationist board members were recalled and replaced with moderates. On June 18, 1959, the federal court declared the Little Rock school closings unconstitutional. On August 12, the city's high schools reopened; three black students entered the new Hall High School, and Jefferson Thomas and Carlotta Walls of the original Little Rock Nine returned to Central High.

The Fallout

During the crisis, the story in Little Rock was on the front page of nearly 70 percent of the nation's newspapers. For the first time in the history of television, the events in Little Rock interrupted regular programming. Even Broadway got into the act. The musical *South Pacific* added the words "Little Rock" to one of the musical numbers and drew jeers from New Yorkers.[66] The international media followed the Little Rock crisis with keen interest, and negative coverage subsided only slightly when Eisenhower ordered federal troops to the city. The embassy in Brussels, Belgium, reported that "Little Rock and segregation was receiving more press coverage than any previous American domestic issue."[67] Many European newspapers argued that the Little Rock crisis, which came in the aftermath of the Soviet invasion of Hungary, had done incalculable harm to American prestige. In an editorial, the *Socialist Tageblatt* declared that "Little Rock was a happy find for the Communists as a means of overshadowing the condemnation of the Hungarian massacre and the new Anti-Semitism in the Soviet Union."[68] The *West African Pilot,* a Nigerian newspaper, asked, "What moral right have Americans to condemn apartheid in South Africa when still maintaining it by law?"[69]

The economic impact of the crisis also reverberated throughout the city and state and would do so for years to come. Historian Elizabeth Jacoway explained that economics, more than any other factor, came to shape the perspectives of most residents: "After a gratifying post–World War II boom of mounting proportions, industrial growth ceased all together in September of 1957, and for four long years no new industry moved to Little Rock. This period of stagnation came to an end only when Little Rock businessmen were able to demonstrate convincingly that peace and order had returned to their city, permanently, and that Little Rock once again offered a safe and inviting field for investment."[70]

In 1959, the Little Rock Branch of the American Association of University Women published a study entitled "Effect of the Little Rock School Situation on Local Business." The interviews of eighty-five businessmen representing numerous industries such as retail, real estate, and insurance spanned November 1958 to January 1959. The overall findings of the report could be summed up by the remarks of one company president: "Anyone who doesn't think the school situation will affect local business adversely has rocks in his head."[71] The next five years proved him correct.

The WEC also published a report in August 1959 that offered some disturbing data. Through their survey research, the group concluded that 36 percent fewer families moved into Little Rock in 1959 as compared to 1957, resulting in a 20 percent decline in home building. In addition, twice as many residents fled the city, and professionals believed that "community cultural standards will suffer if a good public education system is not maintained."[72] Businesses that may have otherwise relocated in Arkansas to take advantage of low labor costs and pro-business tax policies shied away. Historian James C. Cobb found one businessman who explained that "our contacts with Arkansas have given us an unfavorable opinion of that state in comparison to Tennessee, Mississippi, or Missouri. We have no desire to be involved in the segregation problems current in that state."[73]

Little Rock business people were often more concerned with their civic image than about how the crisis and related violence destabilized their community. One leader said, "One lynching and we've wasted two hundred thousand dollars in magazine advertising."[74] In 1950, the city reported $158 million in growth. Eight years later, that number would fall to $25.4 million. Before the crisis, the city boasted an average of five plant openings a year, including a record-breaking eight from January to August 1957.[75] Not until the Little Rock Chamber of Commerce was able to demonstrate that the city had learned its lesson, by issuing documents such as the "Leadership Reports," did the city again become a viable place for investment. In 1962, five years after the crisis began, Jacuzzi Brothers of Richmond, California, moved to Little Rock, effectively ending the city's industrial drought. While city leaders were repairing Little Rock's image, other southern cities, such as Atlanta, Charlotte, Dallas, and Houston, saw explosive growth that far surpassed Little Rock. A half century later, the city has not yet reached its full potential.

The long-term impact of the Little Rock crisis is more difficult to measure. In 1968, Martin Luther King declared that "there is no more dangerous development in our nation that the constant building up of predominately Negro central cities ringed by white suburbs." King's concern was not exaggerated. Twenty years after *Brown,* many school districts continued to resist implementing the landmark decision. In 1973, Atlanta city schools abandoned busing in exchange for African American control of the schools, essentially resegregating public schools. In 1974, the Supreme Court ended a plan that would bus black children into white suburbs in Detroit. In September 2002, the Federal District Court finally ended more than forty years of court-supervised desegregation monitoring of the Little Rock School District (LRSD), with the exception of student achievement. This single act finally ended the crisis at Central High. Two years later, however, the courts reversed the decision, citing inadequate progress, and placed the schools under court supervision yet again. More recently, the Supreme Court allowed Oklahoma City to end busing if it had taken other measures to end discrimination.

Even with these problems, it is difficult to ignore that desegregation, at some level, worked. Less than 14 percent of African Americans had a high school education in 1950. Two generations later, in 1992, the number had jumped to 66 percent.[76] But there was a price to be paid. African American children bore the brunt of busing, evidenced by the example of Las Vegas, which in the 1990s bused black students for eleven years and white students for only one year. Additionally, segregation fragmented close-knit African American communities. Hazel Fournier, a Mobile, Alabama, school board member, explained, "We submerged a culture, a people and a tradition." Finally, desegregation also cost African American teachers and administrators their jobs as their former students moved into formerly all-white facilities.[77]

Remembering Little Rock

The passage of time has dramatically shaped how the events of Central High have been remembered and commemorated. Cold War concerns

over the threat of communism, which shaped the perspective on the crisis at the time, have almost completely disappeared from the discussion.
The heroes of the crisis—the Little Rock Nine—have been repeatedly
honored for their courage. They have become symbols in a movement
crowded with heroes. The rest of the players, with the possible exception of Orval Faubus, have faded into the background. The events at
Little Rock have even overshadowed other watershed moments in the
civil rights movement, placing it second only to Martin Luther King's
1963 "I Have a Dream" speech.

Reporting on the twenty-fifth anniversary of the crisis, the *Arkansas
Gazette* declared: "It is the most discussed the most studied event in
Arkansas history, the one thing about the state that outsiders always
know. Locally, it was a historical watershed. People date things from 'the
crisis': the phrase needs no elaboration. Discussions of political, business, and civic leaders invariably include an assessment of what they did
or didn't do in 1957."[78]

With few exceptions, commemorative events have largely replaced
nuanced debate regarding the impact of the crisis and the long-term
impact of desegregation in America. On October 24, 1987, the Little
Rock Nine returned to Central High School, where the entire student
body, as well as Little Rock's second black mayor, Lottie Shackelford,
welcomed them. Melba Pattillo Bealls said on that occasion, "What we
feel this morning is joyous that we made it, and sad that we had to make
it."[79] Two years later, in July 1989, Orval Faubus paid tribute to his old
adversary Daisy Bates with a warm tribute during a dinner held in her
honor. At the event, which designated Bates "Arkansas's Matriarch of
Integration," and without a hint of irony, Faubus said: "She worked for
a cause—her aim was to help others. She firmly believed that her efforts
were for the welfare of her people and the betterment of conditions in
our country."[80]

Numerous honors have been given to the Little Rock Nine. Artist
George Hunt completed a painting, *America Cares,* in time for the fortieth
anniversary. President Bill Clinton presided over the commemorative
events, and historians Elizabeth Jacoway and C. Fred Williams organized
a symposium entitled "Understanding the Little Rock Crisis: An Exercise
in Remembrance and Reconciliation." Two years later, on November 9,
1999, the day Daisy Bates was buried after her body lay in state in the

Arkansas State Capitol, the nine former students gathered in the East Room at the White House to receive the Congressional Gold Medal for their "selfless heroism." That day, they joined George Washington, Mother Teresa, and Reverend Billy Graham as recipients of the nation's highest civilian honor. In 2005, the U.S. Postal Service issued a commemorative stamp, and a bronze statue of the Little Rock Nine was unveiled on the state capital grounds.

The most enduring legacy of the crisis is the Little Rock Central High School National Historic Site, a facility managed by the National Parks Service that opened in 1997 to coincide with the fortieth anniversary celebration. It is located in a refurbished Mobil service station across the street from the school, and the centerpiece of the site is an exhibition, *All the World Is Watching Us: Little Rock and the 1957 Crisis.* Construction for a new visitor's center, which will be six times the size of the current site, began in June 2006. The formal dedication will coincide with the fiftieth anniversary.

In 2004, Little Rock Mayor Jim Dailey appointed a Fiftieth Anniversary Commission, co-chaired by Virgil Miller (a local banker) and Nancy Rousseau (principal of Central High School), to oversee the celebration scheduled for September 23–27, 2007. The main event will take place on the lawn of Central High on September 25. Additional activities include a film festival, a play by the Arkansas Repertory Theater, the display of the original Emancipation Proclamation at the Clinton Presidential Center, an exhibition organized by the Arkansas Arts Center of the 1957 photographs by Will Counts and Ernest Withers, and a gala hosted by the Little Rock Nine Foundation.

How to Use This Volume

The primary documents (newspaper articles, political cartoons, excerpts from oral histories and memoirs, speeches, photographs, and editorials) collected in this volume are organized thematically to help readers understand what a single historical moment reveals about how historians practice their craft. The documents have not been altered; original spelling and grammatical errors have been retained. The goal is to understand the historical process by (1) seeing how disparate materials are gathered, (2) reading conflicting accounts or differing perspectives,

(3) arriving at conclusions based upon the evidence presented, and (4) determining how historical events are remembered over time.

Five sections that include primary documents representing multiple perspectives follow this introduction. The documents for each section were selected for one of three reasons: (1) they have never been published; (2) they reveal something significant about the event and its aftermath; or (3) they offer an unconventional or unexpected perspective on the Little Rock crisis. The documents encourage scholars to examine the events surrounding Little Rock as a way to understand the complexity of implementing *Brown v. Board of Education,* but also to understand the context of the growing international concern over race and foreign policy. This approach situates the Little Rock crisis squarely in discussions about how domestic issues are influenced by events outside our borders, offering an appropriate segue to current events. There is an annotated bibliography, and the appendixes include a list of key players in the desegregation crisis, a timeline, questions for consideration, and sample assignments.

Notes

1. American Association of University Women (Little Rock Branch), "Effect of the Little Rock School Situation on Local Business," January 24, 1959, 6. Sara Murphy Collection, MC1321, 15:10, University of Arkansas Libraries Special Collections.

2. Harry T. Baker and Jane Browning, *An Arkansas History for Young People* (Fayetteville: University of Arkansas Press, 1991), 244. At the same time, Arkansas also had race-bating politicians such as Jeff Davis (who capitalized politically on the similarity of his name with that of the president of the Confederacy, Jefferson Davis) in its governor's chair at the turn of the century.

3. Jim Lester, *A Man for Arkansas: Sid McMath and the Southern Reform Tradition* (Little Rock: Rose Publishing Company, 1976), 129.

4. Anthony Badger, "The White Reaction to Brown: Arkansas, the Southern Manifesto, and Massive Resistance," in *Understanding the Little Rock Crisis,* ed. Elizabeth Jacoway and Fred C. Williams (Fayetteville: University of Arkansas Press, 1999), 83.

5. Faubus quoted in David Halberstam, *The Fifties* (New York: Ballantine Books, 1994), 668. *Brown I* is *Brown v. Board of Education of Topeka,* 347 U.S. 483; *Brown II* is *Brown v. Board of Education (II),* 349 U.S. 294.

6. Pete Daniel, *Lost Revolutions: The South in the 1950s* (Chapel Hill: University of North Carolina Press, 2000), 252; Virgil T. Blossom, *It Has Happened Here* (New York: Harper and Brothers, 1959), 1–7, 16–18; "National Affairs," *Time,* September 16, 1957, 24.

7. Halberstam, *The Fifties,* 672–673.

8. Roy Reed, "The Contest for the Soul of Orval Faubus," in *Understanding the Little Rock Crisis,* ed. Jacoway and Williams, 100.

9. Sam Faubus was contemptuous of his son's change in position and wrote letters to the editor of the *Arkansas Gazette* under the pseudonym of Jimmy Higgins during and after the crisis. Halberstam, *The Fifties,* 673.

10. Gene Roberts and Hank Klibanoff, *The Race Beat: The Press, the Civil Rights Struggle, and the Awakening of a Nation* (New York: Knopf, 2006), 144.

11. Reed, "The Contest for the Soul of Orval Faubus," 99–100.

12. Waldo Martin Jr., *Brown v. Board of Education: A Brief History with Documents* (Boston: Bedford/St. Martin's, 1998), 12.

13. Reed, "The Contest for the Soul of Orval Faubus," 103.

14. Herbert Brownell with John P. Burke, *Advising Ike: The Memoirs of Attorney General Herbert Brownell* (Lawrence: University of Kansas Press, 1993), 215–218.

15. Halberstam, *The Fifties,* 425.

16. Ibid., 687.

17. Ibid., 690.

18. Stephen A. Ambrose, *Eisenhower: Solder and President* (New York: Simon and Schuster, 1984), 620.

19. Cary Fraser, "Crossing the Color Line in Little Rock: The Eisenhower Administration and the Dilemma of Race," *Diplomatic History* (spring 2000): 245.

20. Howard Zinn, *A People's History of the United States* (New York: Harper Collins, 2003), 428.

21. Halberstam, *The Fifties,* 4–5.

22. David McCullough, *Truman* (New York: Simon and Schuster, 1992), 521; and Ambrose, *Eisenhower,* 157.

23. Martin, *Brown v. Board of Education,* 22; *Sarah C. Roberts v. The City of Boston,* 59 Mass. (5 Cush.) (1850); *Plessy v. Ferguson,* 163 U.S. 537 (1896).

24. Martin, *Brown v. Board of Education,* 197–198; *Brown v. Board of Education of Topeka,* 347 U.S. 483 (1954); *Davis v. County School Board of Prince Edward County of Virginia,* 74 Sup. Ct. 686 (1952); *Gebhart v. Belton,* 33 Del. Ch. 144, 87 A.2d 862 (Del. Ch. 1952), aff'd, 91 A.2d 137 (Del. 1952); *Bolling v. Sharpe of the District of Columbia,* 347 U.S. 497 (1954).

25. Halberstam, *The Fifties,* 190.

26. Dwight D. Eisenhower, *Waging Peace, 1956–1961: The White House Years* (New York: Doubleday, 1965), 148.

27. Dwight D. Eisenhower, quoted in Stanley I. Kutler, "Eisenhower, the Judiciary, and Desegregation: Some Reflections," in *Eisenhower: A Centenary Assessment,* ed. Gunther Bischof and Stephen E. Ambrose (Baton Rouge: Louisiana State University Press, 1995), 89.

28. It was originally called the "Declaration of Constitutional Principles." Martin, *Brown v. Board of Education,* 220 and Roberts and Klibanoff, *The Race Beat,* 146.

29. Anthony J. Badger, "The White Reaction to Brown: Arkansas, the Southern Manifesto, and Massive Resistance," in *Understanding the Little Rock Crisis,* ed. Jacoway and Williams, 90.

30. Ibid., 93.

31. Ibid., 86. The school board in Fayetteville agreed to desegregate four days after the *Brown* decision. See Roberts and Klibanoff, *The Race Beat,* 144. The process,

however, was not entirely peaceful. See John A. Kirk, "Arkansas, the Brown Decision, and the 1957 Little Rock School Crisis: A Local Perspective," in *Understanding the Little Rock Crisis*, ed. Jacoway and Williams, 75.

32. Roberts and Klibanoff, *The Race Beat*, 154.

33. Kirk, "Arkansas, the Brown Decision, and the 1957 Little Rock School Crisis," 70–71.

34. Ibid., 92.

35. Halberstam, *The Fifties*, 668.

36. Kirk, "Arkansas, the Brown Decision, and the 1957 Little Rock School Crisis," 71–72.

37. Ibid., 74.

38. Wilson Record and Jane Cassels Record, eds., *Little Rock, U.S.A.* (San Francisco: Chandler Publishing, 1960), 33–34.

39. Halberstam, *The Fifties*, 669.

40. Kirk, "Arkansas, the Brown Decision, and the 1957 Little Rock School Crisis 80.

41. Ibid., 79–80.

42. Halberstam, *The Fifties*, 668.

43. Amis Guthridge, quoted in "Segregationist Rally, March 20, 1956," *Southern School News*, April 1956.

44. James Eastland, quoted in Halberstam, *The Fifties*, 671.

45. "The Governor's Proclamation, September 2, 1957," reprinted in *Little Rock, U.S.A.*, ed. Record and Record, 36.

46. Halberstam, *The Fifties*, 674.

47. "The Nation," *Time*, September 16, 1957, 24.

48. L. C. Bates (a local NAACP activist) and Benjamin Fine (a reporter for the *New York Times*) were also present at the bus stop. See *Little Rock, U.S.A.*, ed. Record and Record, 40.

49. Grace Lorch, quoted in "The Nation," *Time*, September 16, 1957, 25.

50. Email from Laura Miller to Catherine Lewis, November 10, 2006.

51. Eisenhower, quoted in Brownell with Burke, *Advising Ike*, 209–210.

52. *Saturday Evening Post*, June 13, 1957, reprinted in *Little Rock, U.S.A.*, ed. Record and Record, 62–63.

53. Brownell with Burke, *Advising Ike*, 210–211

54. Eisenhower, quoted in NAACP, Press Release, "Central High School—1957: A Turning Point in History," September 27, 1987. Collection B-12, series II, box 1, file 7, item 22. Special Collections, University of Arkansas at Little Rock.

55. Telegram, Columbia School of Journalism to the Editorial Board of the Tiger, October 8, 1957. Collection B-12, series II, box 2, file 6, item 3. University of Arkansas Libraries Special Collections.

56. Jacoway and Williams, *Understanding the Little Rock Crisis*, 10.

57. Melba Patillo Beals, *Warriors Don't Cry* (New York: Washington Square Press, 1994), 151, 164, 167, 173.

58. Jacoway and Williams, *Understanding the Little Rock Crisis*, 10.

59. Bealls, *Warriors Don't Cry*, 148 and 184.

60. Beth Roy, *Bitters in the Honey* (Fayetteville: University of Arkansas Press, 1999), 234.

61. Record and Record, *Little Rock, U.S.A.*, 114.

62. Ibid., 130.

63. Vivion Lenon Brewer, *The Embattled Ladies of Little Rock, 1958–1963: The Struggle to Save Public Education at Central High* (Ft. Bragg, CA: Lost Coast Press, 1999), 68; and Record and Record, *Little Rock, U.S.A.*, 123.

64. Record and Record, *Little Rock, U.S.A.*, 130.

65. Ibid., 30–131.

66. Roberts and Klibanoff, *The Race Beat,* 163.

67. Fraser, "Crossing the Color Line in Little Rock," 6.

68. Christensen dispatch to the Department of State, September 30, 1957, RG59, 811. 411/9-3057, National Archives, Washington, DC, quoted in Fraser, "Crossing the Color Line in Little Rock," 6.

69. Hunt dispatch to the Department of State, October 14, 1957, RG 59, 811. 411/10-1457, National Archives, quoted in Fraser, "Crossing the Color Line in Little Rock," 7.

70. Doug Smith, "25 Years after LR's Watershed," *Arkansas Gazette,* May 17, 1979, 2B.

71. American Association of University Women (Little Rock Branch), "Effect of the Little Rock School Situation on Local Business," January 24, 1959, 4. Sara Murphy Collection, MC1321, 15:10, University of Arkansas Libraries Special Collections.

72. Women's Emergency Committee to Open Our Schools, "The Little Rock Report: The City, Its People, Its Business, 1958–1959," 1. Sara Murphy Collection, MC1321, 15:10, University of Arkansas Libraries Special Collections.

73. James C. Cobb, "The Lessons of Little Rock: Stability, Growth, and Change in the American South," in *Understanding the Little Rock Crisis,* ed. Jacoway and Williams, 113.

74. Ibid., 118.

75. Ibid., 114.

76. Jonathan Tilove, "Busing: Flawed Solution to Enduring Problem," *New Orleans Times-Picayune,* January 12, 1992, 2.

78. Smith, "25 Years after LR's Watershed," 1B.

CHAPTER 1

Before the Crisis

Arkansas was a relatively moderate southern state, one that had peacefully integrated the state university, several smaller colleges, medical and law schools, several public schools, and the bus system prior to 1957. This is one of the reasons that the desegregation battle over Little Rock's Central High School was so unexpected. While most of the participants in the crisis focused on civil and state's rights, President Eisenhower viewed the conflict through the lens of Cold War politics. Facing widespread international criticism, the administration was concerned that communists would use racial strife in the United States as propaganda to persuade countries that had not yet declared their political allegiance. The documents in "Before the Crisis" present different perspectives on how the racial climate in Arkansas and the South was shaped by race relations in the twentieth century and by America's role in the world community.

DOCUMENT 1:
Speech of Senator Benjamin R. Tillman, March 23, 1900.

Congressional Record, 56th Congress, 1st Session, 3223–3224.
Courtesy Congressional Record.

Benjamin R. Tillman served in the Confederate army, as governor of South Carolina (1890–1894), and in the U.S. Senate (1895–1918) as a Democrat. Known as "Pitchfork Ben," he was censured for assaulting another senator on the senate floor in 1902. In this excerpt from a speech Tillman defends the vigilante violence committed by white constituents against African Americans, arguing that the "hot-headedness" of Southern blacks and Republican mistakes during Reconstruction "put white necks under black heels."

And he [Senator John C. Spooner, of Wisconsin] said we had taken their rights away from them. He asked me was it right to murder them in order to carry the elections. I never saw one murdered. I never saw one shot at an election. It was the riots before the elections precipitated by their own hot-headedness in attempting to hold the government, that brought on conflicts between the races and caused the shotgun to be used. That is what I meant by saying we used the shotgun.

I want to call the Senator's attention to one fact. He said that the Republican party gave the negroes the ballot in order to protect themselves against the indignities and wrongs that were attempted to be heaped upon them by the enactment of the black code. I say it was because the Republicans of that day, led by Thad Stevens, wanted to put white necks under black heels and to get revenge. There is a difference of opinion. You have your opinion about it, and I have mine, and we can never agree.

I want to ask the Senator this proposition in arithmetic: In my State there were 135,000 negro voters, or negroes of voting age, and some 90,000 or 95,000 white voters. General Canby set up a carpetbag government there and turned our State over to this majority. Now, I want to ask you, with a free vote and a fair count, how are you going to beat 135,000 by 95,000? How are you going to do it? You had set us an impossible task. You had handcuffed us and thrown away the key, and you propped your carpetbag negro government with bayonets. Whenever it was necessary to sustain the government you held it up by the Army.

Mr. President, I have not the facts and figures here, but I want the country to get the full view of the Southern side of this question and the justification for anything we did. We were sorry we had the necessity forced upon us, but we could not help it, and as white men we are not sorry for it, and we do not propose to apologize for anything we have done in connection with it. We took the government away from them in 1876. We did take it. If no other Senator has come here previous to this time who would acknowledge it, more is the pity. We have had no fraud in our elections in South Carolina since 1884. There has been no organized Republican party in the State.

We did not disfranchise the negroes until 1895. Then we had a constitutional convention convened which took the matter up calmly, deliberately, and avowedly with the purpose of disfranchising as many of them as we could under the fourteenth and fifteenth amendments. We adopted the educational qualification as the only means left to us, and the negro is as contented and as prosperous and as well protected in South Carolina to-day as in any State of the Union south of the Potomac. He is not meddling with politics, for he found that the more he meddled with them the worse off he got. As to his "rights"—I will not discuss them now. We of the South have never recognized the right of the negro to govern white men, and we never will. We have never believed him to be equal to the white man, and we will not submit to his gratifying his lust on our wives and daughters without lynching him. I would to God the last one of them was in Africa and that none of them had ever been brought to our shores. But I will not pursue the subject further.

I want to ask permission in this connection to print a speech which I made in the constitutional convention of South Carolina when it convened in 1895, in which the whole carpetbag regime and the indignities and wrongs heaped upon our people, the robberies which we suffered, and all the facts and figures there brought out are incorporated, and let the whole of the facts go to the country. I am not ashamed to have those facts go to the country. They are our justification for the present situation in our State. If I can get it, I should like that permission; otherwise I shall be forced to bring that speech here and read it when I can put my hand on it. I will then leave this matter and let the dead past bury its dead.

DOCUMENT 2:
Photograph, Sharecroppers' children on Sunday, near Little Rock, Arkansas, October 1935.

Courtesy Library of Congress.

In the early twentieth century, numerous African Americans and poor whites in Arkansas and much of the South were restricted mainly to low-wage labor or sharecropping, a system of farm tenancy that arose at the end of the Civil War. Many former slaves were forced into this system that often put them in severe debt to the landlord. The landlord provided land, equipment, animals, and seed. The sharecropper provided labor and typically received half of the money that was made by selling the crop. From that share, the landlord deducted expenses and often charged high rates of interest. The

system universally abused the laborer. The Farm Security Administration, created by the Department of Agriculture in 1937, took this photograph of sharecroppers' children. For eight years, FSA photographers took more than seventy-seven thousand photographs to document the lives of poor farmers during the Great Depression.

DOCUMENT 3:
Letter to Brooks Hays from Franklin Delano Roosevelt, September 9, 1938.

from Brooks Hays, A Southern Moderate Speaks *(Chapel Hill: University of North Carolina Press, 1959), 21–22. Courtesy of University of North Carolina Press.*

Born in London, Arkansas, in 1898, Brooks Hays was educated as a lawyer before serving as assistant attorney general of Arkansas (1925–1927). From 1932 to 1939, he was a Democratic national committeeman for Arkansas. During the New Deal, he served as a National Recovery Administration labor compliance officer for Arkansas in 1934 and as assistant to the administrator of resettlement in 1935, and he worked for the Farm Security Administration (1936–1942). He was elected to Congress, serving for seven terms

(1943–1959). During the Little Rock crisis, Hays sought to medi-
ate between President Eisenhower and Orval Faubus, at great personal cost. He lost the 1958 election to Dale Alford, a former
member of the Little Rock School Board and a segregationist. This
letter describes Arkansas Democratic Congressman Hays's
attempt to repeal the poll tax in Arkansas two decades before the
Central High crisis, demonstrating that voices of moderation were
spread throughout the state.

Hyde Park, New York
September 9, 1938

Mr. Brooks Hays
Democratic National Committeeman
Little Rock, Arkansas

Dear Brooks:

Thank you for your interesting letter about the proposal to repeal
the poll tax.

I think we should all remember that free suffrage has come in almost
every state after a long struggle. At the time of adoption of the federal
constitution some form of property qualification was a prerequisite for
voting—and in some states this amounted to a denial of the privilege of
voting to a large proportion of the adult male population of the state.

Gradually, through the years, state after state abolished the requirement of owning real estate, or of owning an equivalent amount of some
other kind of property. Then came efforts to restrict the franchise by
the imposition of poll taxes.

I am glad to know that there is such a general move in those states
which still have them to repeal them altogether. They are inevitably contrary to the fundamental democracy and its representative form of government in which we believe.

The imposition of a poll tax which prevents a large number of otherwise qualified men and women from voting is not far removed from
the effort of some people in the state of Maine two years ago to prevent
men and women who, through no fault of their own, were receiving
relief from voting because of an old law that denied the vote to people
in poor houses.

I am, of course, not advising the voters of the state of Arkansas how to vote on this question—but there is no reason under the sun why I should not talk about the important general principle that applies under our constitutional form of government in every state in the union.

Very sincerely yours,
(signed) Franklin D. Roosevelt

DOCUMENT 4:
Gunnar Myrdal, "An American Dilemma."

from Gunnar Myrdal, An American Dilemma: The Negro Problem and Modern Democracy *(New York: Harper and Brothers, 1944). Courtesy Harper Collins.*

The Carnegie Corporation commissioned Swedish economist Gunnar Myrdal (1898–1987) to direct a study of the condition of African Americans in the United States in 1938. Myrdal hired forty-eight writers, including Ralph Bunche and Kenneth B. Clark, to aide in the research, which was published in two volumes in 1944. Myrdal makes an argument that race relations in America are a moral, not a sociological, problem. Myrdal's work was cited in the *Brown v. Board of Education* decision as an authoritative source on the impact that the concept of "separate but equal" had on the African American psyche. In 1964, the *Saturday Review* asked twenty-seven scholars, "What books published during the past four decades most significantly altered the direction of society?" Myrdal's book was second only to John Maynard Keynes's *The General Theory of Employment, Interest, and Money.* Myrdal shared the Nobel prize with Friedrich von Hayek in 1974.

In their basic traits the Negroes are inherently not much different from other people. Neither are, incidentally, the white Americans. But Negroes and whites in the United States live in singular human relations with each other. All the circumstances of life—the "environmental" conditions in the broadest meaning of that term—diverge more from the "normal" for the Negroes that for the whites, if only because of the statistical fact that the Negroes are the smaller group. The average Negro must experience many times more of the "abnormal" interracial relations than the average white man in America. The more important fact, however, is that practically all the economic, social, and political power is held by whites. The Negroes do not by far have anything approaching a tenth of the things worth having in America.

It is thus the white majority group that naturally determines the Negro's "place." All our attempts to reach scientific explanations of why the Negroes are what they are and why they live as they do have regularly led to determinants on the white side of the race line. In the practical and political struggles of effecting changes, the views and attitudes of the white Americans are likewise strategic. The Negro's entire life, and, consequently, also his opinions on the Negro problem, are, in the main, to be considered as secondary reactions to more primary pressures from the side of the dominant white majority.

The Negro was brought to America for the sake of the white man's profit. He was kept in slavery for generations in the same interest. A civil war was fought between two regional groups of white Americans. For two years no one wanted Negroes involved in the fighting. Later on some two hundred thousand Negro soldiers fought in the Northern army, in addition to all the Negro laborers, servants, spies, and helpers in both armies. But it was not the Negroes' war. As a result of the war, which took a toll of some half million killed and many more wounded, the four million Negro slaves were liberated. Since then the Negro's "place" in American society has been precarious, uncertain and changing; he was no longer so necessary and profitable to the white man as in slavery before the Civil War. In the main, however, the conflicting and vacillating valuations of the white majority have been decisive, whether the issue was segregation in the schools, discrimination with reference to public facilities, equal justice and protection under the laws, enjoyment of the franchise, or the freedom to enter a vocation and earn an honest living. The Negro, as a minority, and a poor and suppressed minority at that, in the final analysis, has had little other strategy open to him that to play on the conflicting values held in the white majority group. In so doing, he has been able to identify his cause with broader issues in American politics and social life and with moral principles held dear by the white Americans. This is the situation even today and will remain so in the foreseeable future. In that sense, "this is a white man's country."

DOCUMENT 5:
Harry S. Truman, Executive Order 9808, December 5, 1946.

President Harry Truman issued Executive Order 9808 to establish a fifteen-person commission charged with (1) examining the condition of civil rights in the United States, (2) producing a written report of their findings, and (3) submitting recommendations on improving civil rights in the United States. In December 1947 the committee published their findings in a report entitled *To Secure These Rights: The Report of the President's Committee on Civil Rights.* As a result, Truman issued two additional Executive Orders (9980 and 9981) on July 26, 1948, which ordered the desegregation of the federal workforce and armed services.

Whereas the preservation of civil rights guaranteed by the Constitution is essential to domestic tranquility, national security, the general welfare, and the continued existence of our free institutions, and

Whereas the action of individuals who take the law into their own hands and inflict summery punishment and wreak personal vengeance is subversive of our democratic system of law enforcement and public criminal justice, and gravely threatens our form of government; and

Whereas it is essential that all possible steps be taken to safeguard our civil rights:

Now, Therefore, by virtue of the authority vested in me as President of the United States by the Constitution and the statues of the United States, it is hereby ordered as follows:

1. There is hereby created a committee to be known as the President's Committee on Civil Rights, which shall be composed of the following-named members, who shall serve without compensation. . . .

2. The Committee is authorized on behalf of the President to inquire into and to determine whether and in what respect current law-enforcement measures and the authority and means possessed by Federal, State, and local governments may be strengthened and improved to safeguard the civil rights of people.

3. All executive departments and agencies of the Federal Government are authorized and directed to cooperate with the Committee in its works, and to furnish the Committee such information or the services of such persons as the Committee may require in the performance of its duties.

4. When requested by the Committee to do so, persons employed in any of the executive departments and agencies of the Federal Government shall testify before the Committee and shall make available for the use of the Committee such documents and other information as the Committee may require.

5. The Committee shall make a report of its studies to the President in writing, and shall in particular make recommendations with respect to the adoption or establishment, by legislation or otherwise, of more adequate and effective means and procedures for the protection of the civil rights of the people of the Unites States.

6. Upon rendition of its report to the President, the Committee shall cease to exist, unless otherwise determined by further Executive Order.

—Harry S. Truman, "To Secure These Rights," 1947

DOCUMENT 6:

Thomas F. Power Jr., Memorandum, August 26, 1947.

U.S. Mission to the United Nations Central Subject Files, 1946–1963, Dependent Areas: Conferences to Eweland, Record Group 84, entry 1030D, box 5, National Archives, Washington, D.C. Courtesy National Archives.

This memorandum was written by Thomas F. Powers Jr., a longtime diplomat who served as director of the United Nations Development Program from 1950 to 1976. Powers, an aide to Eleanor Roosevelt, was present at the founding of the organization in 1945 and later served as a member of the Council on Foreign Relations. The incident Powers references in the memo occurred in 1946 when several New York hotels refused to house United Nations delegates from Haiti, Liberia, and Ethiopia. The

Department of State kept detailed records to document how America was being perceived abroad, and this document provides insight into international criticism of American racial policies.

TO THE UNITED NATIONS
August 26, 1947

SUBJECT: Argentine Representation Regarding Discrimination
Against Delegates in New York

At the meeting of the Secretaries-General this morning, the Argentine Secretary-General stated that he had been instructed by his Government to formally raise the question of discrimination against Delegates by New York hotels. He said he knew that last year a bad situation had been averted only by the intervention of the U.S. Delegation and he desired to know what the situation was at this time.

Mr. Vaughan, of the Secretariat, replied with obvious gratification that all of the Delegations were being accommodated in adequate quarters, and that there was no problem of discrimination similar to that which existed last year. No further discussion of this question took place.

TFPower: jg
cc: Ambassador Austin
    Mr. Rusk
    Mr. Villard
    Mr. Ross
    Mr. Sandifer
    Mr. Timberlake
    Mr. McKeever
    Reference

DOCUMENT 7:

Letter from President Harry Truman to Governor Sidney S. McMath.

Courtesy Special Collections, University of Arkansas Libraries, Sidney McMath Collection, MC899, box 1.

Sidney Sanders McMath was an Arkansas attorney who became widely known as a progressive force in the Democratic Party in the South. He served as governor of Arkansas from 1949 to 1953 and focused his administration on reform, championing rural electrification and highway construction, repeal of the poll tax, honest elections, and African American enfranchisement. Always loyal to President Harry Truman, McMath opposed Faubus's stand on segregation. Truman's letter to McMath upon his election celebrates the state's good fortune.

January 5, 1949

My dear Governor McMath:

I cannot resist the impulse to wish you a successful administration as you assume the duties of Governor of one of the most progressive states in the Union.

I have asked a sterling native of Arkansas, the Secretary of the Treasury, to represent me at the inaugural exercises and to extend my hearty greetings and good wishes to you and to all who will be associated with you in the great task of government.

Our country is blessed by a bounty and abundance unequaled in economic history. Arkansas stands at the threshold of a great opportunity. It can go forward with progress under the enlightened leadership of a man who now assumes office under such happy auspices.

I send all citizens best wishes for happiness and continued prosperity.

Very sincerely yours,
(signed) Harry Truman

Honorable Sidney S. McMath,
Governor of Arkansas,
Little Rock, Arkansas.

DOCUMENT 8:

Cartoon, "Ike at the Dike," by commodore.

from the Chicago Daily Defender, *1952. Courtesy* Chicago Defender.

This cartoon shows the extent to which Eisenhower courted southern white politicians during his 1952 presidential campaign, helping to explain his actions during the Little Rock crisis. The cartoon was originally published in the *Chicago Defender,* an African American newspaper founded by Robert S. Abbott on May 5, 1905, with an initial investment of twenty-five cents. On February 6, 1956, the newspaper changed its name to the *Chicago Daily Defender,* which with a circulation of 250,000 became the largest black-owned daily in the world.

DOCUMENT 9:

Judge Tom Brady, "Communist Masses Howled with Glee on 'Black Monday.'"

from Judge Tom Brady, Black Monday, *1954.*

The movement against *Brown v. Board* of Education, passed on May 17, 1954, was led by Mississippi Court Circuit Judge Tom P. Brady. Brady formed the Citizens' Council in July 1954, comprised of white political and business leaders, to oppose integration. In 1956, the Mississippi legislature formed the State Sovereignty Commission, which helped fund the council's efforts to spy and intimate blacks and whites who supported integration. This editorial is drawn from Brady's manifesto, *Black Monday,* a book that he published using the text of a speech he delivered to the Sons of the American Revolution in Greenwood, Mississippi. Note how Brady counters the Eisenhower administration's concern that racism in America would help communism spread.

Do not erroneously suppose that the segregation ruling by the Supreme Court will satiate the inordinate hunger for power of these minority groups. Each one of their foresworn aims will be relentlessly prosecuted. . . .

It is unwise to prophesy, but socialized medicine, when such a case is prepared and comes for review upon appeal, will be ripe for legal validation by the present U. S. Supreme Court, under the "Open Sesame" interpretation of the Fourteenth Amendment. Such a decision would not be nearly as socialistic as the control and regulation of the schools of your State.

There will be more FHA's and more corruption, more TVA's, et ceteras. The Government will first control and then usurp the banking business, then it will manage and socialize transportation, agriculture and any other private enterprises where totalitarian state will be advanced. We will all become socialized Federal workers, working for the glory of the State.

This is but a part of what lies ahead of "Black Monday." Sovereign States, do you know what lies behind it? The Communists of America have been trying since 1936 to destroy the South. The bait which attracts them is the negro population. Hate campaigns against Southern States were conducted in the North. Abuse and falsehoods were flagrantly utilized. Counsel and advice were given the negro leaders. A bloodless revolution was planned.

The negro was to be placed in office and in control, while the whites were to be driven out. A black empire was to be established in the Southern States of this nation, ruled by negroes. All public offices were to be held by negroes. The most fantastic and preposterous promises were made. The good will which had for eighty years existed between the races has been disturbed. Pilgrimages from the South to the North were encouraged where indoctrinization of the negroes took place. The new converts were returned to the South to disseminate their "new, glorious knowledge," and begin the creation of this fine socialistic Eden. Back of all this was but one motive, not the welfare of the negro, but the splitting away and controlling of a fine section of this nation, the segment which gave to democracy Thomas Jefferson, Washington, Madison, Monroe and Andrew Jackson. It was and is being done in behalf of Communist Russia. If the South, the stronghold of democracy, could be destroyed, then the nation could be destroyed.

This plan failed. The economic superiority of the white man or the innate loyalty of the Southern negro to this country, or both probably, caused the abandonment of the plan by the Communists. Then, too, it was prematurely conceived.

The plan to abolish segregation in the seventeen States, thirteen of which are Southern, was substituted. The medium through which this was to be accomplished was the National Association for the Advancement of Colored People, its affiliate organizations, together with the CIO.

Let us calmly and as impartially as possible review the facts.

In 1936, huge numbers of negroes migrated north to such cites as Chicago, Detroit, Akron, Pittsburgh, Philadelphia and New York. A little later, a migration went to California, the 1st District receiving a tremendous portion. In passing, James Roosevelt moved into this district and it was the block vote of these negroes which recently gave him the Democratic nomination to Congress.

Inflamed with their new power and fired by the promises of the

Roosevelt machine and the CIO, the negro vote switched with the CIO to the Democratic Party, making possible the election of Roosevelt to the presidency. The block vote of the negroes helped keep him there. It is partially responsible for the New Deal and all its socialism. Truman used the negro vote as a stirrup, and rewarded it with the Civil Rights agitation and the appointment of negroes to high offices. Satisfying their inordinate ambitions was one way of paying a political debt.

Catastrophes and epidemics such as the Great Fire of Chicago, the San Francisco earthquake, cholera and meningitis, the yellow fever and influenza epidemics, and the other pestilences which this country has undergone are disastrous and lamentable, but the most destructive force which we are subject to is mental (not insanity) and spiritual illness. This is the essence of communism and its corollary, socialism. They are the political and economic ills which destroy men's souls and decompose nations. The dubious have but to casually examine the economic and political conditions of the nations which have been thoroughly infected with the virus of communism. There is something mysterious about this dread governmental disease. The symptoms are so multiplex. It strikes where least expected with the speed and fury of a forest fire. It is a fanatical religion. It is an obsession. There is an abundance of satanic power embodied therein. It fascinates the quasi intelligent and it enthralls the ignorant. It appeals to rich and poor. To the indigent and maladjusted it is a panacea.

All the powers of darkness and evil are at its command. These are not idle words! Communism has always hitched to and ridden behind the four horsemen of the Apocalypse. Communism is the wine of Circe which transforms men into brutes. Through it is yet largely underground, it is rampant in our nation.

The Communist masses of Russia and Red China must have howled with glee on "Black Monday." They know the unanimous decision of the Supreme Court abolishing segregation in the four Districts and States involved was illegal usurpation of the legislative prerogative of those State Legislatures and of Congress. The hoards of Russia and Red China know that another deadly blow has been dealt our Constitution, that outmoded, effete document which still precariously stands in the way of a new, brave communistic order in this country. They know that the South was struck below the belt, that the long governing principle of *stare decisis* is no longer operative in this country; that sociological criteria have supplanted laws in the deciding of cases in this country by our supreme judiciary.

Those muffled groans which were scarcely audible came from the graves of Chief Justices Marshall, Jay, Lamar, Taney, White, Hughes and Vinson.

The honor and glory, the courage and patriotism, the learning and wisdom of the highest judicial tribunal ever produced on this earth has been socialized and psychologized. Yes, the unanimous decision of the U. S. Supreme Court was to the constitutional rights of the sovereign states what the kiss of Iscariot in Gethsemane was to the Master.

DOCUMENT 10:

National Association for the Advancement of Colored People (NAACP), "Statement of the Emergency Southwide NAACP Conference, Atlanta, Georgia, June 4, 1955 and Directives to the Branches."

The Crisis 62 (*June–July 1955): 337–340, 381.*
Courtesy The Crisis.

The National Association for the Advancement of Colored Persons (NAACP) was founded in New York City in 1909 and was initially called the National Negro Committee. Headquartered in Baltimore, Maryland, the organization has six regional offices to help coordinate the state offices in that region. The organization, in the early years, worked through the courts to overturn Jim Crow statues and fight lynching. In the 1950s, the organization's Legal Department, lead first by Charles Hamilton Houston and then Thurgood Marshall, worked to overturn the *Plessy v. Ferguson* decision that legalized segregation. On June 4, 1955, the NAACP held an emergency statewide conference in Atlanta, Georgia, to adopt a policy statement regarding the implementation of the *Brown* decision, issued the month before. This statement maps out the NAACP's national program to implement *Brown*.

We, the State Conference officials of the NAACP, representing 16 Southern states and the District of Columbia have met here today, on

June 4, 1955, to map a program of action to make full use of the two historic decisions of the Supreme Court desegregating public schools.

We adopt and approve the staff memorandum interpreting the May 31 decision and we authorize our branches in every state to act to secure desegregation beginning next September, by filing petitions with their school boards requesting the "prompt" beginning set forth in the May 31 opinion. In the absence of any affirmative actions by school boards by the opening of schools in September, 1955, our branches will take whatever action is necessary to get the school board to initiate the process of desegregation. To this end, we are sending the following 8-point directive to all of our branches.

To the recalcitrant states determined to flout the Constitution we say: maintenance of segregated schools is unconstitutional and all state laws and practices to the contrary "must yield" to this principle of desegregation. This is the law of the land which applies to every state, county, city, and hamlet. There will be no local opinion on this. Whenever and wherever a state or county refuses to recognize this principle, our answers will be the same as the legal action begun here in Atlanta on June 3, 1955.

Directives to the Branches

On May 17, 1954, the United States Supreme Court in a historic decision outlawed racial segregation in public schools. On May 31, 1955, in another unanimous decision, the Court ordered "good faith compliance" with this decision "at the earliest practicable date" and made the lower federal courts guardians in the enforcement of this order and arbiters as to whether good faith is being practiced by school authorities.

A sampling of sentiment throughout the country indicates a generally favorable reaction to the May 31 decision, with Kentucky, Oklahoma, Maryland, Missouri, Delaware and West Virginia promising full compliance. There will be resistance in the rest of the South in varying degrees, but make no mistake about it, this decision in no way cuts back on the May 17 pronouncement. Indeed, the May 31 decision merely affords to law-abiding public officials an easy method to conform to the Constitution of the United States. The decision places a challenge on the good faith of the public officials, on the militancy of Negroes and on the integrity of the federal courts.

For our part, we must be prepared to meet the challenge in a forthright manner. Our branches must seek to determine in each community whether the school board is prepared to make prompt and reasonable start towards integration of the public schools and whether it will proceed with good faith towards full compliance with the May 31 decision at the earliest practicable date. Promises unaccompanied by concrete action are meaningless; nor can there be concern with the attitudes of individuals towards a change in the school system. Segregated schools are illegal, and the Court is merely allowing school boards time to get their houses in order. It does not allow time to procrastinate, stall or evade. It is the job of our branches to see to it that each school board begins to deal with the problem of providing non-discriminatory education. To that end we suggest that each of our branches take the following steps:

1. File at once a petition with each school board, calling attention to the May 31 decision, requesting that the school board act in accordance with that decision and offering the services of the branch to help the board in solving this problem.

2. Follow up the petition with periodic inquiries of the board seeking to determine what steps it is making to comply with the Supreme Court decision.

3. All during June, July, August and September, and thereafter, through meetings, forums, debates, conferences, etc., use every opportunity to explain what the May 31 decision means, and be sure to emphasize that the ultimate determination as to the length of time it will take for desegregation to become a fact in the community is not in the hands of the politicians or the school board officials but in the hands of the federal courts.

4. Organize the parents in the community so that as many as possible will be familiar with the procedure when and if law suits are begun in behalf of plaintiffs and parents.

5. Seek the support of the individuals and community groups, particularly in the white community, through churches, labor organizations, civic organizations and personal contact.

6. When announcement is made of the plans adopted by your school board, get the exact text of the school board's pronouncements and notify the State Conference and the National Office at

once so that you will have the benefit of their views as to whether the plan is one which will provide for effective desegregation. It is very important that branches not proceed at this stage without consultation with State offices and the National office.

7. If no plans are announced or no steps towards desegregation taken by the time school begins this fall, 1955, the time for a law suit has arrived. At this stage court action is essential because only in this way does the mandate of the Supreme Court that [there be] a prompt and reasonable start towards full compliance become fully operative on the school boards in question.

8. At this stage the matter will be turned over to the Legal Department and it will proceed with the matter in court. . . .

DOCUMENT 11:
"Minutes of the Little Rock School Board of Education Meeting, Little Rock, Arkansas, May 24, 1955."

Courtesy Roy G. Brooks.

The Little Rock School Board met seven days after the Supreme Court's *Brown I* decision to create a plan for a peaceful desegregation. It offers a glimpse of the racial climate from the moderate white perspective, as this board points out some serious impediments and seeks a slow, reluctant, and indefinite schedule for integration. By August 30, 1957, the most overtly racist school board member, Dr. Dale Alford, was calling for indefinite postponement of the plan. The next few years would be difficult ones for the Little Rock School Board, as elections, recalls, and resignations changed the makeup of the board and the positions which it took on this matter.

The Board of Education of Little Rock School District met in Special Session in the "Silver Room" of the Albert Pike Hotel at 12:00 noon on May 24, 1955. Meeting called to order by the President, Dr. W. G. Cooper, Jr.

MEMBERS PRESENT:
Dr. W. G. Cooper, Jr., President; Mrs. Arthur E. McLean, Vice-President;

Mrs. Edgar F. Dixon, Secretary; Mr. R. A. Lile; Mr. Harold Engstrom; Dr. Dale Alford; also, Mr. Virgil T. Blossom, Superintendent of Schools. MEMBERS ABSENT: All members of the board were present.

PLAN OF INTEGRATION FOR THE LITTLE ROCK PUBLIC SCHOOLS

Motion by Mrs. Edgar Dixon, seconded by Mr. Harold Engstrom, approving the following Plan of Integration for the Little Rock Public Schools.

PLAN OF SCHOOL INTEGRATION—LITTLE ROCK SCHOOL DISTRICT

The Supreme Court decision of May 17, 1954, which declared segregated schools unconstitutional has placed before us the most difficult educational problem of our time. A careful analysis of the following has been made.

1. Financial ability of Little Rock School District to integrate its schools.
2. Adequacy of present school facilities plus those to be added from $4,000,000.00 bond issue of March, 1953, plus the amount of money to be realized from the sale of the "old Peabody School Site" on West Capitol Ave.
3. Proper time and method for the integration of the schools of Little Rock School District in a manner consistent with the law as finally interpreted by the Supreme Court and acceptable to both races.

Our review of the three questions raised, reveal the following facts and opinions.

1. Integration of its schools by Little Rock School District will probably place *no serious additional* financial burden on the School District.
2. The facilities of Little Rock School District will be inadequate at the junior and senior high school levels until such time as the three senior high schools and six junior high schools are ready for occupancy.
3. It is our opinion that the proper time for, and method of integration is as follows:

A. <u>Time of Integration</u>

Integration of schools in Little Rock School District <u>cannot be accomplished until completion of the needed school facilities</u> (three senior high schools and six junior high schools) <u>and specific decrees have been formulated by the U. S. Supreme Court in the pending cases.</u>

B. <u>Method of Integration</u>

The method of changing from segregated to integrated school should not be attempted simultaneously in grades one to twelve. Due to the complexity of this problem, an orderly systematically planned process should be followed. In Little Rock School District our research and study causes us to believe that the following plan charts the best course for all concerned.

1. In our opinion integration should begin at the senior high school level. (Grades 10–12) (<u>First phase of program</u>)

2. Following successful integration at the senior level, it should then be started in the junior high schools. (Grades 7–9) (<u>Second phase of program</u>)

3. After successful integration in junior and senior high schools it should be started in the elementary schools. (Grades 1–6) (<u>Third phase of program</u>)

    (<u>Present indications are that the school year 1957–58 may be the first phase of this program.</u>)

The Board of Education's reasons for the adoption of this plan of integration are as follows:

1. Since our school system has been segregated from its beginning until the present time, the time required in the process as outlined should not be construed as unnecessary delay; but that which is justly needed with respect to the size and complexity of the job at hand.

2. It is ill advised to begin this process with inadequate facilities.

3. It is unwise to begin integration until the Supreme Court gives direction through its interpretations of the specific cases before it.

4. By starting integration at the senior high school level the process will begin where fewer teachers and students are involved.

5. In the adoption of a plan of integration (1) senior high school 2) junior high school 3) elementary schools) of sequential order, we provide the opportunity to benefit from our own experience as we move through each phase of this plan, thus avoiding as many mistakes as possible.

6. The establishment of attendance areas at the elementary level (grades 1–6) is most difficult due to the large number of both students and buildings involved. Because of this fact it should be the last step in the process.

We sincerely solicit your understanding and cooperation in the implementation of this plan, in order that the interests of all children may be better served.

> LITTLE ROCK BOARD OF EDUCATION
> William G. Cooper, Jr., President
> Mrs. A. E. McLean, Vice President
> Mrs. Edgar Dixon, Secretary
> Dr. Edwin N. Barron
> Foster A. Vineyard
> R. A. Lile

<u>Motion Carried Unanimously.</u>

There being no further business, the President declared the meeting adjourned.

> (Signed) W. G. Cooper Jr.
> President
> (Signed) Lucy A. Dixon
> Secretary

Attest: <u>JUN 30 1955</u>

DOCUMENT 12:

"The Southern Manifesto: Declaration of Constitutional Principles."

Congressional Record, *84th Congress, 2nd Session, March 12, 1956, 4460–61, 4515–16. Courtesy* Congressional Record.

This document, created in 1956, was signed by nineteen senators and seventy-seven congressmen from Alabama, Arkansas, Florida, Georgia, Louisiana, Mississippi, North Carolina, South Carolina, Tennessee, Texas, and Virginia. All the signers were Democrats, with the exception of Republicans Joel Broyhill and Richard Poff of Virginia. There were several notable southern politicians, such as senators Lyndon B. Johnson of Texas and Albert Gore Sr. and Estes Kefauver of Tennessee, who did not sign the document.

The unwarranted decision of the Supreme Court in the public school cases is now bearing the fruit always produced when men substitute naked power for established law.

The Founding Fathers gave us a Constitution of checks and balances because they realized the inescapable lesson of history that no man or group of men can be safely entrusted with unlimited power. They framed this Constitution with its provisions for change by amendment in order to secure the fundamentals of the government against the dangers of temporary popular passion or the personal predilections of public office holders.

We regard the decision of the Supreme Court in the school cases as a clear abuse of judicial power. It climaxes a trend in the Federal Judiciary undertaking to legislate, in derogation of the authority of Congress, and to encroach upon the reserved rights of the States and the people.

The original Constitution does not mention education. Neither does the 14th Amendment nor any other amendment. The debates preceding the submission of the 14th amendment clearly show that there was no intent that it should affect the system of education maintained by the States.

• • • •

In the case of *Plessy* v. *Ferguson* in 1896 the Supreme Court expressly declared that under the 14th amendment no person was denied any of his rights if the States provided separate but equal public facilities. This decision has been followed in many other cases. It is notable that the Supreme Court, speaking through Chief Justice Taft, a former President of the United States, unanimously declared in 1927 in *Lum* v. *Rice* that the "separate but equal" principle is "within the discretion of the State in regulating its public schools and does not conflict with the 14th amendment."

This interpretation, restated time and again, became a part of the life of the people of many of the states and confirmed their habits, customs, traditions, and way of life. It is founded on elemental humanity and common sense, for parents should not be deprived by Government of the rights to direct the lives and education of their own children. . . .

This unwarranted exercise of power by the Court, contrary to the Constitution, is creating chaos and confusion in the States principally affected. It is destroying the amicable relations between the white and Negro races that have been created through 90 years of patient effort by the good people of both races. It has planted hatred and suspicion where there has been heretofore friendship and understanding.

Without regard to the consent of the governed, outside agitators are threatening immediate and revolutionary changes in our public-school systems. If done, this is certain to destroy the system of public education in some of the states.

With the gravest concern for the explosive and dangerous condition created by this decision and inflamed by outside meddlers:

We reaffirm our reliance on the Constitution as the fundamental law of the land.

We decry the Supreme Court's encroachments on rights reserved to the States and to the people, contrary to established law, and to the Constitution.

We commend the motives of those States which have declared the intention to resist forced integration by any lawful means.

We appeal to the States and people who are not directly affected by these decisions to consider the constitutional principles involved against the time when they too, on issues vital to them, may be the victims of judicial encroachment.

Even though we constitute a minority in the present Congress, we have full faith that a majority of the American people believe in the dual system of government which has enabled us to achieve our greatness and will in time demand that the reserved rights of the States and of the people be made secure against judicial usurpation.

We pledge ourselves to use all lawful means to bring about a reversal of this decision which is contrary to the Constitution and to prevent the use of force in its implementation.

In this trying period, as we all seek to right this wrong, we appeal to our people not to be provoked by the agitators and troublemakers invading our States and to scrupulously refrain from disorder and lawless acts. . . .

DOCUMENT 13:
Resolution of Methodist Women's Society, March 22, 1956, *Southern School News*, April 1956, 8.

Established by a consortium of educators and journalists (including Harry Ashmore at the *Arkansas Gazette*), the Southern Education Reporting Service published *Southern School News* out of Nashville, Tennessee. The monthly publication began on September 1954, four months after the *Brown* decision, and targeted educators, journalists, and government leaders. It was in print from 1965 to 1969 as the *Southern Education Report*. In 1970 it changed its name again to the *Race Relations Reporter* and finally went out of circulation in 1974. The periodical reproduced newspaper articles, speeches, and other important primary documents related to the issue of school desegregation throughout the South. The following resolution suggests that some religious communities in Little Rock fully supported integration.

On March 22 at Malvern a resolution on integration was adopted at the annual meeting of the Women's Society of Christian Service of the Little Rock Methodist Conference. It read:

"We recommend to this body that it call upon the governor of our state to appoint a committee made up of Christian citizens of integrity of both races to study and make recommendations that would guide the people of our state in lessening racial tensions in many areas of our common life, including desegregation of the public schools."

DOCUMENT 14:
Capital Citizens' Council flyer, 1957,

Courtesy Special Collections, University of Arkansas Libraries, Virgil Blossom Papers, series 6, box 21, folder 1.

The Capital Citizens' Council (CCC) was founded in 1956 in Pulaski County to oppose desegregation and blended segregationist rhetoric with demands for states' rights. During the 1957 crisis, the council created a Freedom Fund to aid individuals arrested during events at Central High. The Mothers' League of Central High School, a women's group working to oppose the Blossom Plan, was an auxiliary of the council. The council's membership roles included approximately five hundred names by October 1957, only ten of them having children at Central High School. Amis Guthridge, an attorney who supported segregation, was one of the council's main spokespeople. The council's influence waned by September 1959, and it essentially dissolved in 1962. This flyer offers a perspective from the local and most outspoken segregationist groups in Little Rock on the eve of the crisis.

PEOPLE of ARKANSAS vs. RACE-MIXING!
OFFICIAL POLICY OF THE STATE OF ARKANSAS

"The People of Arkansas assert that the power to operate public schools in the State on a racially separate but substantially equal basis was granted by the people of Arkansas to the government of the State of Arkansas; and that, by ratification of the Fourteenth Amendment, neither the State of Arkansas nor its people delegated to the federal government, expressly or by implication, the power to regulate or control the operation of the domestic institutions of Arkansas; **any and all decisions of the federal courts or any other department of the federal government to the contrary notwithstanding.**"

WHOSE STATEMENT IS THE ABOVE?

It is the statement of Gov. Orval E. Faubus of Arkansas. It is the core of the Resolution of Interposition which he personally fathered. Governor Faubus hired the solicitors who circulated the petition to place this Resolution on the ballot. Governor Faubus filed Resolution and petitions with the Secretary of State on July 5, 1956, and the Resolution was submitted to the people in last November's general election. **THE PEOPLE OF ARKANSAS BY A TREMENDOUS, OVERWHELMING MAJORITY GAVE IT THEIR THUNDERING APPROVAL.**

Sponsored by the Governor of Arkansas, adopted by a tremendous majority of Arkansas voters, **THE ABOVE STATEMENT IS THE WILL OF THE PEOPLE OF ARKANSAS.**

WHAT WAS GOVERNOR FAUBUS' SOLEMN PLEDGE?

Here is the pledge he wrote into the same Resolution, the pledge to which We the People adhered overwhelmingly by our votes. "Therefore, the People of Arkansas, by Popular Vote: . . . . Pledge our firm intention to take all appropriate measures, honorably and legally available to us, to resist any and all illegal encroachments upon the powers reserved to the State of Arkansas to order and control its own domestic institutions according to its own exclusive judgment."

Could the stand of the people of Arkansas be made any plainer? The Governor asked us to support him in his stand with our votes. We did so, by a whopping majority.

Where Governor Faubus or his advisers got the above pledge we cannot say, but he could have taken it from the pledge of Citizens' Councils. The above pledge, **WHICH IS THE WILL OF THE PEOPLE OF ARKANSAS,** is exactly what every member of your Citizens' Council pledges himself to do. Members of Capital Citizens' Council stand by their pledge and demand that Gov. Orval E. Faubus stand by his. **HE ASKED THE PEOPLE TO JOIN HIM IN THIS PLEDGE AND THEY DID SO RESOUNDINGLY.** He has pledged his honor, his pledge has been accepted by the people, and he cannot find any acceptable excuse for backing down on the people of Arkansas now.

WHERE DOES THE GOVERNOR STAND?

Governor Faubus told us last year that if we support his segregation measures, no school district in Arkansas would be forced to race-mix against ist will. We gave him what he asked by huge majorities, and re-elected him Governor.

Now Little Rock, North Little Rock, Fort Smith, Van Buren and other places have been ordered by courts to race-mix or have been betrayed into a race-mixing policy by gerrymandered school boards, subservient to an integrationist school lobby, as was the case at Hoxie. The three largest cities in the state are headed for the same agonizing experience—or worse—that we have seen endured by Hoxie. **THE WILL OF THE PEOPLE HAS SPOKEN AGAINST THIS! WHEN WILL THE GOVERNOR SPEAK?**

As Governor He Can Exercise Our Sovereignty to Protect Our People

THE STATE SOVEREIGNTY COMMISSION AWAITS YOUR 3 APPOINTMENTS, GOVERNOR!

In the 1957 General Assembly a measure sponsored by the Governor created the State Sovereignty Commission to protect the people of Arkansas against encroachment of federal courts. The administration urged this measure as the best to meet the emergency, in place of other measures which the Association of Citizens' Council of Arkansas thought would be more effective.

The Governor's law was passed with the emergency clause and became effective February 26, 1957.

This Commission, created to meet an emergency, has never been activated because the Governor has not made the appointment of three Commissioners.

The people of Arkansas, Governor, the grass-roots people who voted overwhelmingly for your two segregation measures, want you to set aside your other activities until you get these three appointments attended to. They want good sound Arkansas citizens in these places.

AND THE PEOPLE WANT ACT 85 ENFORCED

Act 85 of the 1957 General Assembly, also sponsored by you, requires among other things that all race-mixing organizations register with the State Sovereignty Commission and report names of all their contributors. The act provides heavy penalties for violation. These reports are now due to be made under the law. The people want them made, promptly, or the penalties enforced.

PARENT! SUPPORT THE CITIZENS' COUNCIL!

A small clique of white and negro revolutionaries, supported by wealthy tax-exempt foundations, is trying to **FORCE RACE-MIXING** on the unwilling people of Arkansas—on **YOUR CHILDREN AND OURS.**

They are tightly organized, amply financed, and have been working at their brainwashing project for a long time.

To oppose them and disrupt their vile schemes by using every resource of publicity and of the law is the aim of all Citizens' Councils throughout Arkansas. We need the help and support of all good citizens everywhere in Arkansas!

All Arkansans must realize that if Little Rock, North Little Rock, Fort Smith, and other cities are lost today to the renegades and revolutionaries who would mongrelize the white race, other communities that now seem safe will be lost to the mongrelizers tomorrow.

The black plague of race-mixing will spread in our state like any disease.

Parents, help us to get the truth to every citizen of Arkansas! It is a giant task and must be done without any waste of time!

THE BLACK PLAGUE OF RACE-MIXING MUST BE STOPPED IN ARKANSAS! IT CAN BE STOPPED BY PERFECTLY LEGAL, CON-STITUTIONAL METHODS!

Mail whatever financial contribution you can afford to **CAPITAL CITI-ZENS' COUNCIL, P. O. Box 1977, Little Rock, Ark. Phone MO 6-7256.**

If you wish to join the Citizens' Council, ask for information. We will welcome your help.

HELP FIGHT THE GOOD FIGHT!
MAIL CONTRIBUTIONS NOW!

CAPITAL CITIZENS' COUNCIL
Meets Tuesday, July 16, 1957

Internationally Famous Minister, Editor, Radio Broadcaster
Will Be Principal Speaker

SUBJECT: "Must America Sell Her Birthright to Appease the
Internationalist and Communist?"

The Rev. J. A. Lovell of Dallas, Texas, founder and editor of the internationally circulated magazine Kingdom Digest, Pastor of the First Covenant Church in Dallas, will adress us.

For 27 years the Rev. Mr. Lovell has broadcast his own program over 60 radio stations in the United States. His work as editor and broadcaster has made him widely known throughout the world.

He is chaplain of the large Dallas, Texas, Citizens' Council.

Non-members can obtain guest cards from any member, or phone MO 6-7256.

PLACE: LaFayette Hotel   TIME: 8 P. M., Tuesday, July 16, 1957

Ad paid for by these officers of Capital Citizens' Council
Robert Ewing Brown   Theo A. Dillaha, Sr.   Will J. Smith

**We Need Your Financial, Moral, and Vocal Support NOW!
REMEMBER, SCHOOL OPENS SEPTEMBER 3rd**

Capital Citizens' Council, P. O. Box 1977, Little Rock, Ark.

Gentlemen: I enclose contribution of $_____ to help get your message to all the people.

Name_____ Address _____

City _____ State _____

❑ Check here if interested in learning more about the Citizens' Council, possibly becoming an active member. We will mail full information.

(All Arkansans living in places where there is now no Citizens' Council are eligible to join CAPITAL CITIZENS' COUNCIL, which represents the capital city of our State. Whenever a Citizens' Council is formed in your home town, you can transfer the membership to it.)

DOCUMENT 15:
Memo from E. Frederic Morrow to Governor Adams, July 12, 1957.

Courtesy Dwight D. Eisenhower Library.

A native of New Jersey, E. Frederic Morrow graduated from Rutgers University Law School and worked for the NAACP prior to serving in the army during World War II. Before becoming the first African American to serve in an executive position in the Eisenhower administration, he served as a writer for CBS and an advisor at the U.S. Commerce Department. This memo, marked confidential and sent to Governor Sherman Adams (Eisenhower's chief of staff), represents one of the few times Morrow weighed in on the question of civil rights in a formal manner. Regrettably, he was seldom consulted by the president. After leaving the White House, Morrow became the first African American vice president at Bank of America. In 1960, he published *Black Man in the White House*.

THE WHITE HOUSE
WASHINGTON
July 12, 1957

<u>CONFIDENTIAL</u>

MEMORANDUM FOR GOVERNOR ADAMS

This note is not intended to be presumptions, but informative.

Negro citizens are alarmed over reports that the Administration will "soften" the requirements of the bill on Civil Rights before Congress. The general feeling is that this is a very definite retreat from the Platform of the Administration and the attitude on Civil Rights it has maintained since California. Negroes are primarily concerned with and in Civil Rights legislation, so they would rather have no legislation at all than to have a watered-down version that would merely be giving lip service to democratic ideals.

The rapid manner in which the bill went through the House and the forthright way in which Senator Knowland got the bill before the Senate had the Administration and the Republican Party well on the way toward regaining the confidence and the votes of Negro voters in this country. However, in the last few days the talk of the Administration capitulation to the South has resulted in a complete turnabout in feeling and attitude by Negro leadership.

Any weakening of the Administration bill will make it very difficult for any speaker to appear before a Negro audience in this country in an appeal for support in 1958 or 1960. It is my personal feeling that up till now the Republicans have maintained a strong moral position that win, lose or draw would have resulted in a new strength and new admiration on the part of millions of American voters. As it stands now we are not only threatened with loss of this high moral position, but also with possible loss of legislation and thousands of potential voters.

(signed)
E. Frederic Morrow

DOCUMENT 16:
Editorial, "On Scholarship And Integration."

Southern Mediator, *July 26, 1957. Courtesy Special Collections, University of Arkansas Libraries, Virgil Blossom Papers, MC1364, box 21, folder 2.*

First published in 1938 in Little Rock by the Southern Mediator Publishing Company as the *Southern Mediator Journal* and called "the Southwest's progressive newspaper," this weekly black publication, which later became the *Southern Mediator,* enjoyed wide readership outside the state as well as in Arkansas. Briefly published in Jacksonville, Arkansas, it returned to Little Rock in December 1979, ceasing publication in January of 1984.

If Negro students who are slated to enter Little Rock and North Little Rock high schools this Fall compete successfully with the white students in an integrated school system, they must be above the average in scholarship attainment. That is why it is, in our opinion, highly important that we screen the students and select the caliber of students to start with who will measure up to certain scholarship qualifications for school integration this Fall.

First we believe the student should have a fair understanding of the English language. The student should have a working knowledge and be able to speak English as good or better than his classmates. With this kind of background in English, the student will, in all probability, be able to intelligently engage in conversations with the students and teachers and command the respect of all.

In the second place, we believe it is necessary for the student to have a good background in reading and writing. Unless the students read and spell well, they will never be able to interpret subject matter. To read and spell well is a mark of intelligence and it plays an important part in scholarly attainment.

In the third place, a student should have a good background in mathematics and science. The subject of mathematics and science is precise—in that you must be either right or wrong—you cannot filibuster. Mathematics and science help to develop the thinking faculties. It is important that Negro students will know how to think and think quickly during this intricate period of integration.

The above are qualifications which we believe Negro students should have when integration is started on the high school level here in Little Rock and North Little Rock this Fall. In our opinion, most of the citizens of Greater Little Rock will accept the program of integration because they will obey the Supreme Court of the United States regardless of their belief to the contrary.

If the citizens will work with the program which we have outlined above, it will, in all probability, help develop a peaceful and smooth transition of the public school system.

DOCUMENT 17:
Letter to Arkansas Pastors from Clyde Hart, Arkansas State Baptist Convention, August 20, 1957.

Courtesy Special Collections, University of Arkansas Libraries, Virgil Blossom Papers, MC 1364, box 6, folder 1.

Prior to the desegregation crisis, the Arkansas State Baptist Convention, seeking to deflect the question of integration, focused instead on promoting evangelism among blacks. O. L Bayless, chair of the Arkansas State Baptist Convention's State Mission Committee, appointed Clyde Hart in 1954 as director of Negro Work. Before 1957, several Baptist congregations attempted to develop ties with two African American Baptist groups in Arkansas. In contrast, the American Baptist Association, which represented more than three thousand churches in twenty-four states, passed a resolution declaring that integration was "ungodly and unlawful." Slowly and haltingly, and led by some progressive pastors and convention officials like Erwin McDonald, attitudes shifted, and by 1968 the majority of Arkansas Baptists accepted integration and supported the rule of law.

Arkansas Baptist State Convention
Offices of the Executive Board

B. L. Bridges,   Ralph Douglas,
Executive Secretary-Treasurer   Associate Secretary

Department of Missions
Clyde Hart
Director of Negro Work
209 Baptist Building

August 30, 1957

Dear Pastor Friend:

The next two weeks will be the most crucial period for the citizens of greater Little Rock and Arkansas. All Christians should be much in prayer for our school officials, teachers, students, and parents; that the spirit of Christ and peace might prevail during this school opening period.

Will you please give a moment, somewhere in your services Sunday, in special prayer, beseeching All Mighty God to help us find the right answer to racial problems. Pastors and church members can exercise a great stabilizing influence through the power of prayer.

Sincerely yours,
(signed)
Clyde Hart

DOCUMENT 18:
Excerpt of Interview with Orval Faubus, August 19, 1992,

Courtesy Special Collections, University of Arkansas Libraries, Sara Murphy Collection, MC1321, box 1, folder 19.

Sara Murphy was born in Tennessee in 1924, and in the early 1960s she founded the Panel of American Women in Arkansas to address religious prejudice in the wake of the integration crisis. She worked as an educational and management consultant. In the early 1990s, Murphy conducted numerous interviews with participants in the Little Rock crisis, including former Arkansas governor Orval

Faubus, while she was writing her book, *Breaking the Silence: Little Rock's Women's Emergency Committee to Open Our Schools, 1958–1963.* In this excerpted interview "sm" denotes Sara Murphy, while "of" stands for Orval Faubus. The Murphy Collection was donated to the University of Arkansas by her husband, Patrick C. Murphy, on July 26, 1995.

sm: Did you consider yourself a liberal growing up?

of: Yea, I considered myself a liberal. Very strongly one. I believed in some of the socialist doctrine, old age pensions, employment insurance, and Norman Thomas used to say Roosevelt stole his platform. My dad became a Roosevelt Democrat and he was strong for Kennedy. It was the biggest thing in his life when he met Kennedy, when he came to Greer's Ferry.

sm: Any blacks in Madison County?

of: Yeah, there was one what we call a colony. There's place called Wharton Creek, south of Huntsville, 5 or 6 mi. There was quite a group of black people lived there. For a time they had a school of their own. Then they began to move away to Ozark, Fayetteville, Fort Smith where there were more members of their own race. I remember I was friendly? with them. We got their poll taxes for them because they would vote Democratic. When I ran for county office. We have a two-party county now, strong. We didn't have but one Democratic office when I came home from the war. The elections, I've got the vote for one election back in 1912 in which every race for county office was decided by less than 100 votes. Except one, it was 106. That's how close they were and hotly contested between D and R. When you had some good candidates in the D group that helped a lot, R the same. There were two races, twice in my life, one when I was active, where there was an actual tie. A R candidate for sheriff beat D by 1 vote. Later I saw him, Ark. picnic, and he came by to see me. So many left as the timber industry went down the economy went down, businesses failed businesses failed because there weren't enough people any more. Didn't have enough money to support the bus. That's how it came about that Dad and his group were so strongly courted by the two parties. For along time there was a question as to what I was going to be D or R. The Andersons were D but as I grew older to make a political preference in the state, the D in the solid South so I thought it was rather futile to be a R, no matter how good a candidate you were or how well you performed, your influence would be strictly limited. So I consciously decided to be a D, it wasn't difficult because when Roosevelt came along that's the way I would have gone anyhow, if he'd been a R I would have been one, because I think he saved this nation. So when I decided, Dad started arguing with me, this Socialist stuff, some I agreed with, some I didn't. My mother spoke up and said, you leave him alone. He can be what he wants to. I never did forget that. I would have anyhow.

They were a group that morally and honestly and with integrity nobody had any hesitance in associating with them because everybody knew that. There weren't any criminals in the groups, any who didn't pay their taxes. By Some strong party R and D, they would have been classified as heretics by either, but the majority wasn't that way.

sm: Blacks . . . Northern towns would not allow blacks in town after dark.

of: I never knew of any intolerance there. Black people would come to town, one took the paper, and would come in and renew their subscriptions and I was would put their name in the paper, visitors, made a trip, like anyone else, then the leader moved away and others moved away too. But he'd come back every year for a visit, to see the old country. See the neighbors, come by the office, and I'd get info to put in paper and he'd subscribe again. I will never forget one thing that kind of amused me. That the R kind of got on them for voting D, said we freed you, but this black said yeah, but the D are feeding me now. That was in the Roosevelt area.

Down at Ozark one day, I was eating a Weidekers. The waiter said a man back in the kitchen said he knows you. I said bring him out. It was a black man who used to live on Whorton Creek. He came out and visiting with me. He said I've been bragging about the governor being from my home county.

sm: Tell me about Commonwealth.

of: Dad being a socialist, he was on the mailing list. It was a left wing institution but billed and advertised as a labor school, for people who sought to organize labor unions that work in the factories.

sm: Was it associated in any way with the Myles Horton thing in Tenn.?

of: Yeah. Friendly. Same view. Like a Scotsman hunting up another. Myles Horton came and spoke to classes there. Fine looking young man. Died recently.

The advertising was you could come there and work. It was actually communal living. They had barracks for the women students and for the men students, and separate places. Out from Mena four or five mil. west. At time I went down there, I had finished h.s., and I wanted to continue my education if I could. When I got there I found it had no accreditation with any other institution. I discovered it that it had organized the student body into three groups: communist, socialist and unaffiliated. And the groups seemed to me to be very nearly the same size. More in the unaffiliated, which I belonged because if you were a R or D you didn't belong to anything according to their standard.

I'd say largest group was from NYC. This was during the Depression, 1935. Roosevelt was in 3rd year in office, there were WPA, CCC, NYA workers. And I understand William E. Zeuch, who had been head of the college had been a member of Roosevelt's brain trust. And I learned that two contributors to the school were H.L. Mencken and Justice Vandyce. The school did not have any bad reputation in some circles. And if they had conducted themselves properly, they would not have. When they first located there, they had support from the community, business people. They'd be trading, buying food for all those people up there, taking NY Times, other East Coast papers, both LR papers, put on racks there every morning and they had a fairly well stocked library. I read two or three books by Upton Sinclair, I'd already read some. He was a powerful writer. I remember when he ran for gov. in Calif. He won overwhelmingly in the Dem. primary but was defeated in the election.

I was there 30 or 40 days. Semesters were 3 months. Jan. Feb. March, April, May, June. I was there in April and part of May. I didn't fail to profit some by being there. The communists were as dogmatic as any group of people I have ever seen. Their way was set in concrete and they would not compromise, they made disruptions in classes conducted by socialists or instructors who were not members of the party. I found that whatever philosophy they had was handed down by one man. If they got one with a new viewpoint, the whole change just had to come on down and everybody just had to switch over, no matter what. The thought and ideology was dictated from the top. That's completely contrary to freedom of speech, or anything like that. At that time refugees from Hitler's Germany were welcomed in this country with open arms and there was refugee from Germany there. He spoke broken English. He'd been a powerful leader in the Comm. Party in Germany, could order the workers into the street at anytime. He had great power and influence but when Hitler came to power he began to persecute those groups. This old German fled to America. I don't know what he was doing there. He might have been doing some useful work because we had a place to cook, a laundry, brought in the wood, the barn, farm animals, did the crops, so there was a lot to be done, but he lectured one day, and that was the straw that broke the camel's back, I learned that was part of the communist philosophy, he said: Marriage under capitalism is legalize prostitution. I thought about my mother, she was a country girl, she fell in love with my dad, she never had another sweetheart, she was 16 yr. old, I was born when she was 17, and she was as faithful a mother and wife as anyone would ever find. He was accusing my mother of being a prostitute. The theory was that under capitalism if a woman is married to a man she can't escape because of economics, which lent credence to the argument but it was too extreme. They were dogmatic as they could be. They would crucify someone who disagreed. There were two or three people there who were Trotskyites. It was unsafe for them, the Communists hated them so. They finally killed Trotsky, you know. There were some smart people there, smart as I ever encountered, teachers, professors, lawyers, and a lot of highly educated people, some very talented in music. A lady from Chicago who could play that piano, all the fine music there was, very often they'd have her give a concert. She enjoyed it and she was good. It was a strange mixture, the dogmatic attitude the Communists exercised, they finally gained control after I left there. And it fell apart.

sm: In that gubernatorial race, it was very unfair that Cherry dug that up. That incensed a lot of people.

of: It almost proved my undoing. McCarthyism was still rather prevalent. It had begun to lose some of its luster. Of course, there was the Comm. dictatorship in Russia, which people had learned the evils of the system, and I can understand had people had fear of anyone being elected to high office who sympathetic with or condoned or was a part of any scheme for? But I didn't deny being there. I never shall forget. The day I started speaking after the preferential [presidential?] primary and they were circulating in the crowd this paper put out by Johnny Wells an extreme right wing, and I recognized it and pointed out, that I was just as American as cornbread and black eyed peas on which I was raised, that there was nothing to it. Then we took off for Newport, it was a terribly hot day, and I went in a cafe to get a drink before going out to speak with some of my crew. My son was among them, then just 15 yr. old. I told him I know it's hot but always remember to get things set up before. They had. Cris Button came to the table, said Orval, we weren't going to mention this because it's being circulated by work of mouth but now that you have mentioned it in your speech, we have got to use it. I took a piece of paper and wrote: I was neither a student or faculty member at Commonwealth College. Some of them already knew the story very well. George Douthit said, Orval, if you deny it, they'll beat you to death with it. I said I'm not going to deny it. I was at Commonwealth College. But I can explain why I was there and when I left and why I left. This is all I want to say right now. So that is not for the record for the present time. So they thought they had me, to deny it. So Cherry went home and proved I was there. I answered it later on. But it shocked people. . . . I got back into the Marion Hotel late. The crowd was still around, they were still looking at me, nodding, shaking hands, but they turned away. I could see that I was isolated. Like I had leprosy. But I knew this, that I would have to face that, so I was not surprised, so I went on through the lobby and went upstairs and went to work. And I fulfilled some engagements that I had. And by a statewide radio hookup, where I would reply to the charges and I did that at the Pine Bluff speech which was the turning point in the campaign. After that I began to gain, people began to come back. My headquarters was as empty as the outside of an Eskimo's igloo in a blizzard. One young fellow, said I didn't understand it. But they came back. I knew if I made a case, I could regain them. What I did, the smartest thing I did, was that I consciously placed myself as an observer, observing me as the figure, detached from me just as much as I could make it and then knowing my attitude of fairness and most Amer. people, and I though, what would

I do, I would wait to see what the other man had to say. So I figured everybody was waiting to hear what I had to say and they were. So I figured if I could adequately explain the conditions of those times and pose to the people, would you remember the details of a certain night 20 years ago, and then I recited how come me to be there and the kind of school it was and what I learned about the Communists and why I left it and went back home. I didn't pay tuition.

sm: Then you weren't enrolled.

of: That's debatable. I was there as what might be considered a prospective student. Didn't complete any courses, didn't pay any tuition. Some say well, you were a student, you were a dropout. So that explained my first statement that I had made. Someone wrote a play there, there was a drama man there from LR, one fellow Merrill, from Oregon, he'd been kicked out of college for objecting to ROTC, he raised so much cain they kicked him out. Certain things they would perform in that drama they said, what we need here is a little military training.

sm: That was certainly an injection of McCarthyism. Turned it in your favor.

of: I'd rather been attacked physically, I'd rather somebody had shot at me with a pistol, that's what they were doing to me. That's what you have to face in public life.

CHAPTER 2

During the Crisis

The crisis over the desegregation of Central High School itself began on September 2, 1957, when Governor Orval Faubus announced on television the day before school was scheduled to begin that he planned to call out the Arkansas National Guard to prevent the black students from entering Central High School because of "evidence of disorder and threats of disorder." The actual crisis officially ended on September 25, when the nine black children were escorted to Central High with the protection of the U.S. Army. The events of those three weeks reverberated for months and years after. The documents in "During the Crisis" detail the events from multiple perspectives of both major and minor players.

Document 19: The Governor's Proclamation, September 2, 1957.

Claiming that he had consulted with numerous persons and groups, including Superintendent of Schools Virgil Blossom, and was convinced that violence and "blood in the streets" was likely if the Little Rock schools were integrated, Governor Faubus proclaimed a state of emergency and ordered the Arkansas National Guard to active duty in order to maintain the peace and protect the populace. In a televised speech delivered on the same day, he said that the schools must be operated as they have been in the past, or lives and property were at risk. The effect of the National Guard was not to prevent riot and mob rule, as they did little to restrain the crowd that gathered outside Central High and even later attempted to enter it. Instead, the troops prevented the nine students from entering Central High when they attempted to do so on September 3.

WHEREAS, The Governor of the State of Arkansas is vested with the authority to order to active duty the Militia of this State in case of tumult; riot or breach of the peace, or imminent danger thereof; and

WHEREAS, it has been made known to me, as Governor, from many sources, that there is imminent danger of tumult, riot and breach of the peace and the doing of violence to persons and property in Pulaski County, Arkansas;

NOW THEREFORE, I, Orval E. Faubus, Governor of the State of Arkansas do hereby proclaim that a state of emergency presently exists and I do hereby order to active duty Major General Sherman T. Clinger, the Adjutant General of Arkansas, the State Militia units consisting of the Base Detachment of Adams Field and the State Headquarters Detachment at Camp Robinson, and any other units which may be necessary to accomplish the mission of maintaining or restoring law and order and to preserve the peace, health, safety and security of the citizens of Pulaski County, Arkansas.

IN WITNESS WHEREOF, I have hereunto set my hand and caused the Great Seal of the State of Arkansas to be affixed. Done in office in the City of Little Rock this 2nd day of September, 1957.

DOCUMENT 20:
"What They're Saying About Little Rock: Press and Individuals React With Brickbats and Bouquets."

Arkansas Gazette, *September 5, 1957. Courtesy* Arkansas Democrat-Gazette.

This article, written early in the crisis, offers a survey of reactions around the nation. Harry Ashmore was the executive editor of the *Arkansas Gazette,* the city's main newspaper, and author of a series of Pulitzer prize–winning editorials during the 1957 crisis.

WASHINGTON, SEPT. 4—Senator Richard L. Neuberger (Dem. Ore.) telegraphed today to both Secretary of Defense Charles E. Wilson and Neil McElroy, who soon will succeed Wilson, calling for a review immediately of federal contributions to the Arkansas National Guard.

In a message, Neuberger asked "Is it either advisable from the standpoint of public policy or within the law for such contributions to continue if the Arkansas National Guard is to be an instrument used for avoidance of complying with an order of the federal District Court? This situation calls for a review at the highest level of the Defense Department. Trust you will undertake such action."

Defense Department records show that in the fiscal year which closed June 30, Uncle Sam contributed $3,320,700 in the Army Guard in Arkansas $2,288,220 to the Air Guard.

The acting chief of the National Guard Bureau of the Defense Department, Maj. Gen. Winston B. Wilson, had no comment on the use of National Guard by Governor Faubus.

The president of the National Guard Association of the United States, Maj. Gen. Ellard N. Walsh, retired, also said "no comment."

Newspapers Comment

Eastern newspapers are playing Little Rock as the top news event of the day.

The *New York Times,* in a personality sketch of Governor Faubus in its "Man in the News" column, said he "has always exhibited an almost painful desire for 'legitimacy,' that is, acceptance by the conservative element that opposed him almost to the man in his first campaign."

The *Washington Post* and *Times Herald* said editorially: "It would be tragic indeed if Governor Faubus had responded to a manufactured scare, to a threat of violence fabricated by lawless elements in no sense representative of the community. One wonders whether the governor did all he could do to promote and encourage observance of the law, whether, in this situation, order might not have been coupled with law for the maintenance of both."

The Washington *Evening Star* said in an editorial, "The reasonable inference [from events in Arkansas] is that the governor, despite his earlier disclaimer, intends to bring about a court test of his power to resist the court order. If so, he has embarked on a lost cause. For while the governor has a duty to use the Guard to maintain order, he has no duty to prevent Little Rock's school Board from carrying out its own plan of integration."

Griffin Applauds
From the Associated Press

Georgia's Governor Marvin Griffin commended use of troops to prevent integration of Little Rock's Central High School and said he would have done likewise.

"I would like to extend my encouragement and appreciation to the governor of the great state of Arkansas." Griffin said yesterday at his news conference.

In his formal comment on the Arkansas situation, Griffin added that "one of the guarantees of the Constitution of the United States is the right of the people to bear arms, and it has not been changed."

"The governor of Arkansas is the commander-in-chief of the military forces and preservator of the peace . . ." he said.

"Thus it becomes a matter of whose judgment will prevail—the governor of the state or one of many federal judges, particularly one sent to Arkansas from North Dakota."

"Governor Faubus is within his rights. I remember sitting at the Williamsburg (Virginia, governors') conference and hearing the president call on the governors for restoration of states' rights. This would be a good place for Mr. Eisenhower to make a beginning."

Griffin was then asked "Would you have taken the same action Governor Faubus did?"

"Yes sir," the Georgia governor snapped briskly.

Hailed by Citizens Council

The New Orleans Citizens Council sent Governor Faubus a telegram supporting his stand in the dispute.

The telegram said, in part:

"Should all chief executives in the Southern states take your courageous stand, there would never be any racial strife in the South.

"We urge you to stand firm and keep faith so that you may serve as an example for others to do likewise."

Segregationist Pleased

Circuit Judge Tom Brady, Mississippi segregationist, said at Brookhaven, Miss., Little Rock dispute might determine whether the states become "satellites of an all-powerful federal judiciary."

In a statement praising Governor Faubus for "acting courageously," the author of the pamphlet "Black Monday" said Mr. Faubus exercised "the police powers . . . granted to each state of the Union by the federal Constitution.

"It is not believed that even the present United States Supreme Court will presume to proclaim that its decrees supercede the sacred police powers vested in the state under our Constitution.

"If it does, however, then the fact is that the states as such have been destroyed and are now satellites of an all-powerful federal judiciary and the people of the South are its vassals."

Ike Urged to Intercede

At Washington, the political organization Americans for Democratic Action called on President Eisenhower to intercede with the governor, "and persuade him to desist from his course of forcing segregation at the point of rifles and carbines."

DOCUMENT 21:
Letter from Cardwell B. Smith to Virgil Blossom, September 5, 1957.

Courtesy Special Collections, University of Arkansas Libraries, Virgil Blossom Collection, MC1364, box 6, folder 9.

Cardwell Smith, a native of Arkansas living in California, was one of many individuals to write Virgil Blossom, the Little Rock school superintendent, during the crisis. Cardwell's letter reflected a typical response to the *Brown* decision, one that often conflated desegregation with a communist conspiracy.

1018 Quincy Street
Bakersfield, California

Mr. Virgil T. Blossom   September 6 '57
Superintendent of Schools
Little Rock, Arkansas

Dear sir:

"A house divided against itself shall surely fall." You are bringing division into the house, by your denunciation of the governor for the steps he is taking to uphold the rights of the states. According to the constitution of the United States, the government is not supposed to interfere with the affairs of state. That is impure interference void of constitutionality for the government to step in and tell the states how to run their own affairs.

Don't you respect the rights of your own color not to wish segregation to be shoved down the throats white people who do not want to see it take place. (I mean de-segregation)

Are you not aware that this integration trouble is the result of communist propaganda? It is surprising how many people there are who don't suspect it. As you know, the colored man has had equal rights and facilities for years, but such organizations NAACP and UNESCO, both communist inspired, stirred up the trouble. Is it possible you can't see these things? They are obvious. It's an axiom.

Some of the colored people are intelligent enough to see through this whole thing for what its worth. One Negro educator said that in NAACP, that word ADVANCEMENT could rightfully be changed to AGITATION of colored people.

I was brought up at Paris, Logan County, Ark., and I learn that the colored people there said they were satisfied with the way the school system had been originally, wished there had never been change. They are intelligent.

You aware, are you not, that our leader-appeasers said: "we must integrate the races for fear of criticism from Russia? If you didn't know it you should.

Like it or not; Russia and UNESCO and UN dictate terms to their own whims, and we dance to their music with the attitude of "As you desire, Mr. Kruschev."

(more follows)

Don't you know the Russians have no aim for good of anyone but themselves? They recently landed a jet plane here in our country to attend the UN, the organization of communist Russia, whose head is Mr. Kruschev.

They began their softening-up process in the early '20s, by infiltrating the Negro churches in the southern states, agitating all the time among them, telling them that the white people were imposing upon them and advising them to strike-for-freedom. Seeing they already had equal rights, they were urged not to be satisfied with equal rights, they agitated to them they must take the white man's churches, and throw themselves in the midst of all the affairs of the white man, and ask them quarter in nothing.

I am not necessarily a "Nigger Hater," but I do believe in their staying in their own place. I have had experience with them here in California, to the effect that if you give them an inch they will take an ell. I will cite an example: I worked on the ship yard during II world war. I could be going ahead to do what I was told to do by the foremen, and all-of-a-sudden out of no where some nigger would come tell me there was no use of doing a thing this way or that way and so forth. Needless to say, I never bother anyone whether he is white or black. This is just an example of what a nigger will do when he has an opportunity, and is not restricted.

Back to Russian: They began their exterior softening up process when they began to shoot down our planes. If I re-call correctly, they have shot down around 24 of our planes without provocation, only to get a mild protest. If McArthur had been let alone, and if General Wedemeyer had been listened to, we would not be on the brink of disaster as we find ourselves today. The interior softening up process of Russia is infiltration of our public institutions. The are ruining our schools, teaching that there is no such thing as God, and that man is God, etc.

Instead of the blast you slung at the honorable governor, you should pat him on back, and support him to the limit.

Do you agree, or disagree when I tell you that Russia is dictating terms, and we are carrying out his orders? Yea or nay, that's just what's transpiring. Please wake up.

Very truly yours,
(signed) Cardwell B. Smith

DOCUMENT 22:
Photograph, Integrated Classroom at Anacostia High School, Washington, D.C., September 10, 1957.

Courtesy Library of Congress.

Opening in 1935 as Anacostia Junior/Senior High, the school was converted to a high school in 1943. Shortly after the *Brown* decision, Anacostia, along with all other District of Columbia Schools, opened on September 13, 1954, on a desegregated basis. A few months after integration, serious district-wide conflict arose among the black and white students, resulting in fights and petty theft. Wide disparities in white and black achievement were recorded and racial tension erupted at a district football game in 1962. Racial tension continues to define the schools today.

DOCUMENT 23:
Cartoon, "Right Into Their Hands."

Oakland Tribune, *September 11, 1957. Courtesy* Oakland Tribune.

The *Oakland Tribune,* a daily newspaper founded by George Staniford and Benet A. Dewes in 1874, printed this editorial cartoon criticizing Faubus for providing the communists with a powerful weapon for propaganda. The cartoon summarizes Eisenhower's position in the Little Rock crisis.

Document 24: Editorial, "Tale of Two Cities."

New York Times, *September 14, 1957. Courtesy* New York Times.

Throughout the Little Rock crisis, the *New York Times* attempted to put the events into a broad comparative perspective. In this editorial, Little Rock is compared to the school district in Nashville, Tennessee, which enjoyed clear leadership from the city's mayor, Ben West, who served from 1951 to 1963. Nashville was one of the first cities in the South to desegregate public facilities.

The contrast between the way the school-desegregation issue has been handled this week in Nashville, where there was violence, and in Little Rock, where there was none, reflects as much credit on the Tennessee authorities as it reflects discredit on Governor Faubus of Arkansas.

While the latter was inviting trouble by calling out the National Guard in effect to prevent execution of Federal Law, the responsible officials in Nashville were moving in exactly the opposite direction. Up against the actual bombing of a school building and the invasion of their city by a rabble-rousing racist, the Mayor and the Board of Education took rapid and decisive action on their own initiative to enforce the law. They obtained a Federal court injunction against any attempts to disrupt the "free operations of the schools of the City of Nashville" or to intimidate either children or parents. "We intend to see that no one interferes with the education of our children," said Nashville's determined Mayor, Ben West; and Nashville's schools remained operating under the gradual integration plan that had long been agreed upon.

Meanwhile, Frederick John Kasper, the agitator from Camden, N.J., who had been arrested on vagrancy and other charges was told by a Nashville municipal judge in scathing words that all decent people in the South and throughout the country will applaud: "You are the worst possible vagrant. You have come here to cause trouble. If any blood is shed on the streets of Nashville it will be you and your kind that are responsible here. . . . We hope we may never see you or your likes again."

No one could hope or pretend that integration—even integration on so gradual a scale as that planned in Nashville and in Little Rock—would come easy for the communities of the Upper South, not to mention those of the Deep South. Altering the mores of a people is not a simple thing to do. But the great bulk of the responsible citizens of such states as Arkansas and Tennessee recognize the inevitability of the coming change; and surely only the smallest minority of them is willing to resist to the bitter end. We think Mayor West's statement that "every decent citizen abhors violence; every decent citizen wants peace and good order" clearly represents the prevailing point of view of the people of his section of the country.

The moderate leaders of the South, the ones who want to make this transition period as painless and as peaceful as possible, the ones who are trying to build up decent race relations instead of tearing them down— these are the people who need and deserve every encouragement.

They need it from all of us. And they need it most of all from the President of the United States, who before or after his meeting with Governor Faubus today would do well publicly to proclaim his support of those many sensible citizens of Arkansas who unlike their Governor refuse to panic at the thought of a handful of Negro boys and girls entering a high school that had previously been all white.

DOCUMENT 25:
Editorial, Jane Emery, "Can You Meet the Challenge?"

The Tiger, *September 19, 1957. Courtesy* The Tiger.

Jane Emery, whose family was originally from Kansas, edited Central High School's newspaper, and her editorial written during the crisis encouraged her peers to "keep an open mind" and understand that their behavior during the crisis would be scrutinized. She eventually completed her PhD in sociology at the University of California, Berkeley, and became a professor at California State University, Northridge.

You are being watched! Today the world is watching you, the students of Central High. They want to know what your reactions, behavior, and impulses will be concerning a matter now before us. After all, as we see it, it settles now to a matter of interpretation of law and order.

Will you be stubborn, obstinate, or refuse to listen to both sides of the question? Will your knowledge of science help you determine your action or will you let customs, superstition, or tradition determine the decision for you?

This is the chance that the youth of America has been waiting for. Through an open mind, broad outlook, wise thinking, and a careful choice you can prove that America's youth has not "gone to the dogs" that their moral, spiritual, and educational standards are not being lowered. This is the opportunity for you as citizens of Arkansas and students of Little Rock Central High to show the world that Arkansas is a progressive thriving state of wide-awake alert people. It is a state that is rapidly growing and improving its social, health, and educational facilities. That it is a state with friendly, happy, and conscientious citizens who love and cherish their freedom.

It has been said that life is just a chain of problems. If this is true, then this experience in making up your own mind and determining right from wrong will be of great value to you in life.

The challenge is yours, as future adults of America, to prove your maturity, intelligence, and ability to make decisions by how your react, behave, and conduct yourself in this controversial question. What is your answer to this challenge?

DOCUMENT 26:
FBI Interviews, 1957,

Courtesy Special Collections, University of Arkansas Libraries, Sarah A. Murphy Papers, box 9, folder 5.

Federal Bureau of Investigation (FBI) field agents in Little Rock conducted numerous interviews during the crisis and offered perspectives on those involved or witness to the desegregation efforts. According to Elizabeth Huckaby, the role of the FBI was to observe events, investigate letters sent through the U.S. Postal System that were obscene or threatening, and investigate threats to persons, such as a rock thrown through the window of a Central High teacher's room. Daisy Bates remarked that, although the FBI interviewed literally hundreds of persons and observed, firsthand or via photographs, countless acts of violence, no action was taken against any person by either state officials or the Justice Department.

FEDERAL BUREAU OF INVESTIGATION
INTERVIEW REPORT

Little Rock Police Officer THOMAS OWEN, home address 3205 Kathryn, Little Rock, Arkansas, advised on Central High School on September 23, 1957, and that based on his observations of the crowd assembled at the school who were not students, that he considered Mrs. THOMASON of the Central High School Mothers' League as an agitator. He stated that she was constantly attempting to incite the mob to prevent integration. He stated that he observed Mrs. THOMASON attempting to break through the police line where he was stationed and that she was extremely vehement and hysterical in making her protest against the police having a line around the High School to prevent the entrance of unauthorized persons.

Interview with <u>Officer THOMAS OWEN</u>   File # <u>LR 44-341</u>
on <u>9/24/57</u> at <u>Little Rock, Arkansas</u>
by Special Agents <u>JOHN C. WELCH and WILLIAM FITZPATRICK</u>

FEDERAL BUREAU OF INVESTIGATION
INTERVIEW REPORT

Mr. RAY NEAL MOSLEY, a reporter for the Arkansas Gazette, who resides at 1423 West 3rd Street, Little Rock, Arkansas, was interviewed on September 23, 1957, by SAs MILFORD C. RUNNELS and NORMAN L. CASEY, at which time he stated he is of the opinion and would consider MRS. CLYDE THOMASON a leader in the violence and mob action at Central High School, Little Rock, Arkansas, on September 23, 1957. He stated that MRS. THOMASON was crying and trying to force herself through the police line at Central High School on September 23, 1957. She also tried to go through the police line to get her daughter out of the school building. She also made a public display of contributing money to a policeman who quit his job while on duty.

Interview with <u>RAY NEAL MOSLEY</u>   File # <u>LR 44-341</u>
on <u>9/23/57</u> at <u>Little Rock, Arkansas</u>
by Special Agents <u>NORMAN L. CASEY and MILFORD C. RUNNELS</u>

FEDERAL BUREAU OF INVESTIGATION
INTERVIEW REPORT

RODERICK MacLEISH, Chief of the Washington News Bureau, Westinghouse Broadcasting Company, Washington D.C., on September 26, 1957, advised that he is presently residing at 600 Marion Hotel, Little Rock, Arkansas. He advised that on Monday morning, September 23, 1957, he was at the Central High School in Little Rock at about 6:40 a.m. He observed that at that time there were approximately thirty people present in front of the school, but that during the next thirty minutes the crowd increased to approximately 400.

MacLEISH advised that Mrs. CLYDE THOMASON of the Mothers' League was prominently active in the crowd on September 23, 1957. He stated she shouted at the crowd and made statements of the effect, "Where's your manhood, why don't you do something to get these people," etc. He advised that on Monday, September 23, 1957, he also noticed a man whom he believed to be Mr. CLDYE THOMASON, husband of Mrs. THOMASON, but he just stood around giving ugly looks to reporters. MacLEISH stated that Mrs. THOMAS was seen by him in the crowd at the high school at 14th and Park Streets about 7:10 a.m. on Monday 23. He heard her talking to a group of news reporters and she said, "You ought to be up in Maryland instead of smearing the South. It will happen here. (MacLEISH stated that she was referring here to integration.) They have treated us terrible with all this publicity that'll ruin our homes and school system if they integrate. It will ruin Little Rock." MacLEISH stated someone asked her if there would be violence, and she replied that she hoped and prayed there would be none.

Interview with <u>RODERICK MacLEISH</u>   File # <u>LR 44-341</u>
on <u>9/26/57</u> at <u>Little Rock, Arkansas</u>
by Special Agents <u>ROY M. OSBORN and JAMES L. PUGH</u>

FEDERAL BUREAU OF INVESTIGATION
INTERVIEW REPORT

On September 24, 1957, PHYLLIS DILLAHA, 2510 Bishop, Little Rock, Arkansas, employed as reporter, "Arkansas Democrat," was interviewed by SAs JAMES W. BOOKHOUT and JOE B. ABERNATHY. Mrs.

DILLAHA advised that she was a recent college graduate, and on the morning of September 23, 1957, she dressed as a high school student and milled around with the crowd in the vicinity of Central High School. She stated she did not actually see any acts of violence, and did not know the identity of anyone committing an act of violence or causing anyone else to commit such an act. She further advised that she took no pictures on this occasion. Mrs. DILLAHA advised that the only individual she recognized at the high school was a Mrs. CLYDE THOMASON who was head of the Central High League of Mothers. She added that Mrs. THOMASON was in a hysterical condition, but she did not observe her commit any act of violence.

Interview with <u>PHYLLIS DILLAHA</u>   File # <u>LR 44-341</u>
on <u>9/24/57</u> at <u>Little Rock, Arkansas</u>
by Special Agents <u>JAMES W. BOOKHOUT and JOE B. ABERNATHY</u>

FEDERAL BUREAU OF INVESTIGATION
INTERVIEW REPORT

Mr. ROBERT E. BAKER was contacted at the Arkansas Gazette office, 123 Third Street, Little Rock, Arkansas. BAKER immediately identified a picture of Mrs. CLYDE THOMASON taken from the Arkansas Gazette, September 24, 1957, issue Page 1B, as the woman he had observed at Central High School, Little Rock, Arkansas, on September 23, 1957. He also advised that Mrs. THOMASON is the same woman that he referred to in his article appearing in the Washington Post and Times Herald in Washington, D.C., datelined Little Rock, Arkansas, September 23, entitled "Mob Had Job and Leaders Saw It Done." In this article, BAKER stated that her referred to Mrs. THOMASON as, "One member of the Mother's League of Central High School, a segregationist group formed recently, began shouting hysterically to the police: 'They've got the doors locked. They won't let the white kids out. My daughter's in there with those niggers. Oh, my God. Oh, God.'"

Interview with <u>ROBERT E. BAKER, reporter Washington Post and Times Herald</u>
                                        File # <u>LR 44-341</u>
on <u>9/26/57</u> at <u>123 Third Street, Little Rock, Arkansas</u>
by Special Agents <u>JOHN J. FEEHELEY & JAMES J. ROGERS</u>

FEDERAL BUREAU OF INVESTIGATION
INTERVIEW REPORT

Mr. JERRY FRANKLIN DHONAU, reporter for the Arkansas Gazette, was interviewed on September 27, 1957. He was asked concerning an article written by him in the Arkansas Gazette, issue of September 24, 1957, particularly concerning Mrs. CLDYE THOMASON. He stated that Mrs. THOMASON is Recording Secretary of the League of High School Mothers. He stated that, according to notes he made by him on September 23, 1957, he had first seen Mrs. THOMASON at the corner of 14th and Park Avenue in Little Rock at approximately 6:52 AM.

He stated, according to his notes, he saw her later at the corner of 16th and Park at approximately 7:20 AM. He advised when he first saw her on 14th Street there was a woman with her whose identity he did not know. When he saw her on 16th there were several women with her. It was his recollection she spent most of the morning at 16th and Park. He stated that he recalled she was still in the crowd at the time the four Negro newspapermen were attacked by people in this crowd. He advised that he recalled her talking a great deal but he could not remember any specific statements made by her.

Interview with <u>JERRY FRANKLIN DHONAU</u>   File # <u>LR 44-341</u>
on <u>9/27/57</u> at <u>123 Third Street, Little Rock, Arkansas</u>
by Special Agents <u>FRANCIS FINLEY and WILLIAM H. LAWRENCE.</u>

FEDERAL BUREAU OF INVESTIGATION
INTERVIEW REPORT

CHRIS BUTTON, Chief Photographer, KARK TV Station, Channel 4, Tenth and Spring Streets, Little Rock, Arkansas, advised SA's FRANCIS FINLEY and GILBERT W. STRICKLAND he first heard of the Mothers League of Central High School on the morning after the night that Governor MARVIN GRIFFIN of Georgia made a speech at the Marion Hotel. He said he understood, but was not present when it was announced that night that a Mrs. (FNU) AARON was President of the Mothers League. He said he understood they were holding a meeting on the next night following the night GRIFFIN made the speech at the

Sky Room, Lafayette Hotel, and he went to this meeting for the purpose of taking newsreel pictures. He said he met LOUIS OBERSTE, photographer for KATV Television Studio, Channel 7, and OBERSTE advised him he did not think news representatives were going to be admitted to the meeting but stated he shot some film and when Mrs. AARON stood up and announce that the press and representatives of magazines would be excluded, he left.

BUTTON stated he never attended any meetings nor did he know before Governor GRIFFIN's speech about the organization of any mothers league. He said he has no knowledge whether this League was organized spontaneously on the night of GRIFFIN's speech or was organized beforehand and kept quiet until that night.

He said he believed on Sunday, September 1, 1957 or thereabouts, he heard someone say something about impending violence in connection with the integration of the schools. He said he did not recall who or where this was said. He said the statement he recalled hearing was something to the effect, "That will take care of them," meaning someone would take care of the Negroes trying to get into the schools. He said he has no way of recalling where he heard this.

BUTTON stated he did not do any checking regarding the sales of knives and guns.

Interview with <u>CHRIS BUTTON</u>   File # <u>LR 44-341</u>
on <u>9/7/57</u> at <u>Little Rock, Arkansas</u>
by Special Agents <u>FRANCIS FINLEY and GILBERT W. STRICKLAND</u>

DOCUMENT 27:
Cartoon, "Evidence of Disorder, Threats of Disorder: You Sure of What You See out There, Governor?"

Arkansas Gazette, *September 24, 1957. Courtesy* Arkansas Gazette.

This political cartoon, printed after the Little Rock Nine were removed from school the day before in the face of white protest, parodies Governor Orval Faubus's claim that the Arkansas National Guard was called to Central High to preserve law and order. Maryland Governor Theodore Roosevelt McKeldin accused

Governor Faubus of provoking the crowds: "Governor Faubus wrote the book, set the stage, and directed the play for today's unhappy occurrences in Arkansas."

"YOU SURE OF WHAT YOU SEE OUT THERE, GOVERNOR?"

DOCUMENT 28:
Dwight D. Eisenhower, Executive Order 10730, September 24, 1957.

Courtesy Dwight D. Eisenhower Library.

After the Little Rock Nine were removed from school on September 23, 1997, Congressman Brooks Hays and Little Rock Mayor Woodrow Mann asked President Eisenhower for assistance. Though concerned that the presence of federal troops would exacerbate the situation, Eisenhower finally agreed to issue Executive Order 10730, which placed the Arkansas National Guard under federal control and sent paratroopers from the 101st Airborne Division to assist them in restoring order in Little Rock. This order, directed at Orval Faubus, provided assistance for the removal of an obstruction of justice in Arkansas.

Whereas on Sept. 23, 1957, I issued Proclamation No.3204 reading in part as follows:

"Whereas certain persons in the state of Arkansas, Individually and in unlawful assemblages, combinations, and conspiracies, have wilfully obstructed the enforcement of orders of the United States District Court for the Eastern District of Arkansas with respect to matters relating to enrollment and attendance at public schools, particularly at Central High School, located in Little Rock school district, Little Rock, Arkansas: and

"Whereas such wilful obstruction of justice hinders the execution of the laws of that state and of the United States, and makes it impracticable to enforce such laws by the ordinary course of judicial proceedings; and

"Whereas such obstruction of justice constitutes a denial of the equal protection of the laws secured by the Constitution of the United States and impedes the course of justice under those laws;

"Now, therefore, I, Dwight D. Eisenhower, President of the United States, under and by virtue of the authority vested in me by the Constitution and Statutes of the United States, including Chapter 15 of Title 10 of the United States Code, particularly sections 332, 333 and 334 thereof, do command all persons engaged in such obstruction of justice to cease and desist therefrom, and to disperse forthwith"; and

Whereas the command contained in that Proclamation has not been obeyed and willful obstruction of enforcement of said court orders still exists and threatens to continue:

Now, therefore, by virtue of the authority vested in me by the Constitution and Statutes of the United States, including Chapter 15 of Title 10, particularly sections 332, 333 and 334 thereof, and section 301 of Title 3 of the United States Code, It is hereby ordered as follows:

SECTION 1. I hereby authorize and direct the Secretary of Defense to order into the active military service of the United States as he may deem appropriate to carry out the purposes of this order, any or all of the units of the National Guard of the United States and of the Air National Guard of the United States within the State of Arkansas to serve in the active military service of the United States for an indefinite period and until relieved by appropriate orders.

SECTION 2. The Secretary of Defense is authorized and directed to take all appropriate steps to enforce any orders of the United States District Court for the Eastern District of Arkansas for the removal of obstruction of justice in the state of Arkansas with respect to matters relating to enrollment and attendance at public schools in the Little Rock School District, Little Rock, Arkansas. To carry out the provisions of this section, the Secretary of Defense is authorized to use the units, and members thereof, ordered into the active military service of the United States pursuant to Section 1 of this Order.

SECTION 3. In furtherance of the enforcement of the aforementioned orders of the United States District Court for the Eastern District of Arkansas, the Secretary of Defense is authorized to use such of the armed forces of the United States as he may deem necessary.

SECTION 4. The Secretary of Defense is authorized to delegate to the Secretary of the Army or the Secretary of the Air Force, or both, any of the authority conferred upon him by this order.

DWIGHT D. EISENHOWER

Document 29: Dwight D. Eisenhower, "The Federal Court Orders Must Be Upheld," September 24, 1957.

Courtesy Dwight D. Eisenhower Library.

The evening that President Eisenhower issued Executive Order 10730, federalizing the Arkansas National Guard and authorizing the presence of the 101st Airborne, Eisenhower also delivered a televised address to explain his position to the American people. He argued that Faubus's defiance of the Supreme Court undermined respect for the very nation's foundation, which is reflected in respect for the law. The speech was broadcast over radio and television networks.

My Fellow Citizens . . . I must to speak to you about the serious situation that has arisen in Little Rock. . . . In that city, under the leadership of demagogic extremists, disorderly mobs have deliberately prevented the carrying out of proper orders from a federal court. Local authorities have not eliminated that violent opposition and, under the law, I yesterday issued a proclamation calling upon the mob to disperse.

This morning the mob again gathered in front of the Central High School of Little Rock, obviously for the purpose of again preventing the carrying out of the Court's order relating to the admission of Negro children to that school.

Whenever normal agencies prove inadequate to the task and it becomes necessary for the executive branch of the federal government to use its powers and authority to uphold federal courts, the President's responsibility is inescapable.

In accordance with that responsibility, I have today issued an Executive Order directing the use of troops under federal authority to aid in the execution of federal law at Little Rock, Arkansas. This became necessary when my Proclamation of yesterday was not observed, and the obstruction of justice still continues.

It is important that the reasons for my action be understood by all our citizens.

As you know, the Supreme Court of the United States has decided that separate public educational facilities for the races are inherently unequal and therefore compulsory school segregation laws are unconstitutional. . . .

During the past several years, many communities in our southern states have instituted public school plans for gradual progress in the enrollment and attendance of school children of all races in order to bring themselves into compliance with the law of the land.

They thus demonstrated to the world that we are a nation in which laws, not men, are supreme.

I regret to say that this truth—the cornerstone of our liberties—was not observed in this instance. . . .

Here is the sequence of events in the development of the Little Rock school case.

In May of 1955, the Little Rock School Board approved a moderate plan for the gradual desegregation of the public schools in that city. It provided that a start toward integration would be made at the present term in the high school, and that the plan would be in full operation by 1963. . . . Now this Little Rock plan was challenged in the courts by some who believed that the period of time as proposed in the plan was too long.

The United States Court at Little Rock, which has supervisory responsibility under the law for the plan of desegregation in the public schools, dismissed the challenge, thus approving a gradual rather than an abrupt change from the existing system. The court found that the school board had acted in good faith in planning for a public school system free from racial discrimination.

Since that time, the court has on three separate occasions issued orders directing that the plan be carried out. All persons were instructed to refrain from interfering with the efforts of the school board to comply with the law.

Proper and sensible observance of the law then demanded the respectful obedience which the nation has a right to expect from all its people. This, unfortunately, has not been the case at Little Rock. Certain misguided persons, many of them imported into Little Rock by agitators, have insisted upon defying the law and have sought to bring it into disrepute. The orders of the court have thus been frustrated.

The very basis of our individual rights and freedoms rests upon the certainty that the President and the Executive Branch of Government will support and insure the carrying out of the decisions of the federal courts, even, when necessary with all the means at the President's command. . . .

Mob rule cannot be allowed to override the decisions of our courts.

Now, let me make it very clear that federal troops are not being used to relieve local and state authorities of their primary duty to preserve the peace and order of the community. . . .

The proper use of the powers of the Executive Branch to enforce the orders of a federal court is limited to extraordinary and compelling circumstances. Manifestly, such an extreme situation has been created in Little Rock. This challenge must be met and with such measures as will preserve to the people as a whole their lawfully protected rights in a climate permitting their free and fair exercise.

The overwhelming majority of our people in every section of the country are united in their respect for observance of the law—even in those cases where they may disagree with that law. . . .

A foundation of our American way of life is our national respect for law.

In the South, as elsewhere, citizens are keenly aware of the tremendous disservice that has been done to the people of Arkansas in the eyes of the nation, and that has been done to the nation in the eyes of the world.

At a time when we face grave situations abroad because of the hatred that communism bears toward a system of government based on human rights, it would be difficult to exaggerate the harm that is being done to the prestige and influence, and indeed to the safety, of our nation and the world.

Our enemies are gloating over this incident and using it everywhere to misrepresent our whole nation. We are portrayed as a violator of those standards of conduct which the peoples of the world united to proclaim in the Charter of the United Nations. There they affirmed "faith in fundamental human rights" and "in dignity and worth of the human person" and they did so "without distinction as to race, sex, language or religion."

And so, with deep confidence, I call upon the citizens of the State of Arkansas to assist in bringing to an immediate end all interference with the law and its processes. If resistance to the federal court orders ceases at once, the further presence of federal troops will be unnecessary and the City of Little Rock will return to its normal habits of peace and order and a blot upon the fair name and high honor of our nation in the world will be removed.

Thus will be restored the image of America and of all its parts as one nation, indivisible, with liberty and justice for all.

—Eisenhower's Address on Little Rock, 1957

DOCUMENT 30:
Petition, September 1957.

Courtesy Special Collections, University of Arkansas Libraries,
Virgil Blossom Papers, MC1364, box 4, folder 16.

In the midst of the crisis, a group of Little Rock citizens opposed
to the Blossom Plan for integrating the city's high schools issued
a petition to remove Jess W. Matthews, principal at Central High
School. The petition had little effect, but Matthews was again targeted on May 5, 1959, when members of the school board who
opposed integration attempted to fire forty-four administrators
and teachers. He again survived the purge and stayed at Central,
having served as principal from 1946 until his retirement in 1965.
In 1969, a library was added to the campus and named in his honor.

WHEREAS, Mr. Jess Matthews, principal of Little Rock Central High
School, has surrendered completely to the Virgil Blossom forces and is
working diligently, and with heart and soul to force the will of the NAACP
on the white people of Little Rock in keeping negroes in Little Rock
Central High School; and because his sympathies are so obviously on the
side of the negroes, as evidenced by the following facts:

1. The tight censorship of news clamped on what is happening at
   our tax supported Central High School where our children are
   being educated.

2. His misrepresentative of facts in trying to make it appear that all
   is proceeding beautifully and gloriously under the Blossom plan
   of integration when the fact is that the school and city is
   seething in unrest.

3. In the recent fight between Hugh Williams and Jefferson
   Thomas, Mr. Matthews exonerated the negro and suspended
   the white boy.

4. While scores of white students have been suspended, expelled
   or otherwise disciplined, not one negro student has been disciplined or suspended.

5. Recently a negro girl student assaulted, scratched and clawed a

white girl, making it necessary that the white girl go to the hospital. Mr. Matthews said the negro girl did it accidentally.

We, the undersigned, feel that Mr. Jess Matthews should be discharged and replaced with a person whose sentiments are in harmony with the southern white people whose money supports the Little Rock school system.

DOCUMENT 31:

Telegram from Parents of the Little Rock Nine to Dwight D. Eisenhower, "We the Parents," September 30, 1957.

Courtesy Dwight D. Eisenhower Library.

This telegram, praising President Eisenhower's decision to send federal troops into the city, reflects the parents' collective response to the growing violence. Finally, on October 24, the Little Rock Nine entered the school for the first time through the front door without the troops. The arrival of the troops brought much needed relief to the parents and the children. Minniejean Brown commented, when the 101st airborne troops showed up to take the nine students to school on the morning of September 25, "For the first time in my life, I feel like an American citizen."

LITTLE ROCK ARK SEP 30 1957
THE PRESIDENT
THE WHITE HOUSE

WE THE PARENTS OF NINE NEGRO CHILDREN ENROLLED AT LITTLE ROCK CENTRAL HIGH SCHOOL WANT YOU TO KNOW THAT YOUR ACTION IN SAFE GUARDING THEIR RIGHTS HAVE STRENGTHENED OUR FAITH IN DEMOCRACY STOP NOW AS NEVER BEFORE WE HAVE AN ABIDING FEELING OF BELONGING AND PURPOSEFULNESS STOP WE BELIEVE THAT FREEDOM AND EQUALITY WITH WHICH ALL MEN ARE ENDOWED AT BIRTH CAN BE MAINTAINED ONLY THROUGH FREEDOM AND EQUALITY OF OPPORTUNITY FOR SELF DEVELOPMENT GROWTH AND PURPOSEFUL CITIZENSHIP STOP WE BELIEVE THAT THE DEGREE TO WHICH PEOPLE EVERYWHERE REALIZE AND ACCEPT THIS CONCEPT WILL DETERMINE IN A LARGE MEASURE AMERICAS TRUE GROWTH AND TRUE GREATNESS STOP

YOU HAVE DEMONSTRATED ADMIRABLY TO US THE NATION AND THE WORLD HOW PROFOUNDLY YOU BELIEVE IN THIS CONCEPT STOP FOR THIS WE ARE DEEPLY GRATEFUL AND RESPECTFULLY EXTEND TO YOU OUR HEARTFELT AND LASTING THANKS STOP MAY THE ALMIGHTY AND ALL WISE FATHER OF US ALL BLESS GUIDE AND KEEP YOU ALWASY

OSCAR ECKFORD JR 4405 WEST 18TH LOTHAIRE S GREEN 1224 WEST 21ST ST JUANITA WALLS 1500 VALENTINE W B BROWN 1117 RINGO LOUIS M PATILLO 1121 CROSS H C RAY 2111 CROSS ELLIS THOMAS 1214 WEST 20TH W L ROBERTS 2301 HOWARD H L MOTHERSHED 1313 CHESTER.

DOCUMENT 32:
"What for South?"

New York Times, *September 29, 1957. Courtesy* New York Times.

The *New York Times,* founded in 1851 by Henry Jarvis Raymond and George Jones, was and remains one of the nation's most influential newspapers. It provided widespread coverage of the unfolding crisis in Little Rock. This "Week in Review" section synthesizes the month-long crisis in Little Rock, three years after the *Brown* decision, and predicts the future of the public schools. This article clearly outlines the limitations of the Supreme Court's timetable and anticipates the problems ahead.

Little Rock & After

Three years after the historic Supreme Court decision outlawing school segregation, a crisis of tension has been reached. The future is shrouded in uncertainty.

Two years ago the court set out in broad terms the pace for the elimination of segregation. Integration, the court said, must proceed "with all deliberate speed." It left to Federal District Court: the decision on whether that requirement was being fulfilled.

On the whole the pace of integration since has been deliberate indeed. In the seventeen affected states (plus the District of Columbia), about 3,000 school districts have bi-racial population. Of these just over 700 have been integrated. But the pace has varied widely from state to state. In the border areas there has been swift compliance. Farther South progress has been slower; there has been scattered violence, put down by local and state police. In the Deep South integration has been at a standstill.

Last week the President brought military force to bear to back up the court's requirement of "all deliberate speed." On his order Army soldiers ringed the Central High School in Little Rock and thwarted the efforts of the Governor of Arkansas and segregationist mobs to keep Negroes out.

Mixed Reaction

The reaction to the President's move was general gratification in the North, widespread anger in the South, and all through the U. S. a sense of gravity over the collision of Federal and state power. On the question of how the pace of integration might be affected, opinions differed. Some felt that resistance in the Deep South would stiffen, others that integration would be speeded by the realization that efforts to resist the Federal will by force had proved futile.

What the future holds may become clearer after a critical meeting in the White House this week. The President will discuss the Federal-state crisis with five Governors of the South. The talks may shed light on two fundamental questions. They are:

First, what course will the South now pursue in the broad struggle over integration?

Second, what course will the Federal Government pursue if the South stands firm against change?

Toward the Crisis

`The situation in Little Rock up to last week developed in three phases: (1) the planning for school integration; (2) the intervention of Gov. Orval B. Faubus, and (3) the Federal court action against the Governor. `The *first phase* began after the May, 1955, Supreme Court ruling directing racial desegregation of public schools "with all deliberate speed." The Little Rock Board of Education voluntarily drew up a gradual integration program to begin in 1957 and to be completed by 1963.

For several months the program was explained to Little Rock citizens. During this period the National Association for the Advancement of Colored People challenged the length of time the program was to take. Last April the Circuit Court of Appeals ruled the "all deliberate speed" requirement had been met. Seventeen Negro students, chosen for scholastic ability and personality, were then scheduled to enter Central High School last Sept. 3.

The *second phase* began when the Governor suddenly entered the scene on Aug. 29. A white mothers' club had petitioned State Chancery Court to halt the integration program.

The Governor was a surprise witness. His liberal Democratic background had led to his being considered a moderate on the racial question until he began making segregationist statements in his election campaign last fall. He told the court that if the program were to proceed, mob violence would follow. The court halted the program. In Federal District Court, however, Judge Ronald N. Davies overruled the state court and enjoined "all persons" from interfering with the integration plan.

Guard Called Out

Then, on the eve of school opening Sept. 3, Governor Faubus surrounded Central High School with armed National Guardsmen. He asserted their mission was simply to "maintain order." He was compelled to act, he said, by his legal responsibility to preserve the peace.

Next day came the dramatic scene when the troops barred nine of the seventeen Negro students scheduled to enter the school (the rest made no attempt). When angry mobs threatened the Negro children the school board petitioned the Federal court for a delay of integration.

The *third phase* began on Sept. 6 when Judge Davies dismissed the board's appeal. He directed the United States Government to enter the case, paving the way for a Federal injunction against the Governor. A summons ordered Mr. Faubus to court Sept. 20.

In an effort to avert a Federal-State clash, President Eisenhower and Governor Faubus met—at the latter's request—in Newport Sept. 14. But despite optimistic statements by both sides the troops still barred Negroes from the school.

In court a week ago last Friday Mr. Faubus' attorneys maintained the Federal Government had no right to question the Governor's judgment in exercising his authority. But Judge Davies quickly enjoined the Governor from "preventing by use of National Guard or otherwise the attendance of Negro students" at the school.

That evening Governor Faubus told a radio-television audience he would "exhaust every legal remedy to appeal this order. However . . . I will comply. . . ." The troops were withdrawn.

In the uneasy calm of last week-end, Little Rock—and the nation—watched and waited. The Negro students had made known their intention to enter Central High. Twice on Saturday President Eisenhower expressed hope that the city would maintain order.

President Acts

Last Monday dawned a fine fall day in Little Rock. By 8 o'clock some 500 men and women were milling behind police barricades opposite Central High School. The crowd was in a fighting mood, stirred up, Mayor Woodrow W. Mann charged later, by "professional agitators."

At 6:45 a buzzer could be heard, signaling the start of classes. A United States flag was hoisted up the staff on the school lawn.

"Where are the niggers?" someone shouted. "We'll lynch 'em." others yelled. "There they are:" the shout went up. The crowd rushed after four Negroes who turned out to be newspaper men. After kicking one down on one knee, the attackers kicked and beat another.

While the mob was thus occupied, the Negro students—six girls and three boys—arrived in two cars, and unmolested, entered the school by a side door. "Oh God," said a woman. "The niggers are in school." The crowd roared with rage.

The cry was taken up by six hysterical teen-age girls. Their hysteria swept through the crowd. An elderly man jumped onto a barricade and shouted, "Who's going over the top?" "We'll all go over!" the mob roared, and over they went. Police slowly forced them back, aided by state troopers.

At 12:14 a police officer announced through a loudspeaker: "The Negroes have been withdrawn from the school." They had been dispatched safely to their homes on the advice of school officials who feared worse violence. Thus the first integrated classes in Little Rock public school history had come to an end. They had lasted three hours and thirteen minutes.

That evening President Eisenhower took a strong stand. A moderate on the states' rights question, he had said as recently as July 17 that he could not think of a situation in which it would be wise to use troops to enforce civil rights decrees. But he had not anticipated that a state would resort to force. In a statement Monday evening he said:

I want to make several things clear in connection with the disgraceful occurrence [at] Little Rock. . . . The Federal law and orders of a United States District Court . . . cannot be flouted with impunity by any individual or mob of extremists.

He then signed an emergency proclamation. It said that "by the virtue of the authority vested in me by the Constitution and the statutes of the United States . . . I . . . do command all persons engaged in such obstruction to cease and desist therefrom and to disperse forthwith." He cited provisions of the U. S. Code dating back to George Washington's time and authorizing the President to employ armed force to compel obedience to Federal court orders.

Tuesday morning, a crowd of 300 was still milling abut the school. Although the Negro students didn't attempt further entry, there were mutterings and threats from the throng.

Historic Decision

Later on Tuesday the President arrived at a historic decision. For the first time since Reconstruction days the Federal Government, by executive order, invoked its ultimate power to compel equal treatment of the Negro in the South. The President sent United States Army troops into Little Rock, and he federalized the Arkansas National Guard, thus removing it from Governor Faubus' command. The paratroopers, a thousand strong, were members of the 327th Airborne Battle Group of the 101st Airborne Division.

That night the President flew back to Washington to explain his action. On a nation-wide broadcast he said:

The very basis of our individual rights and freedoms rests upon the certainty that the President . . . will . . . insure the carrying out of the decisions of the Federal courts . . . Unless the President did so, anarchy would result.

On Wednesday morning paratroops, armed with rifles and bayonets, formed a cordon around the school. Inside, twenty-four more stood guard in the corridors.

At 9:25. forty minutes after the start of classes, the nine Negro students arrived in an Army station wagon convoyed by troop-laden jeeps. The students entered the school without trouble.

Outside, the soldiers had their hands full, facing both abuse and token resistance. A man in the crowd was struck by the butt of a rifle wielded by a sergeant, and suffered a scalp wound. The sergeant said the man had grabbed at his rifle. Another was pricked by a bayonet when he refused to move.

At the close of school some students were still protesting the Negroes' presence. But others—including several who extended lunch invitations to some of the lonely nine in the cafeteria—were finding integration less burdensome. One said. "If the parents would just go home and leave us be, we'd work this thing out for ourselves." A teacher said, "The Negro students seem to be getting along very well."

'Let Us Be'

Governor Faubus, in a nationally broadcast speech Thursday night, portrayed Arkansas as under "military occupation." He spoke of "the warm red blood of patriotic American citizens staining the cold, naked, unsheathed knives."

He charged the F. B. I. held "teen-age girls . . . incommunicado for hours of questioning." F. B. I. director J. Edgar Hoover later accused the Governor of "falsehoods."

At the school, the Negroes continued to arrive in the Army station wagon and to enter without molestation. By the week-end, attendance, normally 2,000. had risen form a low of 1,250 to 1,450 in two days. The mobs had been dispersed. No jeers were being heard.

The Questions

The immediate question at the week-end was what would happen next in Little Rock. Beyond that there were the broader questions of what the South generally would do and what the U. S. would do.

In Little Rock the first reaction appeared to be relief. The presence of the troops, it was felt, would put down the ugly spectre of mob violence which had risen over the integration crisis. But there was also a feeling of shock that the situation had reached such a pass. Many felt that Governor Faubus had been vindicated in his prediction that integration of the high school would cause violence. Support for the Governor was increased by resentment of anything smacking of Reconstruction—the last time Federal authority was imposed on the South by Federal troops. Some persons in Little Rock felt that the Governor was to blame for precipitating the crisis, but they appeared to be in the minority.

In Little Rock as elsewhere, a major concern was how long the troops would stay. Washington appeared hopeful it could remove the Regular Army troops promptly and leave federalized National Guardsmen in charge. That might improve the atmosphere in the South somewhat, but it would leave the question of when the situation could be handled without any troops. The President said in his speech on Tuesday that "if resistance to the Federal court orders ceases at once, the further presence of the troops will be unnecessary." It was plain in Washington that Federal officials wanted to remove the troops as soon as possible. The calming of the atmosphere around Little Rock High School during the week raises the prospect that it may be possible to remove them in a few days.

Views on Future

What then? In one view, the integration of Little Rock's schools according to the school board's six-year plan will proceed without further untoward incidents. In this view, since the plan has now been set in motion and the Federal Government has demonstrated that it has the determination and ultimate authority to see that the plan is carried out, there can be no turning back. But there is another view that withdrawal of the troops will be followed by retribution—at least a move by the Arkansas Legislature to thwart integration, and possibly an outbreak of racial violence.

In the South generally the predominant reaction was one of shock and anger over the President's move. The immediate impact was to harden the position of the all-out segregationists and to weaken the position of those moderates who had sought some accommodations to the intent of the Supreme Court's decision against segregation.

Southern spokesmen dwelt on the theme that with "naked bayonets" and "bludgeoning" the Federal Government was trampling the rights of a sovereign state. Senator Richard B. Russell of Georgia, one of the South's most influential leaders, typified this reaction in a telegram to the President. The soldiers in Little Rock, Senator Russell charged, "are disregarding and overriding the elementary rights of American citizens by applying tactics which must have been copied from the manual issued the officers of Hitler's storm troopers." Gov. Marvin Griffin of Georgia said, "The second Reconstruction has begun." The aim of this approach seemed to be to put the South in the more sympathetic underdog role which, in Northern eyes, has been occupied by the Negro students in Little Rock.

Other voices were equally bitter but more calm. James F. Byrnes—who has been a Senator, a Supreme Court justice and Governor of South Carolina—said in a speech on Thursday:

The people of the South deplore violence. It helps no cause. . . . Whenever the tanks and guns are removed, there will remain the same determination on the part of the white people to resort to every legal means to prevent the mixing of the races.

This instinct to draw back from further resort to violence on either side of the integration issue was reflected in a move by the Southern Governors Conference, which was holding its annual meeting last week in Georgia. The Conference created a committee of five Governors and asked the President to meet the committee for a discussion of the Little Rock situation, with particular reference to the withdrawal of Federal troops. The President agreed, but made it clear that he wants to discuss more than the question of removing troops from Little Rock. The assumption is that he wants to discuss how to proceed on integration "with all deliberate speed." The meeting is scheduled to take place in Washington on Tuesday.

Southerners Bitter

While the reaction in the South was one of almost universal bitterness, there were some persons there who held the view that the President had been forced into his action by Governor Faubus and the extreme segregationists. They contended that a show of force against the Federal Government is not the way to resist integration; the legal delaying actions would succeed where force would fail. There also was a feeling among moderates in the South that the President acted too quickly. In this view, the local authorities in Little Rock could have restored order if they had been given more time, and it would have been better to give them more time than to precipitate a crisis of far-reaching consequences in

Federal-State relationships. The Houston (Tex.) Chronicle said: "The President failed to give a good example by using all the resources of law before resorting to force. . . ."

Many observers believe that the trend in the Deep South will be to rely on litigation instead of force. Most Southern states have erected elaborate structures of laws designed to prevent or delay integration. If one of those laws is struck down, the state will be prepared to put another in its place. The experience in Arkansas has solidified the view that this resort to legal stratagems, rather than to the National Guard, is the way to prevent integration. Thus attainment of integration through the courts promises to be a slow process.

There is speculation that economic and social forces may do as much to bring about integration as pressure from the Federal courts or the White House. The South is changing from an agricultural to an industrial economy. Many Southern states are bidding for industry. Racial tensions impede these efforts.

The President, for his part, seems bent on posing for the Governors at their White House talks this week the question of how integration can be kept in motion "with all deliberate speed" without resort to force on either side. He also seems determined to prevent the South from assuming the role of martyr. In a telegraphed reply to Senator Russell yesterday, the President said:

When a state, by seeking to frustrate the orders of Federal court, encourages mobs of extremists to flout the orders of a Federal court, . . . [the President must] take action . . . I completely fail to comprehend your comparison of our troops to Hitler's storm troopers. In one case military power was used to further the ambitions . . . of a ruthless dictator: in the other to preserve the institutions of free government.

The President appears to have wide support in the North, although there is some feeling that he waited too long to assert firm leadership in the Arkansas situation and might not have had to send troops if he had taken a strong stand sooner.

The developments in Little Rock also attracted wide attention abroad. The free-world reaction generally was approval of the Presidents action. The Communist world, on the other hand, took advantage of the opportunity to argue that the racial strife in Little Rock belied American claims of democracy. "The Communists." said the French Communist newspaper L'llumanilé, "are adversaries of racial discrimination."

DOCUMENT 33:

Foreign Service Dispatch, R. Smith Simpson, "Impact in Mozambique of Racial Developments in the United States," September 30, 1957.

RG 59, 811.411.9-3507 HBS, National Archives, Washington, D.C. Courtesy National Archives.

This foreign service dispatch, written by R. Smith Simpson, the American Consul General in Lourenco Marques (the capital of Portuguese East Africa) shows how Mozambique responded to the international coverage of the Little Rock crisis. The State Department collection includes dozens of such letters from Egypt to Denmark to China that confirmed Eisenhower's concern that America's battle over civil rights negatively affected the nation's credibility throughout the world.

FROM: Amconsul Laurenco Marquez
TO: The Department of State, Washington
              September 30, 1957

SUBJECT: Impact in Mozambique of Racial Developments in the United States

The racist manifestations in the United States, climaxed by the mustering of troops in Arkansas, have made a deep impression upon the Portuguese here. The manifestations have received full and prominent front-page treatment. Every development has been followed with keen interest and the Little Rock events themselves have unfortunately become a symbol of Negro-White relations in the United States. There seems to be no question but that our moral standing has been very considerably damaged and in Portuguese view here any pretension of an American to advise any European Government on African affairs at this point would be hypocrisy.

The fact that the news from the United States which appears in the Mozambique press is reported by Reuters probably has not helped us any. But it is not only through the Mozambique press that racial news from the United States reaches Portuguese here. The Johannesburg *Star* and *Time* magazine both have appreciable circulation in this province.

Both have been devoting considerable coverage to U.S. racial developments in recent months.

No comment of local origin has appeared in the Mozambique press and now that Goncalo MESQUITELA has gone to Lisbon on vacation one of our more vocal critics is absent from the local scene. The one article that has appeared is by Dr. Oliveria BOLEO, whom, we are advised, is chief of the division of education in the Overseas Ministry. The article was entitled: "Well preaches Friar Thomas: Do what he says and not what he does." He refers to the blowing up of a school in the U.S. which had admitted Negroes and condemns the disposition to "hunt and persecute and even hang the Negroes, or manhandle Negro priests—which is happening in the United States, where one-tenth of the population is Negro." He concludes: "In this way, the moral standing of this great Nation diminishes whenever she tries to condemn colonialism or racial segregation elsewhere in the world."

The one cheerful ray of light in this black situation has been the firm attitude of President Eisenhower, who has demonstrated, in Portuguese view, a determination to see that American democracy is no farce.

It would be a master stroke if some motion picture producer should issue a "short" depicting the accomplishments and opportunities of the Negro in the United States and this were distributed commercially throughout the world, including Africa. Such a film (or films) may already exist. If so, we would appreciate being advised and what if any arrangements might be made for its exhibition (or re-exhibition) in this part of the world.

CHAPTER 3

Reaction and Response

The politicians, community members, and families directly involved in the crisis published responses and received letters and telegrams from a range of groups, including the NAACP, the National Urban League, moderate Arkansas voters, segregationists, and even baseball legend Jackie Robinson. The international press in London, Moscow, Tokyo, and Paris characterized the Little Rock crisis as an American disgrace and warned that it aided enemies abroad. The documents in "Reaction and Response" present a wide range of responses to the desegregation effort.

DOCUMENT 34:

Letter from Gilbert E. McDonald to Chairman, Parent-Teachers Association, 1957.

Courtesy Special Collections, University of Arkansas Libraries, Virgil Blossom Collection, MC box 13, folder 64 and box 6, folder 2.

This letter from an enlisted sailor, who had no obvious connection to Arkansas or the city of Little Rock, represents one of the many diverse viewpoints on the crisis. The coverage, which was extensive and widespread, offered Americans at home and abroad a chance to comment on the struggle over civil rights.

COMSUECOMNELM/COMHEDSUPPACT
Navy #510, Box 4
c/o Fleet Post Office
New York, N.Y.

Superintendent of Schools
City Hall
Little Rock, Arkansas
Attn: Chairman, Parent-Teachers Association

My dear Mr. Chairman:

I am an enlisted man in the U.S. Navy and am presently stationed in Naples, Italy.

The contribution of the citizens of Little Rock to the history of the United States of America has succeeded in thoroughly shaming and infuriating a majority of military personnel serving overseas.

The enclosed clipping was printed in the 24 September edition of the Rome Daily American. This paper is read by a great many english speaking Europeans who are earnestly trying to understand the principles of democracy as it is allegedly practiced in the United States.

Generally speaking, you people have succeeded in making a laughing stock out of every U.S. citizen overseas who is trying to set a good example of the American way of life.

Perhaps one of you could tell me what to reply when I'm asked to explain your behavior by my European friends.

> Sincerely,
> (signed)
> Gilbert E. McDonald
> Yeoman second class (YN2), USN

DOCUMENT 35:
"Inside Central High School, October 1957."

Southern School News, *November 1957, 6.*

After the initial crisis in September 1957, the *Southern School News* reported on how the desegregation crisis progressed throughout the 1957–1958 academic year. On May 25, 1958, Ernest Green became the first black student to graduate from Central High School. On September 27, Faubus gave Little Rock voters a chance to accept integration or close the city's four high schools. The final vote, 19,470 to 7,561, ultimately resulted in the closure of the schools, leaving thousands of students without an alternative during "the Lost Year."

Classes went on more or less as usual at Little Rock Central High School with nine Negro students attending under the protection of federal troops. Early in October the students took their six-week tests. No results were released but most students seemed to think they were doing as well, or better, than usual. . . .

The work of some students suffered because of their absences. Most of these were those who took part in a student walkout and those who were suspended for incidents involving the Negro students. The walkout, promoted by the League of Central High Mothers, was considered a flop even by the students who participated. Only about 50 left school on Oct. 3. The enrollment at the school is 1,973. The Mothers League had expected at least 200 to 250 to walk out. . . .

The student newspaper, the *Tiger,* urged students to "maintain a sensible, peaceful neutrality." Later on it said, "All the history books will have to say about the events at Little Rock during the 1957–58 school year has not be written; no one knows what new developments will arise in the next few weeks or months. But another sort of history, of more importance to us personally, is our scholastic record. This should receive our full attention, regardless of the events that have taken place or will take place, and regardless of our personal feelings toward what has happened during this historic year at Little Rock Central High."

DOCUMENT 36:
"The Commies Trained Gov. Faubus of Arkansas."

Courtesy Special Collections, University of Arkansas Libraries, Confidential, *February 25, 1958, Virgil Blossom Papers, MC134, box 15, folder 1.*

Confidential, a sensational magazine that covered lurid topics to attract a wide audience, published an article exposing Governor Orval Faubus's time at Commonwealth College. Inclusion of this article suggests that Communist hysteria often had little to do with one's political position. *Confidential* was founded in 1951, enjoying the height of its circulation with 4.5 million readers in 1955. In 1957, the magazine's owners were indicted for mailing obscene materials through the mail by Postal Service. The magazine was sold in 1958, but never regained its wide readership.

Is Faubus unwittingly playing the Red game?—
Or deliberately aiding Soviet propaganda?

Prepared by the Staff of CONFIDENTIAL
Copyright, 1958, Confidential Magazine

When Governor Orval Faubus of Arkansas openly defied the government of the United States on the school integration issue, he handed to the Communists the handsomest gift they could possibly have received from any American.

Four-fifths of the people of the world are colored. All over the world —in Asia and Europe, in Africa and the Middle East—the Communists have invoked the name of the Little Rock to tell colored people that the United States is a land of lynching and repression.

The people of the world know very little of the great steps we have taken toward integration or of the peaceful changes that are going on here.

But thanks to Faubus' actions and the Red propaganda that plays upon them, no American can travel abroad without being asked by every foreigner about Little Rock. Harry Belafonte recently made a European tour. Everywhere he went, he said, that was the first question asked him.

Is Faubus unwittingly playing a pro-Communist game?

Or is he deliberately aiding the Soviet propaganda machine?

These questions may well be asked on the basis of information which CONFIDENTIAL has turned up and which we are now able to make public nationally.

The fact is this:

Governor Orval Faubus studied at a special school operated by the Communist Party for the purpose of training Commie organizers and agitators.

Among the courses taught there was one entitled "The Art of Propaganda."

Faubus was not just another student at the Communist institution. He was an active student leader. He was the head of the student body.

He was the principal speaker at a May Day celebration—the traditional holiday of the Reds.

The institution was Commonwealth College, located at Mena, Arkansas. It was a peculiar "college" indeed. Students needed no academic qualifications to enter. All that was required was a proper "social orientation."

It was also accused before an Arkansas Joint Legislative Committee of being the nest of "free love" in the Communist tradition of disregard of ordinary standards of sexual morality.

Commonwealth was forced out of business in 1940 by an Arkansas court—but it is still listed as "subversive and Communist" by the Attorney General of the United States and it stands condemned as pro-Soviet by the House Un-American Activities Committee.

The school's instructors included several individuals who later were featured in spy probes and Communist investigations.

Among the visiting lecturers was Harold Ware who founded the underground Communist cell in Washington which was later to be exposed by Whittaker Chambers in the Hiss case.

Ware was the son of the famed Communist leader, Ella "Mother" Bloor, who also lectured at Commonwealth. Ware was killed in an automobile accident in 1937.

Some further idea of Commonwealth's "social orientation" may be obtained from the way the place looked.

A visitor about to enter the main door stepped on a large concrete slab. Cut into the slab was the Communist emblem—the hammer and sickle.

Inside the main hall the visitor saw two huge portraits. They were pictures of Lenin and Stalin.

And Commonwealth's attitude was also expressed in a telegram it sent on November 7, 1933, to the Soviet Ambassador, Maxim Litvinoff. The telegram read:

"Commonwealth has long recognized Soviet Russia and its tremendous significance to the future of economic planning. It extends greetings and felicitations to Soviet Russia's able representative and invites him to visit and inspect Commonwealth, a worker's college in Mena, Arkansas, which supports itself by running a kolkhoz or collective farm. Wire answer collect. Commonwealth College, Mena, Arkansas."

The director of the "worker's college" was one Lucien Koch

On February 16, 1935, a Joint Committee of the Arkansas Legislature launched an investigation of Commonwealth after charges had been publicly made that it trained Communist agitators for work in the farm belt. Faubus admitted being there at the time.

Lucien Koch's political approach may be judged by the following testimony before the Joint Commission:

"Q. Do you believe in God?

"A. No . . .

"Q. Do you believe in the Constitution of the United States?

"A. I am convinced that I believe in it more thoroughly than the planters in the Eastern part of Arkansas.

"Q. Do you believe in the Constitution of the United States?

"A. I answered that question . . .

"Q. Do you respect the American Flag?

"A. I refuse to answer that because I consider it as having no bearing on the investigation. I refuse to answer without advice of counsel . . .

"Q. Do you believe in Capitalism?

"A. I do not believe in Capitalism, as it is now operated . . .

Courses taught at Commonwealth included one in "orientation" which stressed the "benefits" of Soviet life over U.S. capitalism; the menace of Fascism and the need for social revolution; the Marxist-Leninist approach to current events; and public speaking and creative writing.

Creative writing consisted largely of preparing copy for mimeographed leaflets to be used in "workers struggles," while public speaking consisted largely of training in soap-box oratory—the best means of "translating revolutionary jargon into American terms."

The teachers were as unusual as were the courses they taught. Among them was Mildred Price who in 1952 was to take the Fifth Amendment when asked by a Senate Subcommittee whether she was a Communist agent.

At Commonwealth, the teachers were not paid salaries. They received room, board, laundry and, as Miss Price testified, about $1.50 a month for incidental expenses.

This, then, was the school which Orval Faubus attended.

Was Faubus an ignorant and unsuspecting kid when he studied at Commonwealth?

He was a full-grown man of 25 years and he had already been teaching school for seven years when he went to Commonwealth. Just five months before he was elected president of the student body the Legislative committee had begun its investigation of the place and news of its probe had been trumpeted to every corner of Arkansas.

Was Faubus just an ordinary student at this training academy for Commies? Here are some of the things the school paper, "*Commonwealth College Fortnightly,*" had to say about him.

In its issue dated "May Day, 1935" the paper carried an article headed "United Front in Student Elections." The story read:

"The united front at Commonwealth was carried to the student body for the first time when all factions agreed on candidates for student body offices.

(Translation from Commie jargon into plain English: In accordance with the Reds' usual custom, there was only one name on the ballot for each office. There were no opposition candidates.)

"Orval Faubus, a young farmer-schoolteacher from Combs, Arkansas, and Arthur Leche of Cincinnati, were each elected to two offices.

"Faubus is both student body present and member of the Disciplinary Committee."

The same issue of the paper announced on Page One: "Gala May Day Program Planned." May Day is the Communists' greatest celebration, marked by Reds all over the world.

The *Fortnightly's* story said:

"The principal afternoon talk will be by Orval Faubus on 'The Story of May Day.'"

Commonwealth also selected Faubus as one of three student delegates to the "All-Southern Conference for Civil and Trade Union Rights," a Communist-inspired meeting in Chattanooga.

The *Fortnightly* reported afterwards that the conference had met with "vigilante terror" and that a "mob of vigilantes" had caused the landlord of the meeting hall to cancel the lease and force the group to meet elsewhere.

The "vigilantes" were members of the American Legion in uniform.

And, ironically enough, among the resolutions on the conference agenda were some which demanded full integration—not just school integration—for Southern Negroes.

What did Faubus do after he left the Communist training academy?

He has always drawn a veil over this period of his life. He went to the West Coast for reasons which he has never specified more than in the vaguest terms.

At any rate, Faubus eventually returned to Arkansas and began his political career.

In 1954, when Faubus was contemplating running for Governor, he went to friends and asked whether or not he ought to admit the Commonwealth connection. He decided not to do so.

In filling out the biography required of gubernatorial candidates, he omitted all mention of Commonwealth, saying merely that he had received "all my higher education in the State of Arkansas."

During the campaign, a reporter for the Arkansas Democrat got a glimmer of truth and asked Faubus whether he had gone to Commonwealth.

"That is not true. I have never been a student or a faculty member at the school and never attended a class there."

Faubus' opponent, the then Governor Frances A. Cherry, knew that statement to be a lie.

He said so, documenting his statements with copies of the *Commonwealth Fortnightly.*

In the course of a few days, Faubus told six different stories about his connection with Commonwealth.

First he had been there only two days, discovered what the place was and then left.

Next, he had been there a week. Then, 10 days. Then two weeks. And so on.

Faubus said he had gone there because he had received a scholarship in the mail. He didn't know who had been so kind as to send it to him.

Being a poor country boy, he said he had walked the 110 miles from Huntsville to Commonwealth. If he had actually done that, he would have passed by the gates of four Arkansas state institutions of higher learning, any one of which might well have admitted him.

Cherry's documented proof did not save Arkansas from Faubus. For one thing, Faubus, then as now, was a superb propagandist, an expert at stirring up the backwoods and so mingling truth with half-truth that the voters lost sight of all essentials.

For another, McCarthyism was in its dying days and people everywhere were inclined to discount charges of Communist influence. Even the liberal Arkansas Gazette, the state's most influential paper, swung against Cherry on the ground that he was "Red-baiting" and supported Faubus, to the everlasting regret of its liberal editor, Harry Ashmore, who has since been one of Faubus' prime targets.

Among those who cheered Faubus' election was the official Communist paper, *The Daily Worker,* which proudly announced that he had "had the backing of labor and liberal elements."

One interesting question asked during Faubus' campaign was whether or not he had committed a felony.

During World War II, Faubus had been drafted, sent to officers' training camp and commissioned. After the war, he retained his commission in the reserve.

Under the law, a reserve officer must sign a loyalty oath each year. The form asks whether he is or has ever been a member of a number of organizations which are listed by name. Among those organizations is Commonwealth College.

To swear falsely on this oath is a Federal crime, punishable by five years in prison.

Faubus had last signed that form in February, 1954.

A group of Arkansas Republicans demanded to know whether or not he had admitted to going to Commonwealth.

They offered to contribute $1,000 to Faubus' campaign if he would make public the oath as he had signed it. And to prove they weren't kidding, they put the cash into escrow at a bank.

Faubus never attempted to collect the money.

Whatever Faubus swore to the Army, one thing is certain:

As a young man, he took some of the training which the Communists designed for their organizers and agitators.

Which brings us back to the original question:

Is he now playing the Communist game unwittingly?

Or is he deliberately aiding the Reds?

DOCUMENT 37:
Photograph, New York City Mayor Robert Wagner greeting the teenagers who integrated Central High School, 1958.

Courtesy Library of Congress.

Born in Manhattan, Robert F. Wagner Jr. served as mayor of New York City from 1954 through 1965. He was active in building schools and public housing and is remembered for establishing the City University of New York system and Lincoln Center. He barred discrimination on the basis of race, creed, or color in housing and was the first mayor to hire African Americans into the city government. He is shown in this 1958 photograph with the Little Rock Nine. Pictured are (*front row, left to right*) Minnijean Brown, Elizabeth Eckford, Carlotta Walls, Mayor Wagner, Thelma Mothershed, Gloria Ray, and (*back row, left to right*) Terrence Roberts, Ernest Green, Melba Patillo, and Jefferson Thomas.

DOCUMENT 38:
Letter from Jackie Robinson to Dwight D. Eisenhower, May 13, 1958.

Courtesy Dwight D. Eisenhower Library.

Jack Roosevelt "Jackie" Robinson was the first African American to play major league baseball, having joined the Brooklyn Dodgers in 1947. He retired after ten years and became a vice president for Chock Full O'Nuts, a company that operated a chain of lunch counters, and a board member of the NAACP. In this letter, Robinson criticizes President Eisenhower for his gradualist plan for civil rights.

The President
The White House
Washington, D.C.

My dear Mr. President:

I was sitting in the audience at the Summit Meeting of Negro Leaders yesterday when you said we must have patience. On hearing you say this, I felt like standing up and saying, "Oh no! Not again."

I respectfully remind you sir, that we have been the most patient of all people. When you said we must have self-respect, I wondered how we could have self-respect and remain patient considering the treatment accorded us through the years.

17 million Negroes cannot do as you suggest and wait for the hearts of men to change. We want to enjoy now the rights that we feel we are entitled to as Americans. This we cannot do unless we pursue aggressively goals which all other Americans achieved over 150 years ago.

As the chief executive of our nation, I respectfully suggest that you unwittingly crush the spirit of freedom in Negroes by constantly urging forbearance and give hope to those pro-segregation leaders like Governor Faubus who would take from us even those freedoms we now enjoy. Your own experience with Governor Faubus is proof enough that forbearance and not eventual integration is the goal the pro-segregation leaders seek.

In my view, an unequivocal statement backed up by action such as you demonstrated you could take last fall in dealing with Governor

Faubus if it became necessary, would let it be known that America is determined to provide—in the near future—for Negroes—the freedom we are entitled to under the constitution.

> Respectfully yours,
> (signed)
> Jackie Robinson

JR:cc

DOCUMENT 39:
Letter from Henry V. Rath to Wayne Upton, September 12, 1958.

Courtesy Special Collections, University of Arkansas Libraries, Virgil Blossom Papers, MC1364, box 4, folder 13.

Before the opening of the school year, in August 1957, Dr. Dale Alford, one of the most segregationist school board members, declared that to "preserve the domestic tranquility" the Blossom Plan and the integration of Central High should be delayed. Dr. William G. Cooper Jr. and R. A. Lile both elected to abide by the court's decision, while Henry V. Rath and Harold Engstrom Jr. made no comment. Rath joined the school board on March 16, 1957.

September 12, 1958

Mr. Wayne Upton
President, Little Rock School Board
Pyramid Life Building
Little Rock, Arkansas

Dear Mr. Upton:

I believe the Little Rock School Board's request for a two and one-half year delay of integration was reasonable and just.

The U. S. Supreme Court, in denying this request, has acted in complete disregard to the social customs of the South. In setting aside Judge Lemley's decision to stay integration, the Court indicated an unwillingness to consider local officials.

I feel that I can no longer effectively serve education and herewith tender my resignation as a member of the Little Rock Board of Education.

> Respectfully yours,
> (signed)
> Henry V. Rath

DOCUMENT 40:
Cooper v. Aaron, 358 U.S. 1, September 12, 1958.

When the Little Rock School Board asked to delay implementation of *Brown v. Board of Education* in 1956, the Supreme Court held a special term to hear arguments. The state's case rested on two main claims: (1) because it was not a party to the original suit, it was not bound by *Brown,* and (2) a governor of a state had the same power to interpret the Constitution with the same authority as the Supreme Court. On September 12, 1958, in *Cooper v. Aaron,* the Court unanimously decided that the desegregation effort at Central High must continue on schedule. In the decision, the Court also reminded the state of Arkansas that since 1803 it has been "the province and duty of the judicial department to say what the law is," thus reasserting its authority.

Opinion of the Court by The Chief Justice, Mr. Justice Black, Mr. Justice Frankfurter, Mr. Justice Douglas, Mr. Justice Burton, Mr. Justice Clark, Mr. Justice Harlan, Mr. Justice Brennan, and Mr., Justice Whittaker.

As this case reaches us it raises questions of the highest importance to the maintenance of our federal system of government. It necessarily involves a claim by the Governor and Legislature of a State that there is no duty on state officials to obey federal court orders resting on this Court's considered interpretation of the United States Constitution. Specifically it involves actions by the Governor and Legislature of Arkansas upon the premise that they are not bound by our holding in *Brown v. Board of Education.* . . . That holding was that the Fourteenth Amendment forbids States to use their governmental powers to bar children on racial grounds from attending schools where there is state participation through any arrangement, management, funds or property. We are urged to uphold a suspension of the Little Rock School Board's plan to do away with segregated public schools in Little Rock until state laws and efforts to upset and nullify our holding in *Brown* v. *Board of Education* have been further challenged and tested in the courts. We reject these contentions.

The case was argued before us on September 11, 1958. On the following day we unanimously affirmed the judgment of the Court of Appeals for the Eighth Circuit. . . . The District Court had granted the application of the petitioners, the Little Rock School Board and School Superintendent, to suspend for two and one-half years the operation of the School Board's court-approved desegregation program. In order that the School Board might know, without doubt, its duty in this regard before the opening of school, which had been set for the following Monday, September 15, 1958, we immediately issued the judgment, reserving the expression of our supporting views to a later date. This opinion of all of the members of the Court embodies those views.

The following are the facts and circumstances so far as necessary to show how the legal questions are presented. . . .

On May 20, 1954, three days after the first *Brown* opinion, the Little Rock District School Board adopted, and on May 23, 1954, made public, a statement of policy entitled "Supreme Court Decision—Segregation in Public Schools." In this statement the Board recognized that "It is our responsibility to comply with Federal Constitutional Requirements and we intend to do so when the Supreme Court of the United States outlines the method to be followed."

Thereafter the Board undertook studies of the administrative problems confronting the transition to a desegregated public school system at Little Rock. It instructed the Superintendent of Schools to prepare a plan for desegregation, and approved such a plan on May 24, 1955, seven days before the second *Brown* opinion. The plan provided for desegregation at the senior high school level (grades 10 through 12) as the first stage. Desegregation at the junior high and elementary levels was to follow. It was contemplated that desegregation at the high school level would commence in the fall of 1957, and the expectation was that complete desegregation of the school system would be accomplished by 1963. Following the adoption of this plan, the Superintendent of Schools discussed it with a large number of citizen groups in the city. As a result of these discussions, the Board reached the conclusion that "a large majority of the residents" of Little Rock were of "the belief . . . that the Plan, although objectionable in principle," from the point of view of those supporting segregated schools, "was still the best for the interests of all pupils in the District."

Upon challenge by a group of Negro plaintiffs desiring more rapid completion of the desegregation process, the District Court upheld the School Board's plan, *Aaron v. Cooper,* 143 F. Supp. 855. The Court of Appeals affirmed. 243 F. 2d 361. Review of that judgment was not sought here.

While the School Board was thus going forward with its preparation for desegregating the Little Rock school system, other state authorities, in contrast, were actively pursuing a program designed to perpetuate in Arkansas the system of racial segregation which this Court had held violated the Fourteenth Amendment. First came, in November 1956, an amendment to the State Constitution flatly commanding the Arkansas General Assembly to oppose "in every Constitutional manner the Unconstitutional [358 U.S. 1, 9] desegregation decisions of May 17, 1954 and May 31, 1955 of the United States Supreme Court," Ark. Const., Amend. 44, and, through the initiative, a pupil assignment law, Ark. Stat. 80-1519 to 80-1524. Pursuant to this state constitutional command, a law relieving school children from compulsory attendance at racially mixed schools, Ark. Stat. 80-1525, and a law establishing a State Sovereignty Commission, Ark. Stat. 6-801 to 6-824, were enacted by the General Assembly in February 1957.

The School Board and the Superintendent of Schools nevertheless continued with preparations to carry out the first stage of the desegregation program. Nine Negro children were scheduled for admission in September 1957 to Central High School, which has more than two thousand students. Various administrative measures, designed to assure the smooth transition of this first stage of desegregation, were undertaken.

On September 2, 1957, the day before these Negro students were to enter Central High, the school authorities were met with drastic opposing action on the part of the Governor of Arkansas who dispatched units of the Arkansas National Guard to the Central High School grounds and placed the school "off limits" to colored students. As found by the District

Court in subsequent proceedings, the Governor's action had not been requested by the school authorities, and was entirely unheralded. The findings were these:

Up to this time [September 2], no crowds had gathered about Central High School and no acts of violence or threats of violence in connection with the carrying out of the plan had occurred. Nevertheless, out of an abundance of caution, the school authorities had frequently conferred with the Mayor and Chief of Police of Little Rock about taking appropriate steps by the Little Rock police to prevent any possible disturbances or acts of violence in connection with the attendance of the 9 colored students at Central High School. The Mayor considered that the Little Rock police force could adequately cope with any incidents which might arise at the opening of school. The Mayor, the Chief of Police, and the school authorities made no request to the Governor or any representative of his for State assistance in maintaining peace and order at Central High School. Neither the Governor nor any other official of the State government consulted with the Little Rock authorities about whether the Little Rock police were prepared to cope with any incidents which might arise at the school, about any need for State assistance in maintaining peace and order, or about stationing the Arkansas National Guard at Central High School. *Aaron v. Cooper,* 156 F. Supp. 220, 225.

The Board's petition for postponement in this proceeding states: "The effect of that action [of the Governor] was to harden the core of opposition to the Plan and cause many persons who theretofore had reluctantly accepted the Plan to believe there was some power in the State of Arkansas which, when exerted, could nullify the Federal law and permit disobedience of the decree of this [District] Court, and from that date hostility to the Plan was increased and criticism of the officials of the [School] District has become more bitter and unrestrained." The Governor's action caused the School Board to request the Negro students on September 2 not to attend the high school "until the legal dilemma was solved." The next day, September 3, 1957, the Board petitioned the District Court for instructions, and the court, after a hearing, found that the Board's request of the Negro students to stay away from the high school had been made because of the stationing of the military guards by the state authorities. The court determined that this was not a reason for departing from the approved plan, and ordered the School Board and Superintendent to proceed with it.

On the morning of the next day, September 4, 1957, the Negro children attempted to enter the high school but, as the District Court later found, units of the Arkansas National Guard "acting pursuant to the Governor's order, stood shoulder to shoulder at the school grounds and thereby forcibly prevented the 9 Negro students . . . from entering," as they continued to do every school day during the following three weeks. 156 F. Supp., at 225.

That same day, September 4, 1957, the United States Attorney for the Eastern District of Arkansas was requested by the District Court to begin an immediate investigation in order to fix responsibility for the interference with the orderly implementation of the District Court's direction to carry out the desegregation program. Three days later, September 7, the District Court denied a petition of the School Board and the Superintendent of Schools for an order temporarily suspending continuance of the program.

Upon completion of the United States Attorney's investigation, he and the Attorney General of the United States, at the District Court's request, entered the proceedings and filed a petition on behalf of the United States, as *amicus curiae,* to enjoin the Governor of Arkansas and officers of the Arkansas National Guard from further attempts to prevent obedience to the court's order. After hearings on the petition, the District Court found that the School Board's plan had been obstructed by the Governor through the use of National Guard troops, and granted a preliminary injunction on September 20, 1957, enjoining the Governor and the officers of the Guard from preventing the attendance of Negro children at Central High School, and from otherwise obstructing or interfering with the orders of the court in connection with the plan. 156 F. Supp. 220, affirmed, *Faubus v. United States,* 254 F.2d 797. The National Guard was then withdrawn from the school.

The next school day was Monday, September 23, 1957. The Negro children entered the high school that morning under the protection of the Little Rock Police Department and members of the Arkansas State Police. But the officers caused the children to be removed from the school during the morning because they had difficulty controlling a large and demonstrating crowd which had gathered at the high school. 163 F. Supp., at 16. On September 25, however, the President of the United States dispatched federal troops to Central High School and admission of the Negro students to the school was thereby effected. Regular army troops continued at the high school until November 27, 1957. They were then replaced by federalized National Guardsmen who remained throughout the balance of the school year. Eight of the Negro students remained in attendance at the school throughout the school year.

We come now to the aspect of the proceedings presently before us. On February 20, 1958, the School Board and the Superintendent of Schools filed a petition in the District Court seeking a postponement of their program for desegregation. Their position in essence was that because of extreme public hostility, which they stated had been engendered largely by the official attitudes and actions of the Governor and the Legislature, the maintenance of a sound educational program at Central High School, with the Negro students in attendance, would be impossible. The Board therefore proposed that the Negro students already admitted to the school be withdrawn and sent to segregated schools, and that all further steps to carry out the Board's desegregation program be postponed for a period later suggested by the Board to be two and one-half years.

After a hearing the District Court granted the relief requested by the Board. Among other things the court found that the past year at Central High School had been attended by conditions of "chaos, bedlam and turmoil"; that there were "repeated incidents of more or less serious violence directed against the Negro students and their property"; that there was "tension and unrest among the school administrators, the class-room teachers, the pupils, and the latter's parents, which inevitably had an adverse effect upon the educational program"; that a school official was threatened with violence; that a "serious financial burden" had been cast on the School District; that the education of the students had suffered "and under existing conditions will continue to suffer"; that the Board would continue to need "military assistance or its equivalent"; that the local police department would not be able "to detail enough men to afford the necessary protection"; and that the situation was "intolerable." 163 F. Supp., at 20–26. . . .

In affirming the judgment of the Court of Appeals which reversed the District Court we have accepted without reservation the position of the School Board, the Superintendent of Schools, and their counsel that they displayed entire good faith in the conduct of these proceedings and in dealing with the unfortunate and distressing sequence of events which has been outlined. We likewise have accepted the findings of the District

Court as to the conditions at Central High School during the 1957–1958 school year, and also the findings that the educational progress of all the students, white and colored, of that school has suffered and will continue to suffer if the conditions which prevailed last year are permitted to continue.

The significance of these findings, however, is to be considered in the light of the fact, indisputably revealed by the record before us, that the conditions they depict are directly traceable to the actions of legislatures and executive officials of the State of Arkansas, taken in their official capacities, which reflect their own determination to resist this Court's decision in the *Brown* case and which have brought about violent resistance to that decision in Arkansas. In its petition for certiorari filed in this Court, the School Board itself describes the situation in this language: "The legislative, executive, and judicial departments of the state government opposed the desegregation of Little Rock schools by enacting laws, calling out troops, making statements vilifying federal law and federal courts, and failing to utilize state law enforcement agencies and judicial process to maintain public peace."

One may well sympathize with the position of the Board in the face of the frustrating conditions which have confronted it, but, regardless of the Board's good faith, the actions of the other state agencies responsible for those conditions compel us to reject the Board's legal position. Had Central High School been under the direct management of the State itself, it could hardly be suggested that those immediately in charge of the school should be heard to assert their own good faith as a legal excuse for delay in implementing the constitutional rights of these respondents, when vindication of those rights was rendered difficult or impossible by the actions of other state officials. The situation here is no different posture because the members of the School Board and the Superintendent of Schools are local officials; from the point of view of the Fourteenth Amendment, they stand in this litigation as the agents of the State.

The constitutional rights of respondents are not to be sacrificed or yielded to the violence and disorder which have followed upon the actions of the Governor and Legislature. As this Court said some 41 years ago in a unanimous opinion in a case involving another aspect of racial segregation: "It is urged that this proposed segregation will promote the public peace by preventing race conflicts. Desirable as this is, and important as is the preservation of the public peace, this aim cannot be accomplished by laws or ordinances which deny the rights created or protected by the Federal Constitution." *Buchanan* v. *Warley,* 245 U.S. 60, 81. Thus law and order are not here to be preserved by depriving the Negro children of their constitutional rights. The record before us clearly establishes that the growth of the Board's difficulties to a magnitude beyond its unaided power to control is the product of state action. Those difficulties, as counsel for the Board forthrightly conceded on the oral argument in this Court, can also be brought under control by state action.

The controlling legal principles are plain. The command of the Fourteenth Amendment is that no "State" shall deny to any person within its jurisdiction the equal protection of the laws. "A State acts by its legislative, its executive, or its judicial authorities. It can act in no other way [358 U.S. 1, 17]. The constitutional provision, therefore, must mean that no agency of the State, or of the officers or agents by whom its powers are exerted, shall deny to any person within its jurisdiction the equal protection of the laws. Whoever, by virtue of public position under a State government, . . . denies or takes away the equal protection of the laws, violates the constitutional inhibition; and as he acts in the name and for the State, and is clothed with the State's power, his act is that of the State. This must be so, or the constitutional prohibition has no meaning." *Ex parte Virginia,* 100 U.S. 339, 347. Thus the prohibitions of the Fourteenth Amendment extend to all action of the State denying equal protection of the laws; whatever the agency of the State taking the action, see *Virginia* v. *Rives,* 100 U.S. 313; *Pennsylvania* v. *Board of Directors of City Trusts of Philadelphia,* 353 U.S. 230; *Shelley* v. *Kraemer,* 334 U.S.1; or whatever the guise in which it is taken, see *Derrington* v. *Plummer,* 240 F.2d 922; *Department of Conservation and Development* v. *Tate,* 231 F. 2d 615. In short, the constitutional rights of children not to be discriminated against in school admission on grounds of race or color declared by this Court in the *Brown* case can neither be nullified openly and directly by state legislators or state executive or judicial officers, nor nullified indirectly by them through evasive schemes for segregation whether attempted "ingeniously or ingenuously." *Smith* v. *Texas,* 311 U.S. 128, 132.

What has been said, in the light of the facts developed, is enough to dispose of the case. However, we should answer the premise of the actions of the Governor and Legislature that they are not bound by our holding in the *Brown* case. It is necessary only to recall some basic constitutional propositions which are settled doctrine.

Article VI of the Constitution makes the Constitution the "supreme Law of the Land." In 1803, Chief Justice Marshall, speaking for a unanimous Court, referring to the Constitution as "the fundamental and paramount law of the nation," declared in the notable case of *Marbury* v. *Madison,* 1 Cranch 137, 177, that "It is emphatically the province and duty of the judicial department to say what the law is." This decision declared the basic principle that the federal judiciary is supreme in the exposition of the law of the Constitution, and that principle has ever since been respected by this Court and the Country as a permanent and indispensable feature of our constitutional system. It follows that the interpretation of the Fourteenth Amendment enunciated by this Court in the *Brown* case is the supreme law of the land, and Art. VI of the Constitution makes it of binding effect on the States "any Thing in the Constitution or Laws of any States to the Contrary notwithstanding." Every state legislator and executive and judicial officer is solemnly committed by oath taken pursuant to Art. VI, cl. 3, "to support this Constitution." Chief Justice Taney, speaking for unanimous Court in 1859, said that this requirement reflected the framers' "anxiety to preserve it [the Constitution] in full force, in all its powers, and to guard against resistance to or evasion of its authority, on the part of a State. . . ." *Ableman* v. *Booth,* 21 How. 506, 524.

No state legislator or executive or judicial officer can war against the Constitution without violating his undertaking to support it. Chief Justice Marshall spoke for a unanimous Court in saying that: "If the legislatures of the several states may, at will, annul the judgments of the courts of the United States, and destroy the rights acquired under those judgments, the constitution itself becomes a solemn mockery. . . ." *United States* v. *Peters,* 5 Cranch 115, 136. A Governor who asserts a power to nullify a federal court order is similarly restrained. If he had such power, said Chief Justice Hughes, in 1932, also for a unanimous Court, "it is manifest that the fiat of a state Governor, and not the Constitution of the United States, would be the supreme law of the land; that the restriction of the Federal Constitution upon the exercise of state power would be but impotent phrases. . . ." *Sterling* v. *Constantin,* 287 U.S. 378, 397–398.

It is, of course, quite true that the responsibility for public education is primarily the concern of the States, but it is equally true that such responsibilities, like all other state activity, must be exercised consistently with federal constitutional requirements as they apply to state action. The Constitution created a government dedicated to equal justice under law.

The Fourteenth Amendment embodied and emphasized that ideal. State support of segregated schools through any arrangement, management, funds, or property cannot be squared with the Amendment's command that no State shall deny to any person within its jurisdiction the equal protection of the laws. The right of a student not to be segregated on racial grounds in schools so maintained is indeed so fundamental and pervasive that it is embraced in the concept of due process of law. . . . The basic decision in *Brown* was unanimously reached by this Court only after the case had been briefed and twice argued and the issues had been given the most serious consideration. Since the first *Brown* opinion three new Justices have come to the Court. They are at one with the Justices still on the Court who participated in that basic decision as to its correctness, and that decision is now unanimously reaffirmed. The principles announced in that decision and the obedience of the States to them, according to the command of the Constitution, are indispensable for the protection of the freedoms guaranteed by our fundamental charter for all of us. Our constitutional ideal of equal justice under law is thus made a living truth.

DOCUMENT 41:
Photograph, Empty hallway at Central High School, September 1958.

Courtesy Library of Congress.

On September 12, 1958, the Supreme Court ordered in *Cooper v. Aaron* that the desegregation effort at Central High must continue on schedule. The Little Rock School Board ordered schools to open on September 15, but Faubus ordered the high schools closed. They remained so for the 1958–1959 academic year and hundreds of students were left without access to public education. Some enrolled in segregationist academies, some left the city and state, but most simply withdrew from school for the entire year.

DOCUMENT 42:
Photograph, African American high school girl being educated via television, September 1958.

Courtesy Library of Congress.

Document 41

Document 42

During "the Lost Year" in Little Rock, when the high schools were closed (1958–1959), Virgil Blossom arranged for instruction to be broadcast over the television for black and white students who were not able to leave the community or afford private school tuition.

DOCUMENT 43:
"Charges of Communist Influence."

Southern School News, *March 1959, 2.*

Representative Dale Alford served on the Little Rock School Board from 1955 to 1958. That year, he became the second write-in candidate to become elected to the U.S. House of Representatives, after defeating Brooks Hays, who had supported the desegregation effort. Trained as an ophthalmologist, Alford served in the U.S. Army Medical Corps from 1940 to 1946, then as an assistant professor of at Emory College of Medicine. Alford was re-elected to the House in 1960 and elected not to run in 1962 because he wanted to run for governor against Orval Faubus. Alford lost and tried again in 1966. Like Bruce Bennett (attorney general in Arkansas from 1957 to 1960 and 1963 to 1966), Alford sought to undermine desegregation efforts, often by arguing that Communist threats were responsible for the racial unrest in the South.

Rep. Dale Alford of Little Rock (D-Ark.) told the U.S. House of Representatives in a speech on Feb. 17 that Communists and their dupes had flitted in and out of Arkansas for years and were responsible for the racial trouble in the state. He said this was part of the Communist plan to create unrest and finally to divide the country. He expressed alarm at the "complacency of some officials" toward this development and concern that the Justice Department "yields" to an organization such as the NAACP. . . .

Without calling anyone a Communist, state Atty. Gen. Bruce Bennett in a speech Feb. 16 implied that the NAACP and the *Arkansas Gazette* were acting as agents of a Communist conspiracy to set up a "Black Republic" in the South. He also said that 15 bills he had submitted to the current Legislature were "designed to harass, to keep the enemies of America busy." Most of them were aimed at restricting the activity of the NAACP.

DOCUMENT 44:

Excerpt from the Women's Emergency Committee to Open Our Schools, "Little Rock Report: The City, Its People, Its Business, 1957–1959."

Courtesy Special Collections, University of Arkansas Libraries, D. Sara A. Murphy Papers, MC1321, box 15, folder 10.

The Women's Emergency Committee to Open Our Schools (WEC) was established on September 16, 1958, by a group of fifty-eight white women to urge Little Rock residents to accept integrated public education for their children. The group advertised their policy and purpose as follows: "The Women's Emergency Committee to Open Our Schools is dedicated to the principle of free public school education, and to law and order. We stand neither for integration nor for segregation, but for education." Their aim was also detailed: "To get the four free public high schools reopened; to get the students back in their classes; to retain our staff of good teachers; to regain full accreditation by the North Central Association."

PUBLIC SCHOOLS CONSIDERED INDISPENSABLE . . .

The citizens of Little Rock stress the importance of the high educational standards that have been maintained by its public school system. An overwhelming majority of the people interviewed in this survey who have children now in school, or who will have children in school in the near future want the public schools opened. One-half of those with no children involved spoke out for public schools. The large majority of all skilled personnel want the public schools open. This attitude reaches 100% among the personnel officers.

Although attitudes toward public education were not solicited during the course of the interview, the following comments on public education were volunteered:

> Frankly, I like Little Rock. I like living here, but I will have to leave town unless the schools are open. I don't intend to pay tuition for my children. I believe in public education.

Each semester that this present school situation continues, the more likely it is that our family will move. We do not care to have our children grow up in a state with the present atmosphere, and we insist that they have the advantages of a <u>large, well-established school system.</u>

I am not afraid to express myself. <u>I believe in public education</u> and would welcome integrated schools in preference to no schools.

My wife and I both fervently hope that all <u>public schools</u> will be open next year. We believe that people who want public schools are not the wealthy or financially successful, but those in every walk of life who want culture—not just education.

If the school closing moves down into junior high and the elementary grades, we will move where we can send our children to <u>public schools.</u>

Our family will be broken up several years earlier. We have enrolled our only child outside of the state. <u>Public schools</u> are necessary to the progress of any community.

Many plant workers are concerned. They are not economically or socially able to do without <u>public schools.</u>

Two of us have moved into the county so that our children can attend <u>public schools,</u> and I will send my child to Central in the fall, even if I have to pay tuition as a county resident.

I would first try to find a school for my three children which I could afford before leaving my company or plant. I would do this from necessity, not from choice, because <u>I believe in public schools.</u> (I attended them with Negroes, and attended college with Negroes, and respect them as equal human beings.)

My daughter (only child) prefers to go to Hall High regardless of its status as far as integration and segregation is concerned.

I would rather my children live in a town where there is no school problem. I may have to send them away, but my daughter wants to graduate from Central High.

I prefer to remain here, but I am most uncertain of the future. I prefer not to send my child away to relatives or a private school, because I believe parental guidance at this time is most important. I have not registered my child for next year. <u>I hope the high schools will be open,</u> but I am not optimistic.

My child did not learn as much as in the previous years under the strained situation at Central, but I think Little Rock schools are better than California schools.

I fear that loss of the North Central Accreditation will lower the standards of the whole community.

I am a native Arkansas and will send my children to <u>public schools</u> when they are open.

My company feels being a good citizen means supporting <u>public education.</u> This company believes a city without public education is not a good location for a plant.

It is harder for a doctor to move than for most people, but if no public schools are available, then we'll move. We have discussed it often.

I think that 85% of the doctors are for <u>public schools,</u> and in private conversation, many wish they were young enough to establish a new practice elsewhere.

If the schools are open I will send my children to <u>public schools,</u> even if integrated—unless there is violence.

Appendix D:
The Little Rock Public High Schools: Reputation, Accreditation

For more than one-third of a century, the Little Rock Public High Schools have enjoyed an enviable prestige and representation for excellence both locally and in the broad circles of educational institutions through the nation. This prestige was earned and maintained through the years by the interest of the citizens, the loyalty of students and alumni, the vision and wisdom of administrators and board members and the devoted efforts of well trained and dedicated classroom teachers. People were appreciative of good schools and accustomed to them.

When the public high schools were closed in September 1958 each of the three general high schools was accredited by the North Central Association of the Secondary Schools and Colleges, the largest and most

influential accredited agency for schools and Tech High was accredited
by the State Department of Education as a Class A School.

The general high school had a large enough enrollment to offer a
curriculum broad enough to serve the interests and needs of all pupils
who earnestly desired a high school education. The college preparatory
curriculum and training at Central which was duplicated at Hall High
School qualified the graduates for admission to any college or university in the United States. Central graduates have attended the most outstanding colleges and universities in the country. The high scholastic
background for and achievement in colleges of these graduates have led
the admissions officers of colleges that select their student bodies to rate
Central High (Hall High) as one of the ten or twelve strongest high
schools private and public in the United States. These colleges and universities offer attractive scholarships to get such students and many
Central High graduates have received substantial scholarships.

It is a matter of record with the National Merit Scholarship Council
that no school has a better record for high achievement in that compe-
tition than does Little Rock.

But the general high schools did not concentrate on training the few
for the select school. A large percentage of graduates attend colleges
and make strong records in the schools of their choice.

The general high schools had strong programs for those pupils who
wanted vocational training. According to business men the Central High
secretarial training was as good as the best in the state. The print shops
offered unusually good training. And other industrial and fine arts programs were structured to teach a skill by which a graduate could enter
a job for a living wage.

What has Little Rock lost?

DOCUMENT 45:
L. C. Bates, 1962 Annual Report, NAACP.

*Courtesy Special Collections, University of Arkansas Libraries,
Daisy Bates Collection, MC82, box 5, folder 1.*

Lucious Christopher (L. C.) Bates, husband of Daisy Bates, founded
the *Arkansas State Press,* a weekly newspaper that advocated for civil

rights until it ceased publication in 1959. L. C. Bates served as a member of the NAACP executive committee of the Little Rock chapter, where Daisy Bates was president. He was one of the plaintiffs in *Cooper v. Aaron,* filed by the NAACP in 1956 to force the implementation of *Brown v. Board of Education* in Little Rock. L. C. Bates worked as an NAACP field secretary in Arkansas, Louisiana, and Tennessee from 1960 to 1971.

1962 ANNUAL REPORT
L. C. Bates, Field Secretary
December 5, 1962

EDUCATION:

Arkansas admitted two hundred, fifty-three Negro pupils to its formerly all-white schools this year compared to one hundred, fifty-two last school term. Thirteen school districts accepted Negroes on a token basis. There were only ten districts last year.

What can be scored a victory is the opening of the New Gosnell School in Mississippi County adjacent to the Blytheville Air Force Base where several months' of negotiation and investigation were carried on. The school opened in September without any incident after the Negroes living on the Air Base followed the instruction of the Field Secretary and took their children to the New Gosnell School and refused to allow them to be loaded into a bus to be taken to a Negro school as was done in the past. Twenty-two children are enrolled in school. Twenty-one are children of airmen and one is the child of a civilian who doesn't even live on the Air Base.

Only one of the thirteen school districts with integrated students faces any kind of litigation. And that is in the Dollarway School where the president of the Arkansas State Conference has asked the court to force the school to accept his daughter as a transfer student.

The Secretary in a letter, has asked the Arkansas Director of the trade schools set up under the War Manpower Commission Act to announce the policy of the school in admitting applicants. Thus far, no reply has been given.

Only three of the school districts have integrated the extracurriculum of their schools. These are in the northeastern part of the state.

HOUSING:

Complaints have been filed with the Federal Housing Administration in an effort to block the program of the North Little Rock Housing Authority to build segregated units in the city. The Housing Authority has announced that four units will be erected. They have been designed as a unit for elderly whites and a unit for elderly colored and a low-rent unit for whites and one for Negroes.

LABOR:

The Secretary worked with the State Employment Security Division during the months of January and February and resulted in the employment of two Negroes for the first time in the history of the State's ESD. They were employed on March 1, 1962. The Secretary conferred with the Personnel Director of the Civil Service Commission of the VA Hospital here and succeeded and getting the VA Hospital to employ a Negro stenographer. This is the first time a Negro woman has been employed in a clerical position since the Hospital was build here. Another break through came when the Secretary sent a Negro woman to the Little Rock Air Force Base to make application for a secretarial position. She was employed and began work in January. This was the first.

It is believed that the time is ripe for Negroes to be placed in responsible and dignified positions, but Arkansas is handicapped in finding qualified people who are willing to make themselves available for positions.

POLITICAL ACTION:

All NAACP units in the state were urged to initiate a stepped-up program to get Negroes to purchase poll tax receipts this year. The work done in, and, by the branches was gratifying because there was a substantial increase in qualified electors this year over last year. A poll tax receipt in Arkansas is a prerequisite for voting in this state. The factor that played an important part in interesting Negroes to purchase poll tax receipts was an announcement that there would be Negro candidates campaigning for various offices.

In several communities there were Negroes running for Justices of the Peace. One of the most significant races and one that made an impact on the Little Rock community was the City Directors' race where a local optometrist ran second in a three-way race. He polled eight thousand votes out of twenty-four thousand. In Fort Smith the acting president of the Fort Smith Branch was nominated and ran fourth for a seat on the school board. A dedicated NAACP worker and a Hot Springs business man is running for election to the school board in that city. In Little Rock a young Negro physician who is a life member of the NAACP is a candidate for the Little Rock School Board. The School Board in Hot Springs and Little Rock will hold elections later this month. There was so much interest manifested in the City Directors' race from the Negro community, that the city press has already admonished whites, that if they do not exert more interest in the school board race this year than in the past, they will wake up and find a Negro doctor on the Board.

During the stepped-up campaign to qualify Negroes to vote, the Secretary made ten or eleven appearances before public groups to encourage poll tax payments.

PUBLIC RELATIONS:

The Secretary has lost no opportunity at any time to win public acceptance for the Association. Every officer and NAACP worker in the state has been carefully instructed to do everything possible to sell the Association to the public at all times. It is the view of the Secretary that if the Association is to grow and gain strength it must have loyal friendly supporters and the policy is to retain friends and supporters and to convert those who view the Association with a vehement attitude, if it can be done without sacrificing principles upon which the Association was built.

The Secretary has made it a policy to acknowledge the service of any individual who cooperates to make any program of the NAACP a success.

YOUTH ACTIVITIES:

There has been little activity by the youth in this section this year. The inactiveness of the youth can be attributed to two things: 1) The lack of interest by adult NAACP leaders; 2) The lack of freedom to participate resulting from fear of the NAACP that dominates many parents. However, the youth picture in Arkansas appears much brighter for the future than it has in the past. During the past sixty days, the youth, in spite of their parents are ready to move. The youth of Pine Bluff—AM&N College—organized a temporary unit in November. It appears that this unit has encountered difficulties on campus at AM&N. Efforts are being put forth to convert the unit into a city unit where the students will have freedom of action.

A temporary unit was formed at Shorter College, North Little Rock in November. This unit has the cooperation of the faculty because Shorter College is supported by the African Methodist Episcopal Church.

The Shorter College group has given encouragement to the stepped-up program for the youth movement over the state. Plans are being formulated to recruit youth workers for the NAACP on a state-wide basis.

The youth were used during the campaign to qualify Negroes to vote, and were used locally to get out the vote during the last election. The job done by the youth was a flawless one.

COOPERATION WITH OTHER ORGANIZATIONS:

The Secretary has cooperated with all of the organizations in the state that are working to improve the status of the Negro and the community, and has instructed the heads of all the state units to work with organizations that have programs aimed toward uplifting the community. And at the same time, the branch leaders have been instructed to make every effort to get their organizations to cooperate with the NAACP. The Arkansas Conference has given more cooperation to organizations in the state than it has received from the organizations. The Secretary has worked with political groups, Greek letter organizations as well as fraternal.

MEMBERSHIP:

There has been a slight increase in memberships in the area where the Secretary has worked—Arkansas, (Baton Rouge, Shreveport, Alexandria and Monroe, Louisiana). The membership increase over the last year is approximately seven hundred, fifty, according to branch secretaries' figures. These figures should, and in all probabilities will, exceed one thousand when tabulated at year's end.

The outlook for 1963 sees quite an increase in membership, Freedom Funds and other NAACP activities in this section because the reports of the nominating committees of many of the branches in key communities, show where new and much younger leadership will take over.

OUTSTANDING ACTIVITIES:

Arkansas Employment Security Division employed two Negroes in March for the first time in the history of the employment division. A Negro girl was employed at the Little Rock Air Force Base as a stenographer for the first time in January. The VA Hospital employed its first Negro girl in July. These employments resulted from personal contact made by the Secretary.

The Mississippi County School Board opened the doors to Negro children at the Blytheville Air Force Base in September after complaints were filed with the Department of the Air Force in Washington, D. C.

The Monroe County Branch organized in July in the midst of white hostility where white people used guns to intimidate Negroes.

The Fort Smith Branch was saved, "new blood" recruited, and all disgruntled persons were moved from offices.

SUMMARY:

Branch Visits	Public Meetings	Branch Meetings	Mail Received	Mail Sent
42	17	21	612	2,172

	Regional Meetings	News Releases	Miles (Auto) Traveled	
	2	86	14,091	

CHAPTER 4

Remembering and Commemorating Little Rock

The documents in this section detail how the Little Rock crisis has been remembered and commemorated since 1957. The documents in "Remembering and Commemorating Little Rock" suggest that the shift in the political climate has shaped the memory and the retelling of the event. Additionally, the documents reveal how commemoration can often substitute for real progress.

DOCUMENT 46:
Interview with Daisy Bates, WLIB Radio, June 4, 1964.

Courtesy Special Collections, University of Arkansas Libraries, Daisy Bates Collection, MC582, box 4, folder 4.

Daisy Bates was elected president of the Arkansas Chapter of the National Association for the Advancement of Colored People (NAACP) in 1952. During the crisis, she guided and advised the Little Rock Nine. In June of 1960, Bates moved to New York, though she remained president of the Arkansas Conference of Branches through 1961. She served on the national board of the NAACP from 1957 through 1970. In 1963, Bates spoke at the March on Washington, one of the few women to do so. Five years later, she moved to Mitchellville, Arkansas, to direct the Economic Opportunity Agency, a federal anti-poverty program. In 1984, she revived the *Arkansas State Press*, selling the paper in 1988. Bates died of a heart attack on November 4, 1999. This interview was heard on WLIB radio, a station in New York City.

It has been ten years since the Supreme Court decision against segregation in the schools.

And it has nearly been seven years since that day I remember so clearly—when I took nine children to school in my home town of Little Rock, Arkansas.

Either way you remember, it has been a long time—too long.

The Supreme Court declared that the desegregation of schools should move with "all deliberate speed." Yet today, only 9 percent of the Negro children attending school in the South have been integrated. Nor can the North be proud of its record, because it, too, is a sorry one.

For example, there are 112,000 Negro children in Arkansas. Only 366 are enrolled in desegregated schools.

There are many reasons that can be offered for the slow progress that has been made. Perhaps "excuses" is the better word.

When I think back on the walk that I took with nine children to Little Rock's Central High in 1957, one thing stands out: it was a long walk.

Haven't we walked long enough? In Little Rock, in Birmingham—and in New York—it is time to remember one word in the Supreme Court decision: speed.

I realize that there are local problems that have slowed down the process of desegregation in the schools—but I also remember that long walk I took seven years ago. How long must our children wait?

The First Lady stated recently, that we are still shamed by one-fifth of our citizens who live on the outside of hope, because they are poor.

To this one-fifth, we should address ourselves today. We can safely say that twenty million Negroes encompassed in this one-fifth live on the outskirts of hope. Not because they are poor, but because of segregation and discrimination which exist in our country.

Many claim that they can see no final and equitable solution to this problem.

That is not so. There are those of us who have felt the anguish of segregation and the pains of discrimination. There are those of us who have labored in the vineyard trying to help a nation mold its morals, religion and politics; not by the sermons we preach, but by the lives we live. If we look around, we would see many signs of freedom. They spark—glittering in the dark of despair like a flock of lighting bugs whirling through the dark night of discrimination.

In the state of Florida, a petite 72-year-old white woman of New England—Mrs. Malcom Peabody, helped ignite that spark in the hearts of

men when she joined 200 Negro youths in a freedom march to imprison-
ment. Mrs. Peabody realized that the same chain which binds the Negro
in Florida, binds her freedom in Massachusetts.

She realized that it takes more than mere observances of form and
propriety to plow up a nation's heart and sow the seeds of true and lasting greatness.

Only deep and abiding faith in our democracy enabled the young freedom fighters to endure the searing stings of water hosed into the stream
of hate, the torture of dungeons, and the painful bits of vicious dogs.

1964 represents a historical challenge to you, to me, and to every
American. The outcome of this challenge depends on WHAT we do
this election year!

We must respect the young—freedom fighters and demonstrators—
call them what you will or may—for their fervent zeal for fighting for
what we believe—freedom and dignity for all mankind.

Therefore, let us resolve now that none will stand by as an idle spec-
tator. Every hour is filled with destiny, and every delay complicates our
difficulties.

DOCUMENT 47:
Excerpt from Interview, Sammie Dean Parker, December 9, 1992.

*Courtesy Special Collections, University of Arkansas Libraries,
Sarah A. Murphy Papers, box 1, folder 32.*

While working on her book on the Women's Emergency
Committee, Sara Murphy interviewed numerous individuals
involved in the 1957 crisis, including Orval Faubus, Hazel Massery,
and Margaret Morrision. She also included Sammie Dean Parker
(Hulett), a Central High Student in 1957 and one of the most vocal
opponents of the desegregation effort, in this group. In the tran-
script, "sd" is Sammie Dean Hulett and "sm" is Sara Murphy. The
following is an excerpt from the complete interview.

---

sd: I just feel like my life . . . you know, as you get older, I'm 51, and as
I've gotten older down through the years I've looked back and I can see
different faces [phases] in my life that there was a crossroads and I could

either go this way or this way. In my situation, a lot of the times, that I could have made choices I wasn't given the right to make those choices myself. It was like someone was always there to tell me you shouldn't do this. I think one of the reasons my parents felt the way they did about my coming to Dallas and working for AA was because of what I had gone through my last year in high school and they were just so devastated to let me out of their sight, so to speak. It was just a trauma for my whole family, a nightmare. I feel like I was used.

sm: How do you feel like you were used?

sd: Where the school situation was concerned, it was like. I have always been an outgoing person. I'm an extravert personality and I have a charisma. People are drawn to me. I was like a leader, not a follower. Therefore, I was . . . when they expelled Minniejean Brown, I believe the NAACP said, get rid of a white girl. And I was that white girl. Why I don't know. I feel like probably the school adm. felt like I was some kind of threat to them in some way. But I wasn't.

sm: That they were using you as an example?

sd: Yes, yes. I think they used me very definitely used me as an example.

sm: What about the governor's office. Did you feel used by them?

sd: I was grateful for the protection after things had gotten to that point. I don't think in a situation like we had there, which was a time bomb, I don't think people can be involved in that type of atmosphere and not be touched by it. Whoever you are. But with me, I had the White Citizens Council, I believe it was, I had the support of all these people. I mean, wonderful, loving, caring, we're talking family, churches, you know.

sm: Did you speak to the WCC?

sd: Oh yes. I was on Television with the attorney, Amis Guthridge. Like a 30 minutes segment when he asked me questions about what had been done to me. All this involved when I was expelled from school. Up to this point, I didn't take a front seat in all of this, I was in the background. When I was expelled they moved me up front and I was visible to everyone. I don't feel like I was used by the governor's office. I feel that I was treated very harshly by the school adm. I'm the type of person, I love school. I had goals I had set for myself. Its like my husband told in there. My goal was to be in the senior play and that's what I was working toward and of course, we didn't have it. A lot of things we didn't have, a lot of things we didn't experience that seniors experience in their senior year because we didn't have the time and plus we didn't have the money at T.J. Rainey h.s.

sm: What church did you go to?

sd: During that time I went to First Church of the Nazarene. It used to be at Maryland and Battery. It's now out on Miss. I'm not a racist. I'm not. I'm the type of person, I love everybody. I really do. I feel that the era I grew up in, we had a housekeeper, a lady who came and did the ironing. But I was never lewd or never ugly to them. As I was growing up, I can remember going to their houses and sitting at their table and eating cornbread when I was a little kid. My dad was an engineer for the Rock Island Railroad and my mother was a hair stylist and she had her business in our home and so we were a pretty busy family. As far as disliking black people, I don't.

sm: Did you mother and daddy feel like you?

sd: Well, here's the whole thing, the bottom line. When they started to integrate the schools, I think what everybody objected to was the fact that they did not start integrating at the kindergarten, first grade level. High school students, we had never gone to school together, we'd never associated with them socially. The nine black students that integrated Central High did not live in LR high school. Are you aware of that? They were brought into LR to integrate that school by the NAACP. I don't recall where. I know one of them was from some place in Minnesota, Minniejean Brown was from New York, Ernest Green, I can't remember where he was from, Melba Patillio, she was in my home room and she was nice, she and I had a lot of conversation. I was not one of these students who put gum in their chairs or their hair or laughed at them when they got hurt, or pushed down the stairs. But Minniejean was the one who pushed people down the stairs. She actually instigated a lot of what went on there. She was what I would call a rabble rouser, a trouble maker. But those students . . .

[lost some tape] . . .

sm: Back to Central High thing, how do you think that experience changed you?

sd: Well, it made me more skeptical of people and their motives. I feel like as I said earlier, that's when my life took a turn. I felt like I didn't get Miss Little Rock because of the publicity I had had. Anybody there knew, it was too close to the time. I think that would have created more negative publicity for the pagaent. I don't know. Whether it is or not that's the way I felt and I think that's important.

sm: Anybody involved on one side or the other did get that kind of branding so it was a liability.

sd: Did we know that then? That blacks were going to monopolize the sports fields? Things would evolve the way they have today? Did we know that? It was different. It's like I said. It wasn't, as far as I'm concerned, as far as them integrated at the high school level, we felt like it's being pushed down our throats. Our parents were opposed to it, our grandparents were opposed to it. We were not raised like that, they're integrating our school. They're not even integrated in the north. We had friends that live in Texas that can tell us that there is . . . one person, friend of mine, lived in Connecticut, and she told me she never saw a black person until hse moved to Dallas. Like I said, I'm not a racist. I am not a bigot, I don't hate black people. I have some very dear friends who are black. Here and in Little Rock. That I've worked with. That I have worked with in the past, that I do now. Some of them I hold a lot higher in my heart than I do some whites. But I think that we would just make . . . Why were we chosen? Why was Little Rock Central High School chosen? Was it because Orval Faubus was governor of Arkansas and he was opposed to it?

sm: I think they didn't think there would be any trouble there. Because they thought it had been a peaceful community up to that time and they did not have a history of conflict between races and they felt like it would be more peaceful there than it would have been in Alabama, Mississippi, etc. REally thought LR would go well. They didn't expect the trouble. And they didn't think Faubus would get involved in it because he had a very moderate record up until that time. So it was a real surprise that the depth of people's feeling that came out of that. You're trying to understand as a historian why did it happen there?

sd: I would give any thing if I had the memorabilia to show you but my husband burned it. Because it was very important to me. There were years that it was tucked away in the attic. I received letters from all over the world. And people would send me money, as much as $20 in one letter. I got hundreds of dollars, just people saying, we're behind you. They had seen me on television. Then NBC or ABC picked it up and carried it nationwide. People were against it. That's all there was to it. They were against it. If they were integrated . . . we didn't have black kids that lived in our neighborhood. How could they go to our school if they didn't live in our neighborhood? And now they've got busing but I hear they're finding out that that's not working. I just feel like I wish I had lived somewhere else.

sm: You wish you hadn't gone through it? Is that what you are saying?

sd: I wish I had lived somewhere else and that I had grown up somewhere else so I would not have been subjected to that.

sm: So that you would not have been involved as a player, an actor in that?

sd: Yeah. I think it took a lot from me. I used to dance on Steve's show. You remember Steve Stephens? Your party on Saturday? Just had a great time. We'd go down there every afternoon. Then of course, when things got so hot, I had a bodyguard to go down there and a bodyguard to follow me home, you know, and it was really bad. But it was not of my doing. You know what I'm saying. It was not of my doing. I feel like I was used. Made an example of.

DOCUMENT 48:
Editorial, Dr. R. W. Ross, "Where is the rest of LRCHS?"

Arkansas Democrat-Gazette, *September 25, 1997. Courtesy* Arkansas Democrat-Gazette.

R. Wendell Ross was to have served as Central High School's student body president for the 1958–1959 school year. During the year the school was closed, he and twenty-eight other students completed correspondence courses so they could continue to play on Central's football team. After graduating from Central High, he completed a degree at Ouachita Baptist University in Arkadelphia, Arkansas. He then enrolled at the University of Arkansas Medical School in Little Rock. After completing his residency in family practice, he served in the U.S. Air Force for three years, part of that time in Vietnam as a flight surgeon. Dr. Ross has worked for thirty-six years as a family physician in Van Buren, Arkansas. He is married to Joy Schnieder and has three children and eight grandchildren.

I find it very ironic that the observance of the 40th anniversary of the integration of Little Rock Central High School today will be a segregated event. Not one former white student who attended LRCHS in 1957, 1958 or 1959 has been invited to participate in this historic and important gathering.

Those of us who were Central High students at that time are not surprised by our exclusion. No consideration then or now was ever given to the contribution and sacrifice that the 2,000 students and faculty (minus about 50 troublemakers) made to the successful integration of that facility.

The recognition of nine African-American students who integrated Central is entirely appropriate and I applaud that. It was wrong that their safety was ever compromised, and the emotional trauma they experienced was painful to me then as it is now.

But if at this time we find it so important to pay tribute to those who sacrificially participated in this great historical accomplishment, then it is morally wrong to not recognize the 2,000 white students of Little Rock Central High School. The majority of us, though not delighted with the difficulties of those days, faced them head-on and as good citizens went out of our way to befriend and help those nine black students.

Volumes could and will be written to verify the truth of my preceding statement. The vast majority of us went to school every day, studied hard, kept the rules, supported Principal Jess Matthews and our teachers and coaches, and, by being a part of the grass-roots moral fiber of our school, community and nation, made it possible for there to be a milieu for the success of the school year in 1997–98 that culminated when Ernest Green became the first African-American to receive his diploma from that institution.

It is also of interest that those of us who were graduating from high school in those years were a part of the great numbers of young men who had finished high school, finished their higher education and went to Vietnam as officers and leaders to fight an unpopular war again at great personal sacrifice for an ungrateful nation.

It was plain to the student body when those events were taking place that Gov. Orval Faubus placed us all in physical and emotional danger simply to bolster his sagging political career. Had our state and federal governments been as thoughtful and wise as our local leaders, such as Mayor Woodrow Mann, they could have planned appropriately and avoided the intolerable situation of anarchy that occurred outside Central in 1957. When we looked from the windows of the school building at the troublemakers outside, only very rarely did we recognize any of our neighbors. They were all rabble who had come from outside Little Rock and Pulaski County.

The following year, my high school was closed and I had to seek an education elsewhere, as did my fellow students, so I would like to use this platform to express my congratulations to and admiration for the white students of Little Rock Central High School in the years of 1958 and 1959 as well as the new African-American students who enrolled there during those days.

I would like to say to them: You are the heroes and you are the success for this great nation.

Men like Orval Faubus and Bill Clinton have always been political opportunists and they always will be. They will make the headlines and their face and name will be billboarded in the press. But it is people like you, who are good citizens, have principles and strong values of decency and what is right, who, when called upon to do the difficult things like Little Rock Central High School and Vietnam, get the job done, and thus become the foundation of this great nation.

It would be nice if someone would acknowledge that. It would be appropriate to be recognized as a positive contributor to that historical event, but the real heroes are never recognized and never honored. Their honor comes from being what they are.

DOCUMENT 49:

Bill Clinton, "Remarks by the President in Ceremony Commemorating the 40th Anniversary of the Desegregation of Central High School," September 25, 1997.

Courtesy William J. Clinton Library.

William Jefferson "Bill" Clinton was born in Hope, Arkansas, in 1946 and was eleven years old during the Little Rock crisis. He was elected forty-second president of the United States in 1992, serving two terms. A graduate of Georgetown University, Clinton was awarded a Rhodes Scholarship in 1968 to study at Oxford University. He completed his law degree at Yale in 1973. In 1976, Clinton served as the Arkansas attorney general, and he won the governor's race in 1978. He lost a re-election bid, but was then re-elected governor in 1982.

REMARKS BY THE PRESIDENT
IN CEREMONY COMMEMORATING
THE 40TH ANNIVERSARY OF THE
DESEGREGATION OF CENTRAL HIGH SCHOOL

Central High School
Little Rock, Arkansas

11:10 A.M. CDT

THE PRESIDENT: Governor and Mrs. Huckabee; Mayor and Mrs. Dailey; my good friend, Daisy Bates, and the families of Wylie Branton and Justice Thurgood Marshall. To the co-chairs of this event, Mr. Howard, and all the faculty and staff here at Central High; to Fatima and her fellow students—(applause)—to all my fellow Americans: Hillary and I are glad to be home, especially on this day. And we thank you for your welcome. (Applause.)

I would also be remiss if I did not say one other word, just as a citizen. You know, we just sent our daughter off to college, and for eight and a half years she got a very good education in the Little Rock school district. And I want to thank you all for that. (Applause.)

On this beautiful, sun-shiny day, so many wonderful words have already been spoken with so much conviction, I am reluctant to add to them. But I must ask you to remember once more and to ask yourselves, what does what happened here 40 years ago mean today. What does it tell us, most importantly, about our children's tomorrows.

Forty years ago, a single image first seared the heart and stirred the conscience of our nation; so powerful most of us who saw it then recall it still. A 15-year-old girl wearing a crisp black and white dress, carrying only a notebook, surrounded by large crowds of boys and girls, men and women, soldiers and police officers, her head held high, her eyes fixed straight ahead. And she is utterly alone.

On September 4th, 1957, Elizabeth Eckford walked to this door for her first day of school, utterly alone. She was turned away by people who were afraid of change, instructed by ignorance, hating what they simply could not understand. And America saw her, haunted and taunted for the simple color of her skin, and in the image we caught a very disturbing glimpse of ourselves.

We saw not one nation under God, indivisible, with liberty and justice for all, but two Americas, divided and unequal. What happened here changed the course of our country here forever. Like Independence Hall where we first embraced the idea that God created us all equal. Like Gettysburg, where Americans fought and died over whether we would remain one nation, moving closer to the true meaning of equality. Like them, Little Rock is historic ground. For, surely it was here at Central High that we took another giant step close to the idea of America.

Elizabeth Eckford, along with her eight schoolmates, were turned away on September 4th, but the Little Rock Nine did not turn back. Forty years ago today, they climbed these steps, passed through this door, and moved our nation. And for that, we must all thank them. (Applause.)

Today, we honor those who made it possible—their parents first. As Eleanor Roosevelt said of them, "To give your child for a cause is even harder than to give yourself." To honor my friend, Daisy Bates and Wylie Branton and Thurgood Marshall, the NAACP, and all who guided these children; to honor President Eisenhower, Attorney General Brownell, and the men of the 101st Airborne who enforced the Constitution; to honor every student, every teacher, every minister, every Little Rock resident, black or white, who offered a word of kindness, a glance of respect, or a hand of friendship; to honor those who gave us the opportunity to be part of this day of celebration and rededication.

But most of all we come to honor the Little Rock Nine. Most of us who have just watched these events unfold can never understand fully the sacrifice they made. Imagine, all of you, what it would be like to come to school one day and be shoved against lockers, tripped down stairways, taunted day after day by your classmates, to go all through school with no hope of going to a school play or being on a basketball team or learning in simple peace.

Speaking of simple peace, I'd like a little of it today. (Applause.)

I want all these children here to look at these people. They persevered. They endured. And they prevailed. But it was at great cost to themselves.

As Melba said years later in her wonderful memoir, Warriors Don't Cry, "My friends and I paid for the integration of Little Rock Central High with our innocence."

Folks, in 1957, I was 11 years old, living 50 miles away in Hot Springs, when the eyes of the world were fixed here. Like almost all Southerners then, I never attended school with a person of another race until I went to college. But as a young boy in my grandfather's small grocery store, I learned lessons that nobody bothered to teach me in my segregated school. My grandfather had a 6th grade education from a tiny rural school. He never made a bit of money. But in that store, in the way he treated his customers and encouraged me to play with their children, I learned America's most profound lessons: We really are all equal. We really do have the right to live in dignity. We really do have the right to be treated with respect. We do have the right to be heard.

I never knew how he and my grandmother came to those convictions, but I'll never forget how they lived them. Ironically, my grandfather died in 1957. He never lived to see America come around to his way of thinking. But I know he's smiling down today not on his grandson, but on the Little Rock Nine, who gave up their innocence so all good people could have a chance to live their dreams. (Applause.)

But let me tell you something else that was true about that time. Before Little Rock, for me and other white children, the struggles of black people, whether we were sympathetic or hostile to them, were mostly background music in our normal, self-absorbed lives. We were all, like you, more concerned about our friends and our lives, day in and day out. But then we saw what was happening in our own back yard, and we all had to deal with it. Where did we stand? What did we believe? How did we want to live? It was Little Rock that made racial equality a driving obsession in my life.

Years later, time and chance made Ernie Green my friend. Good fortune brought me to the Governor's Office, where I did all I could to heal the wounds, solve the problems, open the doors so we could become the people we say we want to be.

Ten years ago, the Little Rock Nine came back to the Governor's Mansion when I was there. I wanted them to see that the power of the office that once had blocked their way now welcomed them. But like so many Americans, I can never fully repay my debt to these nine people. For, with their innocence, they purchased more freedom for me, too, and for all white people. People Like Hazel Brown Massery, the angry taunter of Elizabeth Eckford, who stood with her in front of this school this week as a reconciled friend. (Applause.) And with the gift of their innocence, they taught us that all too often what ought to be can never be for free.

Forty years later, what do you young people in this audience believe we have learned? Well, 40 years later, we know that we all benefit—all of us—when we learn together, work together, and come together. That is, after all, what it means to be an American. (Applause.)

Forty years later, we know, not withstanding some cynics, that all our children can learn, and this school proves it. (Applause.) Forty years later, we know when the constitutional rights of our citizens are threatened, the national government must guarantee them. Talk is fine, but when they are threatened, you need strong laws faithfully enforced and upheld by independent courts. (Applause.)

Forty years later, we know there are still more doors to be opened, doors to be opened wider, doors we have to keep from being shut again now. Forty years later, we know freedom and equality cannot be realized without responsibility for self, family, and the duties of citizenship, or without a commitment to building a community of shared destiny and a genuine sense of belonging.

Forty years later, we know the question of race is more complex and more important than ever—embracing no longer just blacks and whites or blacks and whites and Hispanics and Native Americans, but now people from all parts of the Earth coming here to redeem the promise of America.

Forty years later, frankly, we know we're bound to come back where we started. After all the weary years and silent tears, after all the stony roads and bitter rides, the question of race is in the end still an affair of the heart. (Applause.)

But if these are our lessons, what do we have to do? First, we must all reconcile. Then we must all face the facts of today. And finally we must act. Reconciliation is important not only for those who practice bigotry, but for those whose resentment of it lingers, for both are prisons from which our spirits.

If Nelson Mandela, who paid for the freedom of his people with 27 of the best years of his life, could invite his jailers to his inauguration and ask even the victims of violence to forgive their oppressors, then each of us can seek and give forgiveness. (Applause.)

And what are the facts? It is a fact, my fellow Americans, that there are still too many places where opportunity for education and work are not equal, where disintegration of family and neighborhood make it more difficult. But it is also a fact that schools and neighborhoods and lives can be turned around if, but only if, we are prepared to do what it takes.

It is a fact that there are still too many places where our children die or give up before they bloom, where they are trapped in a web of crime and violence and drugs. But we know this too can be changed, but only if we are prepared to do what it takes.

Today children of every race walk through the same door, but then they often walk down different halls. Not only in this school but across America, they sit in different classrooms, they eat at different tables. They even sit in different parts of the bleachers at the football game. Far too many communities are all white, all black, all Latino, all Asian. Indeed, too many Americans of all races have actually begun to give up on the idea of integration and the search for common ground.

For the first time since the 1950s, our schools in America are resegregating. The rollback of affirmative action is slamming shut the doors of higher education on a new generation, while those who oppose it have not yet put forward any other alternative. (Applause.)

In so many ways, we still hold ourselves back. We retreat into the comfortable enclaves of ethnic isolation. We just don't deal with people who are different from us. Segregation is no longer the law, but too often, separation is still the rule. And we cannot forget one stubborn fact that has not yet been said as clearly as it should. There is still discrimination in America. (Applause.)

There are still people who can't get over it, who can't let it go, who can't go through the day unless they have somebody else to look down on. And it manifests itself in our streets and in our neighborhoods and in the workplace and in the schools. And it is wrong. And we have to keep working on it—not just with our voices, but with our laws. And we have to engage each other in it.

Of course, we should celebrate our diversity. The marvelous blend of cultures and beliefs and races has always enriched America, and it is our meal ticket to the 21st century. But we also have to remember with the painful lessons of the civil wars and the ethnic cleansing around the world, that any nation that indulges itself in destructive separatism will not be able to meet and master these challenges of the 21st century. (Applause.)

We have to decide—all you young people have to decide—will we stand as a shining example, or a stunning rebuke to the world of tomorrow? For the alternative to integration is not isolation or a new separate but equal, it is disintegration.

Only the American idea is strong enough to hold us together. We believe, whether our ancestors came here in slave ships or on the Mayflower, whether they came through the portals of Ellis Island or on a plane to San Francisco, whether they have been here for thousands of years, we believe that every individual possesses the spark of possibility; born with an equal right to strive and work and rise as far as they can go, and born with an equal responsibility to act in a way that obeys the law, reflects our values and passes them on to their children. We are white and black, Asian and Hispanic, Christian and Jew and Muslim, Italian and Vietnamese and Polish Americans and goodness knows how many more today. But above all, we are still Americans. Martin Luther King said, "We are woven into a seamless garment of destiny. We must be one America."

The Little Rock Nine taught us that. We cannot have one America for free. Not 40 years ago, not today. We have to act. All of us have to act. Each of us has to do something. Especially our young people must seek out people who are different from themselves and speak freely and frankly to discover they share the same dreams. All of us should embrace the vision of a colorblind society, but recognize the fact that we are not there yet and we cannot slam shut the doors of educational and economic opportunity. (Applause.)

All of us should embrace ethnic pride and we should revere religious conviction, but we must reject separation and isolation. All of us should value and practice personal responsibility for ourselves and our families. And all Americans, especially our young people, should give something back to their community through citizen service. (Applause.) All Americans of all races must insist on both equal opportunity and excellence in education. That is even more important today than it was for these nine people; and look how far they took themselves with their education. (Applause.)

The true battleground in education today is whether we honestly believe that every child can learn, and we have the courage to set high academic standards we expect all our children to meet. We must not replace the tyranny of segregation with the tragedy of low expectations. I will not rob a single American child of his or her future. It is wrong. (Applause.)

My fellow Americans, we must be concerned not so much with the sins of our parents as with the success of our children, how they will live and live together in years to come. If those nine children could walk up those steps 40 years ago, all alone, if their parents could send them into the storm armed only with school books and the righteousness of their cause, then surely together we can build one America—an America that makes sure no future generation of our children will have to pay for our mistakes with the loss of their innocence. (Applause.)

At this schoolhouse door today, let us rejoice in the long way we have come these 40 years. Let us resolve to stand on the shoulders of the Little Rock Nine and press on with confidence in the hard and noble work ahead. Let us lift every voice and sing, "till earth and heaven ring," one America today, one America tomorrow, one America forever.

God bless the Little Rock Nine, and God bless the United States of America. Thank you. (Applause.)

DOCUMENT 50:
Governor Mike Huckabee, "Never Again Be Silent When People's Rights Are at Stake."

Arkansas Democrat-Gazette, *September 27, 1997. Courtesy* Arkansas Democrat-Gazette.

Governor Huckabee delivered this speech after President Clinton's opening remarks on September 27, 1997, at the ceremonies in Little Rock scheduled to celebrate the fortieth anniversary of the desegregation crisis. Born in 1955 in Hope, Arkansas, Huckabee became governor July 15, 1996, upon the resignation of Governor Jim Guy Tucker. In November 1998, he became the state's forty-fourth governor and only the third Republican governor in the state since the time of Reconstruction. He won a second four-year term in 2002. Huckabee is currently contemplating a run for the 2008 presidential nomination.

Thank you very much, mayor, Mr. President, Mrs. Clinton.

We welcome the world to Arkansas today because 40 years ago the world watched as a most unfortunate event happened on this very campus. Forty years ago there was a lot of tension that filled the air in Little Rock, Ark., and on the campus of Central High School. And today we come back exactly 40 years later and we recognize that there is still some tension.

There were those who perhaps hoped this event wouldn't take place because it only might open up old wounds. But we come today because it is important to have tension every now and then. After all, it is tension that builds our muscles and gives us strength. And if it is necessary for us to have some tension in order that we can change things, then tension can be a very necessary and positive thing for us.

In the Proverbs it says that "he who conceals his sins does not prosper. But whoever professes and renounces them will find mercy." Today, we come to confront the pain of the past, to celebrate the perseverance of some very courageous people and to continue the path to prosperity.

It is important that we confront the pain of the past because, frankly, there are some times when as we look back on our history we are disturbed, and we ought to be disturbed. The children of Israel wandered for 40 years in the wilderness, and in many ways Arkansas and the rest of the nation has wandered for 40 years in the wilderness as it relates to race relations.

Essentially, it's not just a skin problem, it's a sin problem. Because we in Arkansas have wandered around in ambiguity, all kinds of explanations and justifications. And I think today we come to say once and for all that what happened here 40 years ago was simply wrong. It was evil, and we renounce it.

What the people did who tried to hold those nine from entering the doors of this high school may be forgivable, but it is not excusable. I remember those photos, and they will always haunt me as I look back and see the faces of those teenagers—the same age as my own children—and realize those teenagers were simply reflecting the values and the teachings they got at home.

And what is really tragic that we today come to renounce is the fact that in many parts of the South it was the white churches that helped not only ignore the problems of racism, but in many cases actually fostered those feelings and sentiments. And today, we call upon every church, every pulpit, every synagogue, every mosque in every part of Arkansas and the rest of the world to say never, never, never, never again will we be silent when people's rights are at stake.

We come today to celebrate the perseverance of some extraordinary people. The nine who have been introduced today had the courage to risk their very lives for an opportunity that the white students in Little Rock took for granted in 1957. And we celebrate them today.

But I'm so glad the mayor made mention of some heroes we often forget, and that's the parents of the Little Rock Nine. As a parent of a high school student here in this school, I will tell you that I often have anxiety about my daughter going to school, or my son, and the reason is very simple: I'm wondering if they are going to get into trouble, make bad grades, and that happens.

But I cannot even begin to imagine the anxiety on the part of the parents of the Little Rock Nine whose greatest fear was not that their son would come home having had an argument with a fellow student or a teacher, not the fear of coming home with an F, but the fear of never coming home because of a mob. That, my friends, is something that I cannot even begin to comprehend.

But these brave parents not only had to comprehend it, they had to live with it. And they had to live with the deprivation—economically and physically—that they often faced because many of their lives were forever changed by those who haunted them and taunted them through levels of racism that we read about and see the photos of. Photos that we will never forget, and we shouldn't.

We come today also to continue the path to prosperity. I say "the path" because we haven't arrived. And let's be very honest and very clear and very certain about it. We've come a long way in 40 years—a long way. But we're not home yet. We're a long way from the time when we can say all things are as they should be. But we can also say that all things aren't as they once were, and that should give us hope and that should give us courage and that should give the commitment to continue on today.

I know that when Mayor Dailey and I sat down a little more than a year ago and first talked about what we hoped might be some way to commemorate the events of 40 years ago—and I use the word commemorate, not celebrate—we celebrate progress, but we don't celebrate what happened 40 years ago, but we mark it, and hopefully we move from it. But when we sat down, we had a great anxiety and fear that we would end up with little more than simple ceremonies and testimonies of those of us who are politicians coming to congratulate ourselves for all the things that we had done.

And I will tell you today what I believe is in the heart of every person on this platform, and I think I can say with genuine sincerity that none of us here would for one moment claim that we are the ones who have moved this generation in the 40 years so much as it is the courage of individual citizens like these parents, the Little Rock Nine and those who came after them. And for those white students at Little Rock Central who understood it was the right thing to do to welcome those classmates and to accept them and to receive them. And for every one of them who had to put up with the jeers and with the insults, a heartfelt thanks.

We celebrate the progress, but now we must navigate the future. Some have asked: how long are we going to deal with this Central crisis situation? Are we going to have to relive it every few years? And I know there were some who were frankly made to feel very uncomfortable about all of these activities because some felt that it would just resurrect feelings and anxieties.

Well, let me tell you how long we will deal with it—until justice is the same for every human being whether he or she is black or white, we will deal with it. Until the same rules apply to get a bank loan for every person regardless of who he or she is, we will deal with it. As long as there are whites who turn around and see a black person coming and bring fear to their hearts, we will deal with it. And as long as there are blacks who look and see and have resentment toward a white person, we will deal with it. We will deal with it until the dream of Dr. Martin Luther King lives in all of our hearts, and that is that we will judge people by the character of their hearts and not by the color of their skin.

Let me remind us: Government can do some things, but only God can change people's hearts. Government can put us in the same classrooms, but government can't make classmates go home and be friends when school is out. Government can make sure that the doors of every public building are open to everyone. Government can ensure that we share schools and streets and lunch counters and buses and elevators and theaters. But let us never forget that only God can give us the power to love each other and respect each other and share life, liberty and the pursuit of happiness with every American, regardless of who he or she is.

Today, as we dedicate the Little Rock Central Visitor Center, I will tell you that last Friday my daughter and I went there. We walked through that exhibit and it brought memories to me of the time when Sarah was 11 and we went through Yad Vashem in Jerusalem to visit that incredible place that is dedicated to the memory of the victims of the Holocaust—another one of our history's horrors. And as we went through Yad Vashem, she saw the pictures of the horrible treatment and of the extraordinary injustices of the evil that was marked by that time. I never will forget when we came to the end of that exhibit and there at the guest book, she stood and took my pen and started writing her name and address. And underneath there was a space for comments.

As long as I live I will remember as my daughter paused and then wrote words that will forever be in my mind. She wrote simple words. I wondered as we went through it, did she understand the message of it, did she get it? If there was any doubt, it was erased as I looked as those words. Because those words simply said, "Why didn't somebody do something? Why didn't somebody do something?"

In silence, we left and I knew she got it. Today, as the world once again revisits Little Rock and the great state of Arkansas and its great people, I hope that never, ever, ever does someone have to ask why didn't someone do something. As for those who go through that visitor center and may ask why didn't someone do something, I hope they will take a good, long look and realize that today we celebrate nine people who did do something.

God bless you, and God bless America.

DOCUMENT 51:
Excerpt from Interview with Ernest Green, New York City, January 26, 1973.

Courtesy Special Collections, University of Arkansas Libraries, Sara Murphy Collection, MC1321, box 1, folder 25.

Ernest G. Green was the first black student to graduate from Central in 1958. After completing his bachelors and masters degrees at Michigan State University, Green became the assistant secretary of Housing and Urban Affairs under President Jimmy Carter. He later moved to Washington, D.C., where he worked as a managing partner and vice president at Lehman Brothers. This remembrance offers an opportunity to see how the event is retold forty years later. The full name of the interviewer is unknown.

Pagan: Tell me about some of these incidents in the halls. I'm interested in the degree of hostility.

Green: The degree of hostility varied. I suppose, because I was the oldest, it was unlikely that somebody was going to walk up. I remember that when somebody did that once, on the steps going down, tried to push me, and I pushed them back. It was the little things. The lockers were always broken into. I mean, we must have changed lockers a zillion times. And each time the School Board would buy us the books, which got to be whacky. I ended up, one, you never kept anything of any consequence in your locker. You wouldn't put notes if you were writing a term paper. I mean you just knew that they would eventually break into it. And as the troops began to be pulled back, then the little hostilities like that, in some cases . . . I remember one of the girls was called up one night and told that she was going to be squirted in the face with acid in a watergun. And sure enough some guy came up to her with a water pistol. Well, it had water in it. Now you know that kind of thing is psychologically unnerving. It's a little bit like guerrilla warfare. And because we were so outnumbered, suppose some of the kids felt more threatened than maybe I did. The fear and the physical problem never really bothered me. I never saw it as a problem initially. I suppose now if I had to think back on it . . .

Pagan: What percentage of the whites showed hostility to you, wither by derogatory terms or by acts of harassment?

Green: Probably about ten percent. The rest of them were somewhat removed from it, and then there would be five or six percent of the students who tried to be extremely friendly. The vast majority of them just stayed away. The harassment was really carried on by a small cadre of people. Central had that year, you had Blossom's daughter, you had the principal's daughter, you had . . . I remember a lot of prominent families in Little Rock, their kids were still going to Central. They weren't out at Hall. And I think the attitude was that, for the most part, that we were just going to endure it, not get involved one way or the other. And that was my assessment of what went on there.

Pagan: As the year went on did things get any better say, after Christmas? Did things begin to slack off?

Green: Well, after the incident with Minnijean some of the more avid segregationist thought that they had been strengthened somewhat. They continued some harassment. Well, we had the Christmas break, you know, of course we weren't in school but we used to run into some of the students downtown. But as we got towaards graduation, and I guess the big thing was whether I was going to get out of there and all of that symbolism that was attached to my graduating, why, then they did began to slack off. And I think the crowning point was, well, I knew I had to last out the academic year and get the diploma and all that people attached to it. And the other part was that the other students, we developed a certain solidarity among ourselves, because we were all thrown in there together. I guess, well, about March or April, some to the resisters became resigned to the fact that we were there and there was not much that they could do about it. And it did towards the end of the year begin to slack off.

Pagan: You were, I suppose, glad to have the troops there. Did the troops help you . . .

Green: Well, initially, we used to go to class with them, with a paratrooper at our side. But they removed the troops completely from the school around Jan or Feb and I think the fact that this was the first time that one could remember that the American govt. had brought in its military weight to back up a social edict, and particularly one that involve blacks and whites. And that had a great psychological impact. There's no question about that. I think in terms of black people in the South feeling that the government was really going to enforce the laws, this gave them some hope on that.

Pagan: Tell me about Mrs. Bates during the crisis. How would you characterize her leadership?

Green: Superb. Daisy Bates symbolized the greatest quality of leadership. She held the group together. She was the person who kept the parents in touch with what was going on. She was the linkage with what was really going on inside, and . . . last night I saw Wiley Branton who was a lawyer, NAACP lawyer and is now in Washington, . . . but Daisy was the leader. She was the one who helped us in times of . . . coordinating all of the activities. There was so much, just the news stuff alone. If there hadn't been one person coordinating all of that it would have been extremely chaotic. We never would have done anything. We would have just spent time being interviewed. The whole business of the troops. We were escorted to school every day by the army. We went around in an army jeep and all that. Now, when you figure the cost that the govt. put out that year, why, they figure the diploma cost about a million bucks when you figure all the time and payment of troops and bivouacking and all of that stuff. But I have nothing but praise for Daisy. She was superb, she was an inspiration, she helped us and helped the parents. Her house was shot at. You know, the advertising on her newspaper began to draw back, her paper was boycotted. She endured tremendous personal damages. My mother was a school teacher, most of the other parents . . . there was never any economic threat against our parents as there was against Daisy.

She suffered a great deal, there's no question about that. She went through a great deal.

Pagan: Tell me about the feeling in the black community. This is a very hotly debated topic. Did the black community favor integration at this time?

Green: Well, I think when you look at that question of whether we went to school with whites or not . . . the black community, particularly older people in Little Rock had great problems understanding why we were going there because it was disruptive certainly. Now you know, if you had lived in Little Rock during the last forty or fifty years that was unthinkable, for a black person to be going to Central High School. What they did understand, I think, was that there were nine youngsters, teenagers, who were making some sacrifice to make some changes not only for themselves but for the rest of the black community in Little Rock. And we got tremendous support. And the thing that everybody in Little Rock knew was that Central High School was invariably better than the black school. Materials, availability of courses, access to further education, the whole thing. And they could understand that. And the thing about the South, the South has really never in some cases been able to maintain our school system well, let along a dual school system. And it just was working against . . . particularly hard on blacks in terms of where you could go and what you could do.

Pagan: Did blacks encourage you and give you moral support?

Green: Yes, sure, definitely. In a number of cases, civic organizations had special parties for us and arranged things for us. I remember one of the black sororities arranged for us to . . . they bought season tickets for us to go to the auditorium for music concerts. Churches and that sort of thing were very supportive of us. My friends in Horace Mann, in the black high school, were extremely helpful and encouraging.

Document 52: Ron Wolfe and Mary Hargrove, "A Product of the Old South."

Arkansas Democrat-Gazette, *October 5, 1997. Courtesy* Arkansas Democrat-Gazette.

This article presents a diverse range of responses to the desegregation crisis in Little Rock on the occasion of the fortieth anniversary of the event. James Eison, who graduated from Central High in 1958, frames his understanding of the events within what he terms his "Southern heritage."

"We come here today to say once and for all that what happened here 40 years ago was wrong. It was evil, and we renounce it."

—Gov. Mike Huckabee on the 40th anniversary of the Little Rock
Central High School integration.

"I'm angry at the judgments. . . . We were the products of our time and should not apologize."

—James Reed Eison, class of '58, Central High School.

The school day had barely begun on Oct. 3, 1957, when Jim Eison and 50 other white students marched out of Little Rock Central High School and across the street toward the effigy of a black student hanging from an oak tree.

They had left to protest the presence of their school's first nine black students. They hadn't planned on the effigy—at least, Eison hadn't. He just saw it there, and he couldn't resist it.

Some of the boys kicked and punched the straw-filled dummy that was dressed in bluejeans and an orange sweater. Rebel yells split the air amid shouts of, "Kill 'em, kill 'em!"

One boy stabbed the dangling figure in the back with a penknife. Cameras snapped and whirred, and a photographer asked Eison what he was thinking. "Oh, if that were only a real one!" Eison cried.

Someone set the effigy on fire, and it burned until the police pulled it down and stamped out the flames while the crowd booed.

Seventeen-year-old Eison—the crew-cut son of a university professor —made national news that day. Maybe it was just Eison's luck that the cameras caught him. Maybe it was the shirt he was wearing, white with bluebirds, that grabbed their attention. Maybe he just said the wrong thing at the wrong time.

"There I was in history," Eison remembers.

And here he is now, watching a new kind of history—watching as his classmates and others not even born at the time apologize for the hatred and violence 40 years ago.

It's all history, and history is Eison's life. He is curator of the Arkansas Museum of Science and History in Little Rock. But somewhere in this 40th anniversary of Little Rock's racial flash point, he feels the call for him, too, to say he's sorry.

He feels the pressure. He sees 7,500 people, the mayor, the governor, the president of the United States, gathered peacefully at Central High, condemning the past.

Hazel Bryan Massery made headlines Sept. 23 with her apology to Elizabeth Eckford, the black whom she had taunted when they were students at Central High. Forty years later, the two women stood side by side at the school, making amends.

But not Eison. "I don't want to be like Hazel Massery and say I'm sorry," he says. "I can't turn against Arkansas. I just cannot tuck tail on my Southern heritage."

So he tries to explain why.

Eison says he won't betray his beliefs, his Southern upbringing, and the one thing that, for him, is inviolate—history.

Question: *You're speaking out for history's less popular side . . . what makes the risk worth taking?*

Eison: *My training's in history, my field's in history, and my life's been in history. And it just offended my sense that I keep hearing—your newspaper keeps reporting—that this is history. If you're going to call it history, you've got to tell all the sides.*

"I was very hesitant to do this interview," the 58-year-old Eison admits. His crisp white shirt and soft tan jacket mark this an important occasion. He more often sports T-shirts and sandals.

"I'm seeing the class of '58 declared as racist, and I'm irritated to hear [others] telling how we felt," Eison says.

"I was a product of my day and time, and I was acting from my early upbringing," he says. Does it embarrass him now to be reminded what he said about the effigy? The question hangs for only a moment.

"Of course, that's something I wouldn't say today, I assure you," Eison says. "Even if I felt that way, I wouldn't lower myself now to say something that crude.

"The sentiment was true. I'd rather I hadn't said it, but at the same time I'm stubborn enough that I don't like people to make statements and then apologize. I think that's weak."

So he holds his ground. No polishing the scars off history. No apology.

Q: *Your background and family?*

E: *My people from my mother's side were from Heber Springs. They came into that area in 1890, and my great-grandfather was a circuit judge there. There were no blacks in Cleburne County.*

On my father's side, we date back to 1789 in our area near Union, S.C. Our people were ardent Southerners and Confederates.

Both of my great-grandfathers on paternal and maternal sides were slave owners. After the war—my paternal great-grandfather, his slaves stayed with him.

What I can really remember, there was one of the grandchildren of the original slaves alive, and she was very old. She would come by the house [in South Carolina], I remember now 1947–48, she would come by the house and she'd say, "Mrs. Eison, I'm out of sugar" or "I'm out of flour."

Now here's what would seem strange to people today to understand . . . these blacks considered themselves some way still connected with you, and some of them bore the name Eison.

Mrs. Eison, my grandmother, would never have turned these people down from a sense of pride. She was expected by her society, even though it wasn't talked about, to provide them with whatever they needed.

The historian's business isn't sympathizing with those who feel sorry after the fact, Eison says, but with setting down the truth as much as he knows it—history as he saw it, and not the more forgiving history that he finds distorted by memory, cowardice and political correctness.

The objects of his passion for history surround him in his office that is a relic itself: historical documents, big faded paintings, old pottery, bones, swords and a thick file of newspaper stories about recent happy times at Central High.

Eison joined the museum in 1963. He has a bachelor's degree in history and sociology from the University of Arkansas at Little Rock, a knack for fixing old clocks, and a pure disdain for sound-bite verdicts.

"'The governor said 'evil.'" Eison's blue eyes flash the way he remembers his father, Col. Frederic Eison's did. "Well, I differ with these assessments and judgments of the people who lived 40 years ago in the class of '58 at Little Rock Central High School," he says. "I want to caution people against judging people of the past, unless they were here and understood the situation."

And saying this—being "hellbent and determined" to tell his story without apology—he imagines how his father would explode now, reading today's newspaper, reading *this.*

"He would absolutely throw a fit," Eison says. "He'd say, 'You'd better mind your own business.'"

His father died 25 years ago, but Eison still refers to the man as Col. Eison and still remembers the colonel's rule against calling attention to the family. But the Army Corps of Engineers colonel also said, "Segregation is a dead issue."

That taught him that his father wasn't always right.

Q: *Did your family have money?*

E: *Yes, we did. But we lost everything except our name and a little bit of property and our house after the Civil War.*

Now, my father was educated in South Carolina at Clemson; he was a graduate. I remember that after World War II, one of the first things he did on our first trip back and he was still in uniform was [to go see his black friends] even before he met all the proper people in the white society. I remember the relationship and the joy. And he gave them all money, too.

Col. Eison said as children, they had all played together. They'd gone to church together . . . [blacks] sat up in the balcony. There was this division and, of course, they did not go to school. But there was no racism as we call it today.

Oct. 3, 1957: Eison's memory is vivid as flame. These are moments, scenes he keeps ordered and tagged like museum treasures. He can minutely describe clothes, colors, hair, facial expressions, voice tones, the sound of boot cleats in the school hallways as soldiers marched the blacks to class.

The school world of 1957 is there for him like a painting under glass, all there with its white bobby sox and ankle-high pants, crew cuts, frocks, gloves, pretty blond girls and jeering hatreds.

He remembers how his "liberal" grandmother had angered him that year, telling him, "It's not going to hurt you to sit by them." Col. Eison had warned even before, "Desegregation is coming whether you like it or not. It's coming."

But when it came, it hurt and scared the Eison boy in ways he couldn't name, and still can't.

"It challenged a way of life," he says. "Just how it was challenging, I don't know." But it threatened something so deep, so dear to him, that nothing good about desegregation could make up for the loss.

He describes a "beautiful middle-class existence" at 2411 Wolfe St., a 30-minute walk from the school. He was the only child of Col. Eison, an engineering professor at the University of Arkansas at Little Rock, and Anna Bernice Reed Eison, a former teacher who owned Eison's Antiques.

"I had everything, parents at home, our house had beautiful antiques and a maid. I had every material thing you could want. And security," he says.

But not enough security, not enough protection to ward off this vague but awful change. Something—fate, life, time—*something* meant the end of life as he knew it, life steeped in white-columned images of the Old South and its grand codes of honor; something that ordered the South to move forward; something that didn't care how much the South yearned to go back. Something called desegregation.

Something had to be stopped.

Eison remembers, "We'd been warned not to walk out by the authorities, and we knew the world was watching at that time." The world was waiting just outside the school—waiting with cameras poised.

He didn't count how many other boys and girls joined the walkout. The news said 50 to 75, hardly a representative number of the 1,520 students attending that day. But it felt like a lot.

"People were cheering us on," he remembers. "Spectators—there were grown-ups. As you know, a lot of people came from the outside. I remember a lot of women. We walked down the front steps and went across the street.

"Someone had made this [effigy] and thrown the rope over the limb, and this one boy was hitting it and different people were throwing rocks. My best friend ran up with a pocketknife and stabbed it. And, boy, the photographers were taking pictures. Just click, click, click.

"I don't remember why this photographer turned to me, but he did and he said, 'How do you feel about it?' And that's when I said, 'Well, I wish he was a real one.'"

Eison also answered with his name and age, although "common sense would tell you not to do that," he says. "But I was carried away in the excitement. I felt like a big man. I was flattered by all the attention, I guess."

He walked out on school that day—past the assistant principal who was frantically trying to take names—in a show of "intense dislike" for blacks, and with practically no idea why.

"I didn't know anything about blacks," Eison says. "I didn't know anything about their history, what they had achieved or not achieved. Very few people did, either, very few.

"But the reason I maybe felt like I did—remember, I saw and observed these people on the streets, probably a lot of it came through my eyes. And then, another part of it probably came from peer pressure. A kid that age, you follow the crowd."

Q: *Talk about Central High School. How did you feel when you heard the school would be integrated?*

E: *Well, I was a teen-ager, and I don't remember whether I read the papers or not or watched TV. I don't remember being really aware of it until school started that year, and hearing the students talk about it.*

Q: *So your parents and you didn't talk about it previously?*

E: *Mother didn't say much. I do know she didn't believe in [integration], but there was no racial thing said.*

Mother had a [black] maid come two days a week, and she would always give her more, pay her more than what she asked. Why, I don't know. Maybe 'There but for the grace of God go I,' or the attitude of being fair.

If you didn't live back then, you couldn't possibly know how these [black] people were. They have made tremendous advancements . . . but back then, many were dirty, visibly so. And I remember being in the 10-cent stores and would pick things up, and mother would say, 'Put that back. Every Negro in Little Rock's touched it.'

This sounds so awful today, but I told you how she behaved with them. But still, I also know how these people looked.

I do remember, too, their values were so different than ours or your better whites. For example, we used to laugh about it . . . a black could get him a Cadillac and some fancy clothes, they thought they had it made. Then you'd go down to the black part of town, and there were these fancy Cadillacs, and the house would be just falling down . . . that's the difference in value.

Q: *But these blacks who were in the school were not the kind of blacks you had observed, so why would you feel that [dislike] about these blacks?*

E: *It was said that the black community trotted out its cream of the crop . . . the general rumor was that they were forced to be there and they didn't want to go.*

Q: *Weren't there wealthy blacks at that time?*

E: *Oh, yes, but we didn't know so much about it. Now that black history's been dug out . . . there were dentists, doctors and black-owned businesses.*

There were some with a little bit of education and could read, and I'm sure they were fine people.

If you went to the class of '58 when all this was going on and you asked, "Do you have a Negro working at your house?" I'd bet you . . . most of them would say, 'Oh, yes.' And you'd say, "Do you think about him or her this [racist] way," and they'd probably say something like, "Well, she isn't a Negro."

What I'm getting at here is that your Southern people and the class of '58 . . . the [blacks] that worked for you and that you had close connection with, you liked and loved as individuals—not as a race.

Eison's parents were shocked to see their son on the TV news that evening the effigy burned. The TV news did not report what he'd said. Local newspapers didn't, either, but a national wire service did.

Eison hadn't known his father ever to break the well-mannered Southern gentleman's code by swearing. But that night he learned "the man could cuss until a blue haze came over. Boy, he was mad. You talk about eyes shooting sparks."

And that was before the young Eison confessed that he had been suspended from school for the walkout.

"My mother was saying, 'Now, Ted,' 'Now, Ted,' trying to calm him down," Eison remembers. Col. Eison "would probably have physically done something to me if she hadn't been there."

"He was from genteel people," Eison says. "He was from the Old

South and had been brought up [to believe] genteel people did not call attention to themselves. Plus, he was afraid for our reputation. I had trained attention on us, and he didn't care for that at all.

"Outside of that, I can't tell you what he might have thought."

Eison's school suspension ended with his promise of no more trouble. But others made no such promise. President Dwight D. Eisenhower's troops protected the blacks inside Central High School.

"I do believe they would have been killed if it hadn't been for the troops," Eison says. But the guards couldn't stop all that happened.

He was in gym class with one of the black boys—probably Terrence Roberts, he says, but their faces blur in memory. He watched as some white boys urinated in a balloon, stuck the neck of the balloon into Roberts' locker and "squeezed it and squirted all that stuff in there on his clothes. I saw that."

He watched as some whites caught another of the black boys "and turned him upside down and stuck his head in the commode."

The hallways were crowded. The black girls wore long, full skirts. The guards couldn't see everything—the ink that was thrown, the skirt that was slit with a knife.

Eison shared a study hall with black student Melba Pattillo, and he saw white students smear glue on the underside of her desk, "so when she slid into the desk—she had on a felt dress, seems like it was a red felt dress—she got that stuff all over."

Q: *Was there ever a time you felt sorry for those kids?*

E: *No, I didn't. I can't remember feeling any kind of human sympathy about the fear they must have felt.*

Q: *What about now?*

E: *Now, I can picture myself in the same situation. You know how children are very selfish creatures. There is no sympathy in them. True sympathy comes from living long enough and experiencing enough things that hurt you or make you unhappy, and it takes time for you to develop a sense of sympathy.*

The quality of mercy was for later years. He saved the jobs of two blacks working at the museum who were about to be unfairly fired, Eison says. He sponsored nine Cuban refugees from Fort Chaffee, helping them find homes and jobs and taking them to English classes.

That, he says, should prove he's no racist. He expects some people will call him one, anyway.

"They are going to say all the things they are supposed to say," all those right and righteous things, Eison expects.

He knows he is not saying what is expected of him, but "there's a great many people out there that have views that are not being expressed today because they are afraid or it's unpopular."

Q: *What is a racist to you?*

E: *A racist is someone who is beyond reason. For example, people who want to fight the Civil War again, people who want to put the blacks back into slavery.*

Q: *Are you a racist?*

E: *I don't want you to write me off as a racist, because I don't think I am.*

Q: *What will the reaction be to your comments?*

E: *I suspect I'm going to get some flak . . . maybe some hate mail.*

Q: *Do you think anything will happen to your job?*

E: *I don't know if the mayor's going to be so pleased.*

At his high school class reunions, Eison says, "the one thing we never talked about was this [1957–58 school year]. At least, not that I've heard, and I've asked others if they discussed it, and they said 'no.'"

"At the time it was going on, it split families and everything," he says. But afterward, it became "the one taboo," the subject nobody talked about in Little Rock's polite society—until it built to such a happy commemoration.

Commemoration of what, he wonders.

"I don't believe what has happened to our schools as concerns the blacks. I don't believe that this is what the integrationists of 1957 and 1958 thought would happen," Eison says. "I've heard some of the same people who stood up [to me] in '58 and said, 'Oh, you're just a racist,' and I've heard the very same people say, 'Public education is just ruined.'"

Q: *If it hadn't been an effigy that day, if it had been a real black person instead, what would you have done then?*

E: *I wouldn't have had anything to do with that. If it had been a real black* *person—that's just out-and-out murder. . . . Had this been a real lynching, I wouldn't have been part of it, if nothing else from fear of Col. Eison.*

When I look back now, I can't understand the intensity. It fades.

Q: *Over the years, your feelings have changed somewhat?*

E: *Well, yes. And this I'm very strong on. You can't have a country whose Constitution says that all people are created equal under the law—and you know not all are equal, but I said 'under the law'—you can't say that and say, 'except for these people.' You can't do that.*

Segregation happens, like it or not, Eison says. "Birds of a feather do flock together." The wealthy hang with the wealthy. The country-clubbers close their gates to the likes of him. The rednecks knock back their beers in smoky strip joints where Eison could go if he wanted, but why would he? They aren't his people.

In fact, his people are hard to find.

His classmates, he wonders—the others who couldn't like being called racists today when they don't believe they are, those who did what they did with no sense of doubt—where are they? Why aren't they defending themselves as loudly as when they stormed out of Central High along with him?

"Did these people just die?" he asks. "Are they all gone? Have they changed their minds?"

Or is he speaking for them?

In the silence they share.

No apology.

DOCUMENT 53:

"Little Rock Nine and Daisy Bates."

Courtesy Senate Congressional Records.
Senate Congressional Records, *November 9, 1999.*

Forty-two years after the desegregation crisis, the Little Rock Nine were given the Congressional Gold Medal, the highest civilian award given by Congress, by President Bill Clinton. The effort to recognize their efforts was led by former Senator Dale Bumpers (Democrat, Arkansas). Speaking of the role Daisy Bates played in the crisis, U.S. Senator Blanche Lincoln of Arkansas told the honorees: "I know she was a guardian angel of sorts for you. I know she is with us today in spirit."

Mrs. LINCOLN. Mr. President, mere words seem inadequate to honor the courage of some people and so I am humbled to lend my voice to the chorus of praise for the Little Rock Nine, who today will receive the Congressional Gold Medal, and I will also speak in remembrance of Daisy Bates, a daughter of Arkansas and a civil rights activist.

Receiving the medal today are: Jean Brown Trickery, Carlotta Walls LaNier, Melba Patillo Beals, Terrence Roberts, Gloria Ray Karlmark, Thelma Mothershed Wair, Ernest Green, Elizabeth Eckford, and Jefferson Thomas. As teenagers, when they bravely walked through the doors of Central High School in Little Rock, they led our Nation one step closer to social justice and equality. While it is still painful to look at pictures from that time, where white teens sneered at their black peers, seeing the harsh face of hatred opened our Nation's eyes and propelled the civil rights movement forward.

Before the "Crisis of 1957," as some call the events at Central High, Little Rock was not associated with the pervasive segregation of the Deep South. In fact, Little Rock was considered quite a progressive place and some schools in Arkansas had already integrated following the Brown v. Board of Education decision in May of 1954. So, when nine students sought to integrate Central, few Arkansans envisioned a confrontation with the National Guard at the schools entrance. And I doubt many imagined the long-lasting, profound effects of this confrontation on the entire State. While the country witnessed countless images of this face-off, they were not necessarily aware of the continuing abuse endured by the Little Rock Nine, or the fact that Central High School had to be closed because the atmosphere was so hostile.

Now, we all know that the high school years aren't easy for any teenager. For these men and women, high school was inordinately difficult. In addition to enduring the verbal taunts and even beatings, some had to uproot to other schools in the middle of the school year. Luckily for Carlotta, Thelma, Ernest, Jefferson, and the others, a woman named Daisy Bates entered their lives as a "guardian angel" of sorts.

According to Daisy's own accounts and those of the Little Rock Nine, the students would gather each night at the Bates' home to receive guidance and strength. It was through the encouragement of Daisy Bates and her husband, L.C., that these young men and women were able to face the vicious and hateful actions of those so passionately opposed to their attendance at Central. Ironically, Daisy Bates passed away last Thursday. She was laid to rest this morning, the very day the Little Rock Nine will receive their medals. I know she is with us in spirit—acting again as a guardian angel to these brave men and women. This great woman leaves a legacy to our children, our State and our Nation: a love of justice, freedom, and the right to be educated. As a result of her efforts, the newspaper Mrs. Bates and L.C. published was forced to close. She and L.C. were threatened with bombs and guns. They were hanged in effigy by segregationists. But Daisy Bates persevered. She did all this, withstood these challenges, because she loved children and she loved her country. She had an internal fire, instilled in her during a childhood spent in Huttig, AR. And this strong character shone through as she willingly took a leadership role to battle the legal and political inequities of segregation in our state and the nation.

Many have called that confrontation at Central High an historic moment, a pivotal moment, a defining moment.

But it was more than just one moment. When these nine men and women walked into Central High School, they opened more than a door, they opened the flood gates. For them and for the rest of our country, the battle didn't end at the schoolhouse steps. Their struggle lasted for years and, in reality, it still continues. My husband and I are both products of an integrated public school system in Arkansas. We are personally grateful to the Little Rock Nine for making our school experience rich with diversity. I truly value the lifelong lessons that I learned at an early age and I might not have had the wonderful privilege of studying with children of all races were it not for the Little Rock Nine. There is still much work to be done to bring complete civil rights and equality to our Nation.

Today, as we pause to remember Daisy Bates and to honor the Little Rock Nine, I hope we will be renewed and refreshed in or efforts. I'm encouraged by the words of Daisy Bates' niece, Sharon Gaston, who said, "Just don't let her work be in vain. There's plenty of work for us to do." I hope my colleagues will join me in extending appreciation and commendation to the Little Rock Nine. And in remembering a matriarch of the civil rights movement, Daisy Gaston Bates.

DOCUMENT 54:
Julia Silverman, "Plan for Civil Rights Museum at Central High Still in Limbo."

Arkansas Democrat-Gazette, *February 10, 2000. Courtesy* Arkansas Democrat-Gazette.

The following article details the complicated history of commemorating the event. While Central High School Museum was converting the Mobil service station into a visitors' center in 1997 (to coincide with the fortieth anniversary of the integration of Central High) several members of the planning committee wanted to develop a civil rights institute, similar to the one in Birmingham. The group supporting that effort hoped that it would function not just as a museum, but also as a center that would address current race relations issues. But the plan, as the article details, was not feasible. In November 1998, the Mobil station was named a National Historic Site, and the transition to placing it under the management of the National Park Service began in 2000. Since the publication of the article, the NPS planned and developed a new, larger visitors' center that began construction in 2006.

In Hollywood, they call it "development hell."

It's the term for projects long in the works, lingering in limbo and awaiting a ruling on their future.

Such is the current fate of a much-discussed but little-publicized plan to build a full-fledged museum and civil rights institute adjacent to Little Rock Central High School.

At a January meeting, a group of downtown neighborhood activists said the idea had languished long enough. They pledged to forge ahead with plans to secure money and blueprints for such a museum.

Others involved in the revitalization of Central High—the site of a historic civil rights conflict involving federal troops, the Arkansas National Guard, nine black students and Gov. Orval Faubus in 1957—are more cautious.

Such a museum, which theoretically would include permanent exhibits on civil rights, oral histories and archives from the Central High standoff, remains a goal. But it's one that is still far from becoming a reality, said Virgil Miller, who chairs the Central High Museum Board.

"The Central High Institute" is the working title for the project that some hope would include space for an ongoing discussion of race-based issues, complete with visiting scholars, guest lecturers and a scholarly journal; it is a proposal that's been floating around since 1994 and could cost as much as $80 million.

Even its staunchest supporters, many of whom live around the school, acknowledge that they face an uphill climb.

For starters, across town plans are humming along for the Clinton presidential library, which President Clinton has said will focus at least in part on improving race relations. Some Central supporters say it's siphoning off attention and momentum from their cause.

"Do we want to see three years of planning go down the drain?" asked downtown activist and Central High Museum Board member Ethel Ambrose at the January meeting. "Do we want a president to take what has taken place here and try to express it, or do we want it to come from the community?"

Some members of the board, like Miller and state Sen. Bill Walker, say they are currently focused on other projects, such as maintaining the three-room Central High Visitor's Center, unveiled by Clinton on Sept. 25, 1997, for the 40th anniversary of the desegregation crisis, and opening a commemorative garden near the school to honor the Little Rock Nine and their mentor, Daisy Bates. Ideas also include restoring a nearby drugstore and a local diner that was a hangout for Central High students, sites that could serve as stops on a walking tour aimed at recreating history, Walker said.

Also, designation of the school as a National Historic Site in 1998 meant that much of the refurbishing is on hold while the National Park Service works on its "master plan" for the area, due in October.

In addition, last year the Central High Museum Board's nine members halved their meetings to six a year, because day-to-day operations at the visitors' center ran smoothly enough to allow less-frequent meetings, Miller said.

All these factors contribute to a lack of museum momentum that frustrates some of those who consider Central High a natural habitat for a civil rights institute. Although the most recent outline for the plan dates from 1998, and there has been no sustained fund-raising drive to speak of, they say they are actively trying to refocus efforts on building such a facility.

"If the Central High Museum Board plans on doing a museum, then we will help them," said Little Rock architect Bill Asti, a neighborhood activist. "If not, then that's OK too. We will continue to try and bring the idea of a human rights institute at Central High to fruition."

Others are less certain that a free-standing museum is within the realm of possibility.

"No one has stepped forward to take the lead in fund-raising for this," said Skip Rutherford, who serves on the Central High Museum Board and is local coordinator for the presidential library. "Let's not take on a dream we are not sure we can reach."

Rett Tucker, a partner in the Moses Nasari Tucker real estate agency who serves on the Central High Museum Board, also said the costs of running a museum were prohibitive. He pointed to the faltering Arkansas Children's Museum and Aerospace Education Center in Little Rock to prove his point.

"We should not ask the next generation to assume this burden," Tucker said.

DOCUMENT 55:
Spirit Trickey, "Guiding My Mother's Place in History."

The Crisis 112, no. 4 (July/August 2005): 52. *Courtesy* The Crisis.

Spirit Trickey, the daughter of Minnijean Brown of the Little Rock Nine, is an interpretive park ranger at the Little Rock Central High School National Historic Site. This article examines how the Little Rock crisis has affected the children of the students who integrated the school in 1957.

I am standing in a swirl of fourth-graders by an exhibit, filling in details about the 1957 school desegregation crisis in Little Rock, Ark. I ask the children if they have any questions.

"Are any of the Little Rock Nine still alive?"

"Yes." I reply with a smile.

"Have you ever met any of them?"

I pause and then proudly point to a place in a large black-and-white photograph of the nine students who integrated Little Rock Central High School. "As a matter of fact, this young woman is my mother," I announce. Their eyes widen and a few even gasp. I work for the National Park Service as an interpretive park ranger at the Little Rock Central High School National Historic Site Visitor Center. My mother, Minnijean Brown Trickey, is one of the Little Rock Nine.

My service at the place where my mother made headlines is a unique experience that merges the past and present. When I began working here three years ago, I had no idea how much I would learn. I knew that the confrontation at Central High, which remains a working school, was a part of U.S. history, but I was unaware of the magnitude and complexity of the event.

In 1954, the Brown v. Board of Education decision outlawed segregation in public schools. Three years later, my mother was among the nine students who participated in the integration effort at Central High. Gov. Orval Faubus, warning that "blood would run in the streets" if Blacks entered the building, directed the Arkansas National Guard to surround the school. When the Black students arrived on Sept. 4, 1957, the guard turned them away. The troops remained until a federal court order required them to leave.

On Sept. 23, after facing a violent White mob of mostly adults, the Little Rock Nine entered the school. President Dwight D. Eisenhower responded to the chaos by federalizing the Arkansas National Guard and sending 1,000 members of the U.S. Army's 101st Airborne Division to enforce the law, maintain order and protect the Black students, who continued to be verbally and physically harassed throughout the school year. After a while, the taunting got to my mother.

Minnijean Brown was suspended from Central High after spilling chili on two White boys who tried to block her path in the cafeteria. Then in February 1958, she was expelled for "verbal retaliation after provocation," according to her expulsion notice.

She finished high school at New Lincoln School in New York, while living with Kenneth and Mamie Clark, the social psychologists whose work influenced the Brown decision. She married my father, Roy Trickey in 1967. Both were students at Southern Illinois University and active in the Student Non-Violent Coordinating Committee. Later that year, they moved to Ontario, Canada.

We were an activist, outdoorsy family, concerned with issues of education, the environment and human rights. My five siblings and I were dragged, sometimes literally, to every lecture, workshop and protest my parents attended.

The first time I can recall hearing about my mother's role in the integration of Central High was in 1987. I was 7 years old and we came to Little Rock when then Gov. Bill Clinton commemorated the 30th anniversary of the crisis.

A few years ago, I could never have imagined living in Little Rock. Then in 2001, longing to spend more time with her family, my mother, now divorced, moved home. I decided to relocate with her and the move helped me land my dream job. In the summer of 2002, I was hired as a park guide at Central High.

Countless African Americans visit the school site and weep openly about their own experiences of living through the Jim Crow era. Every day I hear a new story. One of my favorites is about a visitor who was a member of the 101st Airborne unit assigned to protect the Little Rock Nine. He said the troops were in awe of the students' courage.

My mother remained pretty quiet about the crisis for many years, but she became very vocal after my older brother, Isaiah, was beaten in 1994 by a police officer in Toronto. She wanted to make sure the civil rights strides she had fought for nearly 40 years earlier were not in vain.

My job at Central High has exposed old wounds. My mother has had to relive many painful memories. She has no regrets about her role in the integration effort, though, and is proud of my work.

Today, a diverse student body attends Central High. Every day that I enter the majestic school building, I discover a little more about the history of my family, my city and my country.

DOCUMENT 56:
Photograph, "Testament."

Courtesy Catherine Lewis.

On August 31, 2005, a bronze statue of the Little Rock Nine was unveiled on the state capital grounds in Little Rock. At the ceremony, State Senator Irma Hunter Brown (Democrat, Little Rock), who helped pass the legislation that made the monument possible, spoke on behalf of the former students. John and Kathy Deering, two artists from Little Rock, designed the sculpture, entitled "Testament." Carlotta Walls Lanier, who was one of the Little Rock Nine, said that the statue was "proof of changing times, and the change of heart for many of us who have been left to deal with the legacy of those turbulent days forty-eight years ago."

DOCUMENT 57:

Bill To Mint Coin Marking 50th Anniversary of LR Central High Desegregation Sent To President Bush," December 18, 2005.

Courtesy Senator Blanche Lincoln, Senator Mark Pryor, and Congressman Vic Snyder.

Senator Blanche L. Lincoln, Senator Mark Pryor, and Congressman Vic Snyder sponsored a bill to mint a commemorative coin to mark the anniversary of the desegregation crisis. At the same time, the U.S. Mint will cast a coin to mark the four hundredth anniversary of the founding of Jamestown. Proceeds from the Little Rock coin will be donated to the National Park Service's Little Rock Central High National Historic Site.

Washington, D.C.—A bill introduced by U.S. Representative Vic Snyder, and companion legislation sponsored by Senators Lincoln and Pryor in the Senate, was sent to President Bush to sign into law today. The legislation instructs the Secretary of the Treasury to mint coins in commemoration of the 50th anniversary of the desegregation of the Little Rock Central High School. President Bush is expected to sign the bill.

"The 1957 crisis in Little Rock, brought about by the desegregation of Little Rock Central High School, was an important part of the march toward freedom and opportunity in America," Congressman Vic Snyder said. "A 2007 commemorative silver dollar issued by the U.S. Mint will honor the 50th anniversary of these very significant historical events and the brave Arkansans who made them possible, and at the same time, raise some funds to help the Little Rock Central High School Historic Site tell this story."

"The Little Rock Nine's struggle to receive an equal education was one of the defining moments of the Civil Rights movement and changed American history by providing a foundation upon which to build greater equality," Pryor said. "A commemorative coin is a deserving tribute to recognize their courage and influence, and I'm pleased sales from this coin will go toward improvements and programs at the Visitor's Center to help share their incredible story and inspire others to fight injustice."

"I am proud to have worked with Senator Pryor and Congressman Snyder in this important way to highlight the sacrifice and courage of the Little Rock Nine and their families," U.S. Senator Blanche Lincoln said. "This Congressional coin pays tribute to their principled stand that has shaped this nation for half a century on our march toward greater equality for all. I salute these brave Americans for their role in this ongoing movement."

Congress may authorize two commemorative coins for each year. One of the two 2007 coin positions has already been filled for the 400th anniversary of Jamestown. The Central High Desegregation 50th Anniversary commemorative coin will fill the other.

In 1957, Little Rock Central High School was the site of the first major national test for the implementation of the U.S. Supreme Court's *Brown v. Board of Education of Topeka* decision and became the international symbol of the end of racially segregated public schools. The desegregation of Central High by nine African American students was influential to the Civil Rights Movement, and recognized by Dr. Martin Luther King, Jr. as such a significant event that in May 1958 he attended the graduation of the first African American from Little Rock Central High. Moreover, it changed American history by providing an example on which to build greater equality, and ultimately a better America.

Proceeds from a $10 surcharge on each commemorative coin would benefit educational programs and capital improvements at the Little Rock Central High National Historic Site. If all of the authorized 500,000 coins are sold, the proceeds would total $5 million, but the anticipated number of coins that will be sold is indeterminable.

To learn more about the commemorative coin program, visit www.usmint.gov. Visit the Little Rock Central High School National Historic Site website at http://www.nps.gov/chsc/

CHAPTER 5

Desegregation Only Went So Far: The Limits and Legacy of Little Rock

The documents in "Desegregation Only Went So Far: The Limits and Legacy of Little Rock" examine the long-term impact of the desegregation efforts of the 1950s and 1960s. They detail continued legal battles, unlikely friendships that crossed racial boundaries, and the half-century struggle to create desegregated schools in America.

DOCUMENT 58:
Cartoon by Bill Mauldin, "Inch By Inch," 1960.

Courtesy Estate of William H. Mauldin.

This cartoon depicts the slow progress that desegregation efforts were making throughout the nation six years after the passage of the *Brown* decision. Bill Mauldin (1921–2003) built his reputation on his two characters, Willie and Joe, average infantrymen during World War II who were featured in numerous publications at home and abroad. In 1943, he was featured on the cover of *Time* magazine. After the war, Mauldin began drawing political cartoons, and after a brief hiatus he began drawing in 1958 for the *St. Louis Post-Dispatch*. He covered the civil rights movement with a fierce wit and once said, "I was a born troublemaker and might as well earn a living at it."

Document 59: Linda Charlton, "Maryland County Begins School Desegregation Plan."

New York Times, *January 30, 1973, 13. Courtesy* New York Times.

This article, detailing the desegregation efforts of Prince Georges County, indicates how long it took districts outside of the Deep South to implement desegregation plans. The African American population in the county grew after World War II, and by 1970 over half of all the blacks in suburban Washington, D.C., lived in Prince Georges County. The Maryland effort comes nineteen years after the passage of *Brown v. Board of Education*. Several factors, including segregated housing patterns, white flight, and covert racism complicated the district's efforts.

INCH BY INCH

Maryland Park, Md., Jan. 19—Last week, Gene Dunlap's son Scotty was a sophomore at Crossland High School; today he was a sophomore at Central High School, and at lunchtime he called his father to bring over his gym shoes so he could try out for the basketball team.

That was how Mr. Dunlap came to be passing through Central's crowded cafeteria about 11:30 A.M., with Scotty's gym shoes in a bag, and stopped to tell the principal, William L. Chesnutt, that he thought "things are going to work out pretty well," on the first day that a court-ordered desegregation plan for suburban Prince Georges County's schools was in effect.

Misunderstanding Discerned

The parents who have fought the plan, which involves the transfer of 33,000 students, including 12,000 who previously walked to school, "just misunderstood the whole thing," Mr. Dunlap said. "Let the kids work it out themselves, and everybody's going to benefit." Until now, about 48 per cent of the county's students rode buses to school; now, it is about 56 per cent.

That's not the way Vernon Fleming sees it. Mr. Fleming, none of whose six children is affected by the plan, is the head of an antibusing group that calls itself Taxpayers Against Busing.

To Mr. Fleming and the 500 or so persons he says are members of the group, the whole thing is part of some unidentified conspiracy—"a nationwide group"—by "outside people, not Prince Georgians," who will "use any means that they can to further their own ends." So he and his group are looking into the possibility of setting up private schools for their children, and meanwhile two of his children who were in the county's public schools are staying home.

"My children are not wards of the state and they never will be as long as I live," he said.

But, according to the county school board, the boycott urged by Mr. Fleming's group and other antibusing factions was not very successful today; absenteeism was reported only 5 per cent above normal.

Officials of the 162,000-student school system, the 10th largest in the country, had urged compliance with the Federal court's orders, as had state and local officials, with varying degrees of fervor.

The desegregation of the county's schools, which this latest plan is intended to bring about, has been a slow, piece-meal process since the 1954 Supreme Court decision, in large part because of a "freedom of choice" policy that was in effect for a decade. The public schools in the county in 1954 were officially segregated; there were 24 separate black schools. Now there are about 40,000 black students, or about one-quarter of the total.

As blacks began to spill over the county line from Washington, whites began moving farther out, perpetuating a pattern of de facto segregation that was challenged successfully in March, 1972, by eight black parents.

Central High School, which had 84 white students out of a total of 1,100, will have 58 per cent white students and 42 per cent black. It was not working out that way today, partly because absenteeism was up from its normal 25 per cent to about one-third, and partly because the confusion of rescheduling left groups of students unaccounted for.

Problems for Students

Some of Central's old students had a very clear perception of what is meant by quality education, and by the lack of it. "This was a dirty school last week," a sophomore said. "We had some broken windows. Now the windows are fixed and clean."

And James Ross, an 18-year-old senior, said he thought the plan, if it worked, would be a good thing because it would mean that his 10-year-old brother won't get "the same high school education I got."

For both black and white students, there were distresses to be endured beyond the ride on the bus—the break-up of school teams, and of friendships. "My parents didn't want me to come today," said a white girl, a sophomore, standing with two classmates in the Central cafeteria during the late-morning lunch break. "They wanted me to go to school in Virginia, but I'd be even more lonely without any of my friends."

The class pictures along a corridor wall illustrate the underlying demography: The first graduating class, the class of 1926, was just about all white, and so was the next one. Year by year, more and more of the faces were black and by 1969 it was the white faces that were the tiny minority.

For Mr. Chesnutt, Central's principal for the last three years, the black-and-white scene in the cafeteria was heartening. For Mrs. Virginia Dillard, co-chairman of Citizens for Community Schools, an antibusing group that, as do the other such groups, disclaims any racist intent, today was a day of mourning "for the loss of freedom which is the right to go to your neighborhood school."

"If you keep people segregated," Mr. Chesnutt mused "yes, they're going to develop a separate culture. You're either going to split your society inside out or you're going to integrate. The kids here, they were proud of being a black school—they didn't want to go to whitey's school, but the parents weren't sympathetic to the kids. They told them they had been bused for segregation, and at least you're being bused for a good reason."

DOCUMENT 60:
Valerie Smith, "Eight Soviets Take Trip to Central High, Get Lesson in Civil Rights."

Arkansas Gazette, *May 5, 1989. Courtesy* Arkansas Democrat-Gazette.

Little Rock's legacy has a twist of irony, as evidenced by the visit of Soviet officials to Central High School in 1989. Most of the participants had long forgotten that anti-Communist hysteria shaped the debates over desegregation in the 1950s.

Eight Soviet officials Thursday got a lesson in civil rights from representatives of a city that is living that lesson.

As part of a three-day tour of Arkansas, the visitors stopped at Central High School for an hour-long panel discussion on the subject with Mayor Floyd G. "Buddy" Villines, former Mayor Lottie Shackleford, *Arkansas Gazette* columnist Deborah Mathis and Little Rock lawyer Phil Kaplan.

More than 100 students, along with a handful of government officials, security personnel and interpreters, crowded into a first floor-classroom to watch the discussion.

Villines explains '57 crisis

Villines began by explaining the significance of the 1957 desegregation crisis at Central High and noting that the struggle for equality in education is not finished.

"The events of 1957 signaled for the first time since the Civil War that the federal government would ensure that all people would have basic rights," Villines said. It was the "beginning of what I hope will be a continued march or move for social and economic equality."

'An eruption of old passions'

Mathis, a 1971 graduate of Central, recalled her experience as the first black editor of the school newspaper.

"What happened in 1957 was an eruption of old passions, old frustrations and old fears—on both sides," she said.

Separatism was the safe option then—and some people continue to choose it today, by fleeing from black schools and resisting desegregation, she said. Unless Little Rock residents continue to fight for civil rights, "what has been could be again," she said.

Kaplan, who was discriminated against early in life because he is Jewish, said, "There are issues other than race that divide people."

He said the U.S. legal system had made it possible to correct inequalities, and that laws and court rulings during the last 40 years had effectively advanced the cause of civil rights.

"But jut because you write a law doesn't mean people overnight are going to change," Kaplan said.

Shackelford, who was a senior in 1957 at Horace Mann High School, said Little Rock residents shouldn't be ashamed of their history, but should be proud that they accepted the need for change.

Ask about minorities there

The Soviet visitors had other plans for the lunch hour, so there was little time for questions from the students.

Marcus Murry, 18, a senior asked if minorities in the Soviet Union had problems with representation.

Larisa Mezhinskaya, a senior assistant within the Procuracy (Justice Department), responded in English that the country had made "great achievements" in improving relations with the 130 nationalities that exist within the Soviet Union.

Galim Yelemisov, procurator (attorney general) for the Republic of Kazakhstan, said through an interpreter that nationalities were "exploited and oppressed" at the turn of the century.

But, since the 1917 revolution, conditions in his country have improved to the point where there is no racism and the literacy rate is 100 percent, he said.

The United States Information Agency, corporate sponsors and the National Association of Attorneys General arranged fro the Soviets' visit.

DOCUMENT 61:

Tom Gordon, "Desegregation Case Finally Pays Off for Students in State."

Birmingham News, *August 28, 2005, 1A. Courtesy* Birmingham News.

This article offers a detailed analysis of how desegregation battles of the 1950s and 1960s affected minority university students in Alabama in the twenty-first century. The *Birmingham News*, founded in 1895, has a circulation of 148,000, making it the largest and most influential newspaper in Alabama.

MONTGOMERY—Heather Hall is on track to receive a physical therapy degree next spring, and the 24-year-old white Dothan resident will get it from a school where such a degree program was not even offered a few years ago: historically black Alabama State University.

The doctorate that Hall expects to receive is a direct result of the state's 24-year-old higher education desegregation case. So are the other two degree programs offered at ASU's College of Health Sciences. So is the building housing the college, the John Buskey Health Sciences Center.

The new ASU degree programs are only a part of what the sweeping case, commonly known as Knight vs. Alabama, has wrought. Part of it has focused on further desegregating Alabama's higher education system, adding more blacks to the ranks of students, faculty members and administrators at the state's majority-white institutions.

But the case also is about using courses and resources—and restraints upon historically white colleges—to build up the state's historically black and long-neglected universities, ASU in Montgomery and Alabama A&M in Huntsville, while not taking away their institutional identities.

"This is probably the only case where the federal court has basically said that historically black institutions have a right to exist," said state Rep. John Knight, the lead plaintiff in the case. "When we started this case, that was a big question mark."

ASU's physical therapy program, which began six years ago, is one of the answers to that question. Twenty-five students, eight of them

white, have graduated from the program. Eight more are due to graduate next spring. Like Heather Hall, three of the prospective graduates
are white, and all of them have benefited from another byproduct of the
higher ed case: academic scholarships.

Hall, a graduate of nearby Huntingdon College, said she could have
studied physical therapy at the University of Alabama at Birmingham or
the University of South Alabama. But when she was looking at schools,
she said, ASU was offering the only doctorate and had superior facilities.

"It has been amazing," she said recently. "I feel that my education
has been the best I could get . . . anywhere."

Transition ahead.

Over its lifetime, the desegregation case has seen three trials and
two major court orders totaling about 1,300 pages. The orders are due
to expire Sept. 30, but the plaintiffs, a group of people with ties to A&M
and ASU, can file objections before that deadline.

Meanwhile, the parties involved are trying to negotiate a transitional
agreement. They hope that would run for about five years and allow the
state's colleges and universities, and the lawmakers who make budgetary
decisions in Montgomery, to put mechanisms in place to help preserve
what the court case has achieved and continue to remove the higher ed
system's vestiges of segregation.

"The whole philosophy behind the transitional agreement is to insti-
tutionalize in the political process, away from federal court supervision,
not only the programs the court has established and the financial support
for them, but the promise of progress on all fronts in the future because
nobody really contends that we have reached the end of the road when
it comes to ending vestiges of segregation," said Jim Blacksher, the
Birmingham attorney who filed the suit that started the case in 1981.

'Overall, a success'

Birmingham attorney Robert Hunter, who has represented the state
for most of the case, said the road's end may not have been reached, but
that a lot of ground has been covered.

"A lot of good has been accomplished under the decrees," said
Hunter, who said the growth in the number of degrees issued to black

students is just one example. "That's the real success of the whole enterprise, and that's what inspires us all to do what we can to continue that success."

Joe Whatley, who helped represent Alabama A&M in the case, called it "overall . . . a success story."

"You know, we didn't achieve perfection but . . . if you expect perfection, you're never going to get there," Whatley said. "You learn more and more as you get older and older that incremental change for the positive is about all we can achieve in this world."

Virtually all of the changes involve numbers—of dollars, students, faculty and administrators—and much of the focus has been on A&M and ASU, which have successfully argued they were historically shortchanged in funds and other resources.

From fiscal 1993 to 2005, the state has appropriated nearly $181 million to carry out the orders by the case's presiding federal judge, Harold Murphy of Rome, Ga. Most of the money has gone to A&M and ASU for such uses as diversity scholarships, physical facilities and multimillion-dollar endowments to support various academic activities, and to set up the courses that Murphy's orders have enabled them to establish. The sum also includes legal fees, among them nearly $4.6 million paid to the plaintiffs attorneys.

"There's no question that more has been spent in Alabama than in any other state on (college) desegregation remedies to this point," Blacksher said.

More to do

Despite the success stories, unresolved issues remain:

In one of his orders, Murphy told some historically white universities to boost their numbers of black administrators and faculty. The plaintiffs say more efforts are needed.

"We're not talking about specific numbers," said Rep. Knight, a special assistant to ASU President Joe Lee. "We're just talking about continuously making progress. . . . As I view the numbers and where we are, I think that we have probably made less progress in that area than in any other part of the case itself."

In Montgomery, when they thought Murphy's deadline was July 30, attorneys for Alabama State asked the judge to order additional funding for the academic programs ASU has so far established under his 1995 decree and to continue for 10 years the state-funded diversity scholarships he ordered.

Blacksher said another issue that has arisen since the case's last trial is how the growing costs of higher education are making it harder for many black students and low- and moderate-income white students to get an education. To counter the trend, the state should substantially boost its need-based financial aid for college students, he said.

"In 1990, the average tuition for a state university was about $1,700 for a year, and now a year's tuition is in excess of $4,500 and total costs average about $12,000," Blacksher said. "One of the things we want the state to do is to agree, over a reasonable period of time, to bring their financial aid at least in line with the Southeastern region."

The plaintiffs have pending at the 11th U.S. Circuit Court of Appeals a claim that the state's property tax structure, with its built-in limits on the amount that can be collected, has severely shortchanged the state's higher education system and limited black access to it. If this appeal leads to a ruling that the tax structure is racially discriminatory and must be fixed, Hunter said, the fallout in Montgomery will be something to see.

"Can you imagine what would be going on in Montgomery if the Legislature were to be charged with devising a new tax system for Alabama?" he said.

Many changes

Things are much different in Alabama's public colleges and universities than they were when the higher ed case began. Some changes—the new courses and additional funds for A&M and ASU, the scholarships designed partly to attract white students to their campuses and the extension service mergers—are direct results of Murphy's two major decrees.

Some of the changes, such as the growth in numbers and percentages of black students at the historically white schools, likely would have happened if the case had never arisen, partly because of the declining pool of white college-age students.

Knight said some results have not been what he hoped they would be overall, and cited the A&M and ASU diversity scholarships as an example.

"I don't know if it has been as successful as the intent of the court was when it was ordered," Knight said.

At A&M, for example, white enrollment in the fall of 1991 was nearly 200 students higher than it was in the fall of 2004. However, the number of whites getting degrees at A&M and ASU was higher in 2003–04 than it was in 1991–92.

At A&M, the number of whites getting undergraduate degrees and post-baccalaureate certificates in professional fields went from 17 to 28. At ASU, the number went from zero in 1991–92 to 22 in 2003–04.

At A&M, the court-ordered courses in engineering have seen substantial enrollment growth. They have yet to attract substantial numbers of white students, partly because A&M's sprawling neighbor, the University of Alabama in Huntsville, has a substantial engineering curriculum of its own.

Arthur Bond, dean of A&M's School of Engineering and Technology, said the courses are fully accredited and are boosting the national pool of black engineering graduates as well as the offerings available in the high-tech Huntsville area.

"When a person wants to study engineering in Huntsville, they have a wider selection thanks to us," Bond said. Thus far the school has had about 75 electrical engineering graduates and about 40 mechanical engineering grads, both black and white, he said.

Touching nerves

One of the biggest changes stemming from the case is the merger of the extension service operations at A&M and Auburn, which Murphy ordered in 1995 and the Legislature approved during a recent special session. In line with that, the state has allocated nearly $17 million to help A&M establish a more urban, nontraditional extension program.

After the 1991 trial, Murphy ordered an end to program duplication between black and white institutions in the Montgomery and Huntsville areas. He also ordered the state to give A&M and ASU about $30 million in capital funds, as well as preference over their geographic competitors in the establishment of new, high-demand academic programs.

These directives touched a nerve in Montgomery, where ASU was a fixture before its two major counterparts, Troy University at Montgomery and Auburn University Montgomery, took root. ASU unsuccessfully sued to prevent the arrival of AUM in the late 1960s.

The directives also touched a nerve in Huntsville, where A&M was a presence long before UAH was built and before Calhoun Community

College, a two-year school, aggressively moved into the area. At times during the case, Murphy let it be known he was thinking about ordering the merger of the institutions in Montgomery and those in Huntsville.

$1 million carrots

Also after the 1991 trial, Murphy told ASU to set up a plan to draw more white students. He told Auburn University, the University of Alabama, UAH and Jacksonville State University to do more to hire high-level black administrators and directed Auburn and some other historically white schools to do more to hire black faculty.

In part of his 1995 decree, which he modified later, Murphy ordered that ASU and A&M each receive at least $1 million in state money for the next 15 years to bolster their endowments. To spur their fund-raising efforts, Murphy dangled before each school the prospect of up to $1 million more in state money each year if they tapped enough non-state funds to match the initial yearly appropriation.

In the years that have followed, A&M has raised enough to receive nearly $5.5 million in additional state money while ASU has raised enough to get nearly $7 million.

Adding prestige

Murphy also ordered that the schools each receive $1 million over 10 years for diversity scholarships and authorized ASU to set up the only allied health science degree program in Montgomery, a master's degree in accounting program and its first ever doctoral programs. (Approval of one of those programs, in microbiology, is pending with the court.) Murphy also ordered that A&M be authorized to set up undergraduate programs in mechanical and electrical engineering.

Those programs, Knight said, have "added to the prestige" of both universities. But he said the governing boards of trustees at each school could have used the new courses, money and other gains from the case as a springboard to an aggressive round of fund-raising.

"Both schools have lost some opportunities because of limited vision coming from the governing boards of these institutions," he said. "I think that the court established the foundation and the groundwork for the institutions to be able to [do] many things that we have not taken advantage of at this particular time."

DOCUMENT 62:

Jeffrey Robb, "Dream of Integrated Schools Fading, Racial Segregation Is Nationwide, No Clear Solution Found, By the Numbers Desegregation Rulings."

Omaha World-Herald, *November 1, 2005, 1A. Courtesy* Omaha World-Herald.

Jeffrey Robb's article puts the desegregation battles of the 1950s in a broad context, surveying how school districts around the nation worked over the next fifty years to implement *Brown v. Board of Education*. The *Omaha World-Herald* was founded in 1885 and is Nebraska's largest daily newspaper. It has a circulation of 192,000, making it the largest employee-owned paper in the United States.

A half-century after a landmark victory for civil rights and against segregated schools, racial separation is slipping back into classrooms across the country.

In the new post-busing era, many school districts are letting segregation return or undertaking failed strategies to stop it. For those still striving for integrated classrooms, no clear, effective solution has been established since school districts nationwide generally put forced racial busing in the past.

For a generation of students in Omaha and other large cities, the U.S. Supreme Court's Brown v. Board of Education decision meant classrooms of color, if not a daily bus ride across town. But today, courts and school districts have stepped back from Brown in favor of broader choice for parents as to where children attend school.

Omaha joins big city districts in the trend, stressing parental choice and struggling with integration. Across the country, the trend raises questions about how much value school leaders place on desegregation.

"If you leave people to their own devices, then things can turn out badly," said Richard Kahlenberg, who studies integration issues for the Century Foundation, a public policy research group. "Integration is something you have to work hard to achieve. It's not going to happen automatically."

For years, the solution was automatic, through a court mandate: busing.

Today, one trend, at play in Omaha, is toward neighborhood schools, which tend to create homogeneous classrooms if the neighborhoods aren't integrated. Magnet schools, which Omaha also uses, are widely employed by school districts, but aren't always a lure to white, middle-class families.

In some places around the country, buses still transport kids long distances, although that is seldom forced.

While race once ruled as the dominant factor in student assignments, districts today aren't even clear whether they can consider race. Courts in the 1990s struck down that option, but three recent federal rulings have allowed its use.

Another trend in integration is more about breaking up concentrations of poverty than racial divisions. Some districts, including Omaha, have turned to socioeconomic integration—assigning students according to family income—to change the makeup of their schools and address low test scores in the inner city.

To many scholars and educators, integration's impact on educational quality takes the issue beyond a philosophical goal. As districts struggle with the achievement gap between whites and minorities, the affluent and the poor, integrated schools generally are considered to be a boost to educational quality.

Racial separation is factoring into the Omaha Public Schools' "one city, one school district" plan. The OPS leadership says the district's expansion plan would balance racial disparities between Omaha and the Millard, Ralston and Elkhorn districts.

Omaha Superintendent John Mackiel acknowledges shortcomings in his own district's level of integration, six years after it ended forced racial busing in favor of parental choice.

In OPS, one of every four black elementary school students last school year attended schools with 90 percent minority enrollment. Ten years ago, when forced busing was in effect, no black OPS elementary students were in such segregated schools.

Outside the Omaha district, meanwhile, nearly every white student in Douglas and Sarpy Counties attends schools that are at least 65 percent white.

National numbers also show that the level of school integration is slipping to a point not seen in decades. According to a recent study by the Harvard University Civil Rights Project, white students are being exposed to fewer blacks in school, while an increasing number of black students are attending more segregated schools.

To some, that represents a startling shift from one of the country's great civil rights achievements.

Jonathan Kozol, an author who will speak in Omaha Friday, said segregation has returned to the United States' public schools "with a dramatic sweep and vengeance." In the last 15 years, he said, the Brown decision has been dismantled.

"We have to rebuild the entire movement, the political movement, the national will to resurrect the dream that's been ripped apart," said Kozol, author of the recently released "The Shame of the Nation: The Restoration of Apartheid Schooling in America."

Although the Brown decision came down in 1954, the first court-ordered busing plan didn't come down until 1971. By the 1990s, courts said school districts had addressed past discrimination and allowed them to halt busing.

That was a welcome change to many parents and communities, who disagreed with kids being transported across town to achieve racial balance. In many communities, busing led to white flight from cities and to strife, even violence.

Today, legal uncertainty surrounds the use of race in student assignment plans.

As school districts revamped their student assignment plans in the 1990s, courts ruled that broad racial balancing was a means to address school district discrimination, not make up for a community's housing patterns.

But a 2003 Supreme Court ruling that supported affirmative action in a university may have opened the door to racial considerations again, even if to a smaller degree.

Since that ruling, three federal appeals courts have decided that school districts could consider race as one part of their student assignment plans. The issue might end up being decided at the Supreme Court.

"It's unresolved right now," said Gary Orfield, director of Harvard's Civil Rights Project.

In general, today's student assignment plans focus on broader parental choice of children's schools.

Oklahoma City, whose release from court control in 1991 set a precedent for dozens of districts, changed to neighborhood schools.

Charlotte-Mecklenburg County, N.C., the first district ordered to bus students, moved to more choice through extensive magnet school programs.

Although those districts are clear of civil rights violations in the eyes of the law, both have seen increasing racial separation. Both districts had an influence on Omaha's post-busing student assignment plan.

Wake County, N.C., which includes Raleigh, is drawing attention for assigning students according to family income. But as part of its plan, Wake employs a degree of mandatory busing.

Some say the enrollment arrangements aren't as important as the housing policies that determine where families live. The belief is that more affordable housing creates new housing options for low-income and minority families, along with a ready opportunity to integrate neighboring schools.

Omaha reflects another issue getting close attention nationally: segregation among school districts in a single metropolitan area. In the busing era, the Supreme Court kept desegregation plans within main city districts in all but a few cases.

But some districts, such as Minneapolis, now operate voluntary interdistrict transfer programs, similar to a formalized application of Nebraska's option enrollment law. The coalition of suburban districts fighting OPS says a transfer program is the solution to the dispute.

Kozol, the author, said he believes merging urban and suburban districts is the best option, which a court ordered with Louisville and Jefferson County. The OPS plan, which is short of a full merger but would grant the Omaha district more authority over public school students within the city limits, takes a similar approach.

Omaha school leaders stress their commitment to neighborhood schools, parental choice and the voluntary use of magnet programs.

According to Orfield of the Harvard Civil Rights Project, that approach can work at magnet schools. But the more districts rely on voluntary participation, the more skillfully they need to recruit students and create better, more attractive programs. Absent that, he said, forced participation—even busing—becomes more necessary.

Too often, Orfield said, a school district's plan is simply a return to segregated schooling, either because districts are abandoning their integration efforts or say they can make those schools work.

"If you don't do anything about this problem, you're just betting on something that has never worked," Orfield said.

Kahlenberg, senior fellow at the Century Foundation, which studies such issues as inequality, foreign policy and homeland security, agreed that strictly voluntary involvement can hinder integration.

Kahlenberg, who favors socioeconomic integration, said the most successful integration plans force every parent to rank their child's choice of schools. Schools then consider demographics or income to balance the classroom makeup.

That means some students might not get their top choices.

But if choice is placed entirely with parents, Kahlenberg said, segregated schools are the end result. He advocates a somewhat limited choice of schools, a concept called "controlled choice."

That's a concept Omaha rejected in its post-busing plans.

Said Kahlenberg, "The goal here is to honor choice and integration."

World-Herald staff writer Paul Goodsell contributed to this report.

By the numbers According to a 2003 study by the Civil Rights Project at Harvard University, school integration is slipping to a point not seen since before school districts were forced to bus students to balance the color of classrooms. The study found that: Whites are being exposed to fewer blacks in school. The percentage of white students nationally in schools attended by the average black student has fallen below levels not seen since 1970. More blacks are attending schools that are mostly minority. Between 1991—which marked the beginning of the end for many desegregation plans—and 2001, the percentage of blacks in mostly minority schools rose from 66 to nearly 72. That's a level not seen since the early 1970s. In the Midwest, the percentage went from 70 to 73. More blacks are attending schools that are intensely segregated—more than 90 percent minority. Some 37 percent of blacks, up from 34 percent, attend such schools. That, too, hasn't happened since the early 1970s. In the Midwest, the numbers went from 39 to 46 percent. More than one-fourth of black students in the Midwest attended schools that were almost entirely minority. Almost 28 percent go to schools that were 99 percent to 100 percent minority.

Desegregation rulings

Brown v. Board of Education of Topeka, Kan. (1954)—In a landmark decision, the U.S. Supreme Court rules that segregation in public schools is unconstitutional, invalidating the notion—upheld in the 1896 Plessy v. Ferguson decision—that separate is equal.

Swann v. Charlotte-Mecklenburg Board of Education (1971)—After years of school district inaction after the Brown decision, the Supreme Court forces changes, determining that federal courts can order school districts to desegregate, including through forced busing.

Milliken v. Bradley (1974)—In a case out of Detroit, the Supreme Court restricts the reach of desegregation plans. Unless outlying districts engaged in discrimination, desegregation plans are limited to the main city school district and can't stretch into neighboring districts.

United States v. School District of Omaha (1975)—Two years after the Department of Justice sued the Omaha Public Schools, the Eighth Circuit Court of Appeals rules that OPS was discriminating and ordered that Omaha schools be integrated. Busing went into effect in 1976. OPS was released from court control in 1984 but continued busing until 1999.

Oklahoma City Board of Education v. Dowell (1991)—The Supreme Court sets parameters for districts to be released from court control, establishing a means for districts nationwide to stop forced busing. As districts leave court control, courts hold that schools cannot balance by race after they addressed past discrimination.

Grutter v. Bollinger (2003)—This Supreme Court case deals with affirmative action in higher education, not desegregation in K-12 education. The court rules that the University of Michigan Law School can take race into account in its admissions. The court finds that the university has a compelling interest in attaining a diverse student body and that the educational benefits of diversity are substantial.

Parents Involved in Community Schools v. Seattle School District (2005)—This is the most recent of three Circuit Court of Appeals rulings supporting the use of race as a factor in student assignment plans. The others arise out of Louisville, Ky., (McFarland v. Jefferson County Public Schools) and Lynn, Mass., (Comfort v. Lynn School Committee). In the Seattle case, the Ninth Circuit Court of Appeals rules that the district can factor in race as a tiebreaker for determining students' high school placement. All three cases apply the Michigan Law School case as a precedent for diversity in a K-12 setting.

Sources: Harvard University Civil Rights Project, Cornell Law School, Circuit Courts of Appeal

DOCUMENT 63:

Seth Blomeley, "Desegregation Payments Questioned: Does It Ever End?"

Arkansas Democrat-Gazette, *November 11, 2005. Courtesy* Arkansas Democrat-Gazette.

The Federal District Court, in September 2002, finally ended more than forty years of court-supervised desegregation monitoring of the Little Rock School District (LRSD). This officially ended the 1957 desegregation crisis, making the LRSD the school district with the longest desegregation litigation in the nation. But there was one area—program evaluation—that had not yet been resolved. In early November 2005, U.S. District Judge William Wilson Jr. held a hearing on whether the Little Rock School District should be held in contempt of court because of a delay in reporting whether black students were benefiting from certain academic initiatives. This article discusses the money paid to three school districts, including Little Rock, to settle desegregation lawsuits.

The state has paid $660 million to the Little Rock, the North Little Rock, and the Pulaski County Special school districts since 1989 as part of a court settlement in desegregation lawsuits, and legislators wondered Thursday if those payments will continue in perpetuity.

"Does it ever end?" asked Rep. Bruce Maloch, D-Magnolia, during a meeting of the Legislature's Desegregation Litigation Oversight Subcommittee.

A 2001 agreement between the state and the school districts binds the state to continue payments through the end of fiscal 2008, which means through June 30, 2008. But lawyers in the case said those payments could last longer.

"That's not an agreement that the funding will end, but it's an agreement that the state can challenge the continuation of funding at that point," said Chris Heller, lawyer for the Little Rock district.

Maloch wondered "whether there's any incentive" for the district to end the desegregation case and stop getting extra state dollars.

"There's a huge incentive for us," Heller responded. "The desegregation case has been a detriment to the school district. We've done everything we can do to end the litigation." John Walker of Little Rock, attorney for the Joshua intervenors, the class of black students in the district, also attended the meeting.

"The state's likely future obligation is subject to dispute," Walker said. "This case will continue to last until Little Rock seriously addresses the remediation of the academic achievement disparity between African-American students and white students. You're looking at these figures, and you're asking where did all this money go. You'd at least be expecting to see some results. It's our position that black children are not being taught, and white students are being taught." Legislators were reviewing payments to the districts as another school lawsuit, one about overall school funding to all districts across the state, remains pending before the state Supreme Court. One issue in that case concerns funding to help students from low-income families, often black students.

"I don't begrudge a nickel of the money that goes to trying to achieve the goals you set out," said the subcommittee's co-chairman, Sen. Jim Luker, D-Wynne. "But I come from an area that doesn't enjoy the benefit of all that extra funding. We still have a large number of students that are low income and a high percentage of minority students." Walker responded that the gap between white and black students in Little Rock on test scores should have improved because of the extra money but the achievement gap remains. He said legislators should demand accountability from the districts.

Heller said that black students in Little Rock score better than black students in other districts in Arkansas.

Sen. Gene Jeffress, D-Louann, a retired teacher for the Camden-Fairview School District, took issue with Walker's saying that teachers aren't teaching black students.

Walker said Camden-Fairview was an example of a district seriously trying to help black students. That district has received about $10 million from the state since 1989 because of a desegregation lawsuit.

Heller said it was "completely ridiculous" for Walker to say teachers aren't teaching black students. Heller said such a statement would particularly offend black educators, who make up half of the teachers and administrators in the Little Rock district.

Rep. Linda Chesterfield, D-Little Rock, a retired teacher who taught briefly in the Little Rock district before spending most of her career in the Pulaski County Special district, asked Little Rock Superintendent Roy Brooks whether the achievement gap between white and black students has diminished since he took the job a year ago.

"I can't answer that question," Brooks said.

"You haven't looked at the statistics?" Chesterfield asked.

"I don't know the answer to that question," Brooks responded.

Brooks said the achievement gap is a national problem, not exclusive to Little Rock.

Chesterfield said the subcommittee would look at test scores of black and white students at its next meeting. A co-chairman said that would be about 60 days.

The state budget will send $57 million for desegregation payments in the current fiscal year, fiscal 2006, and $58.6 million in fiscal 2007.

U.S. District Judge Bill Wilson in 2002 declared the district desegregated or unitary in all parts of its operation except for evaluations the district promised to make in its 1998 desegregation plan regarding whether programs are helping black students enough. In 2004, Wilson found that the district had failed again to comply with the provision and gave very detailed instructions on the completion of the evaluations, including Oct. 1, 2005, and Oct. 1, 2006, submission dates.

An appeal regarding that issue in the case by Little Rock is pending at the 8th U.S. Circuit Court of Appeals.

DOCUMENT 64:
"On the Path of Progress: Guiding Principles and Goals, 2005–2006."

Courtesy of the Little Rock School District.

The Little Rock School District currently serves twenty-six thousand students and operates thirty-one elementary schools, eight middle schools, five high schools, an early childhood center, a career-technical center, an accelerated-learning center, and two alternative learning centers. This document was adopted by the Little Rock School Board on December 15, 2005, and articulates the goals and vision of this large, urban district.

On the Path of Progress
LITTLE ROCK SCHOOL DISTRICT VISION STATEMENT

The Little Rock School District will become the highest achieving urban school district in the nation.

LITTLE ROCK SCHOOL DISTRICT MISSION STATEMENT

The mission of the Little Rock School District is to equip all students with the skills and knowledge to realize their aspirations, think critically and independently, learn continuously, and face the future as productive contributing citizens.

The mission is accomplished through open access to a diverse, innovative and challenging curriculum in a secure environment with a staff dedicated to excellence and empowered with the trust and support of our community.

OVERVIEW

An organizational audit completed in March 2005 provided the Little Rock School District with an outline of best practices used by successful school districts around the country. Among the findings was the need for LRSD to develop a smaller and more responsive central administration. An administrative reorganization began on July 1, 2005, and eliminated more than 100 positions. The reorganization enabled the district to more sharply focus on its schools, the hub of its core business, and to establish administrative line authority to run the schools and staff authority to support them. The final phase of the district restructuring began in late July 2005 as the Board sought to link its core beliefs, as detailed in the 2003 LRSD Strategic Plan, to employee performance. By October 2005, the Board and the district's senior administrative team had developed a series of guiding principles and measurable goals. These principles and goals, which are rooted in the 2003 LRSD Strategic Plan, are the heart of the district's new employee performance accountability system and were formally adopted by the Board on December 15, 2005.

The guiding principles and measurable goals clearly define the educational expectations of the Board and the community at large. The net result is an accountability system that will enable the Board and the community to gauge how well the district is performing against expectations. The Superintendent's Monitoring Report, which contains the evidence of the progress the district is making against its goals, is compiled annually in July and is available to the public.

GUIDING PRINCIPLE ONE

We expect all students to reach their full potential related to meaningful work, higher learning, citizenship and service to others.

Goal A: Students will demonstrate continued and improved academic achievement.

Goal B: Students will be provided a comprehensive and rigorous curriculum.

Goal C: Students will demonstrate positive citizenship and service to others.

GUIDING PRINCIPLE TWO

We effectively manage resources in order to achieve the district's mission.

Goal A: District resources will be allocated in an equitable manner.

Goal B: A positive fund balance will be maintained to ensure the fiscal solvency of the district.

Goal C: District facilities will be operated in an efficient and effective manner.

GUIDING PRINCIPLE THREE

We encourage parents to be knowledgeable about and participate in their child's educational program.

Goal A: The district will support outreach programs that engage parents in their child's education.

Goal B: Parents will feel welcome at school.

Goal C: Staff will assist parents in accessing those school resources necessary to support their child's education.

GUIDING PRINCIPLE FOUR

We are committed to providing a safe and orderly learning environment.

Goal A: Schools will promote a safe learning environment.

Goal B: School facilities will be clean, secure and well maintained.

Goal C: Students will treat each other with respect and demonstrate socially acceptable behavior.

GUIDING PRINCIPLE FIVE

We expect all employees to be responsible for providing or supporting quality educational experiences for all students.

Goal A: A qualified and well-trained staff will provide an effective and supportive environment for students.

GUIDING PRINCIPLE SIX

We are committed to building effective community partnerships.

Goal A: Meaningful private and public relationships will be established and the community will feel valued and recognized for its contribution.

Goal B: Schools will establish partnerships to address local school and economic issues.

BOARD OF DIRECTORS
Robert M. Dougherty, President
Baker Kurrus, Vice President
Bryan Day, Secretary
Larry Berkley
Tom Brock
Dr. Katherine Mitchell
Tony Rose
Roy G. Brooks, Ed.D., Superintendent of Schools

Little Rock School District
810 West Markham Street
Little Rock, AR 72201
(501) 447-1000
www.LRSD.org

DOCUMENT 65:

Laurel Drake, "'Love and Ice Cream': A Tale of Central High Pals, Friendships Forged in the Tense 1960s Spring Back in 2005."

Memphis Commercial Appeal, *January 8, 2006, MD10-11.*
Courtesy Memphis Commercial Appeal.

This article describes the cross-racial friendships that developed in Memphis, Tennessee's newly desegregated Central High School. It offers a perspective on how desegregation efforts were viewed by students who did not take a firm stand on either side of the desegregation issue.

This is a story about friendship—high school friends and the strength of those bonds of friendship.

Members of the Central High School class of 1971 spent their high school years during a time of great upheaval: the Vietnam War, the integration of Memphis City Schools, the assassination of Dr. Martin Luther King Jr. in 1968. This period of time brought about an explosion of music still often heard but only on "oldies" stations. This was the age of Black Power and the Equal Rights Amendment for women. Like the war in Iraq today, public dissent against the war in Vietnam was common and widespread. The issues in 1971 were no less complicated than they are now. The class of 1971 came of age during these times.

Art Boone, Devoe Mack, Renee, Shelley Moore, Chris Drake, Bill— all good friends. This group of friends visited each other at their homes. They studied together at the library at McLean and Peabody. As seniors, they occasionally skipped school and held barbecues at Meeman-Shelby Forest State Park. They played tennis at Southwestern College—it was free then. Chris would visit Devoe at his job at the dry cleaners at Jackson and Maple. Mostly they all hung out together with each other and with many other friends at Central.

At that time, the integration of Central High School was fairly new. Devoe remembers that the class of 1971 was the second integrated class at Central High School—a class of almost 300 students. Twenty percent of the class were African-Americans. The class of 1971 did not have a prom because of the worries of racial problems. Chris and Shelley can remember nasty epithets from other students thrown at them for having black friends. For his part, Devoe also remembers being called an "Uncle Tom" for having white friends. Their friendship endured.

On one memorable day, Chris and Art were suspended for an act of civil disobedience. The sports teams were not yet admitting black students to their rosters and black students protested this quietly by not attending the pep rallies, opting to attend study hall instead. One day during such a study hall, an assistant principal came in and asked the three white students who were there to leave so that he could speak with the black students. Chris and Art and the other white student refused to leave, saying that whatever had to be said could be said with them there. Whatever the assistant principal had planned to say, he never got the chance, because the white students stayed in the room. Devoe remembers someone finding him elsewhere in the school and asking him to the study hall to help restore calm. Such was the racial climate that pervaded those years; small events seemed larger.

Then they graduated from high school and went in all directions. Devoe was the salutatorian of his class and received a four-year academic scholarship to University of Pennsylvania in Philadelphia. Bill went to University of Virginia. Chris went to Lake Erie College and Art took a year off and later went to the University of Tennessee. Renee went to Washington University in St. Louis. Shelley went to New Hampshire. They still kept in touch from time to time but that contact stopped altogether a few years later, as is sometimes the case when people get busy with their lives.

Fast forward to July, 2005: Art's younger sister Becky had just moved to Laramie, Wyo., and had lunch with Shelley, who had lived there for a while. During their lunch, all the old names came up. Whatever happened to all these people? They looked up Devoe Mack.

Devoe was shot in Philadelphia in 1993 by a 16-year-old boy who was trying to rob him. He was a quadraplegic in a nursing home in Memphis, dependent on Medicare. At the time of the shooting, he was divorced and had his own real estate business. He returned to Memphis after he was shot because his mother wanted to care for him. After she died in 1997, he was cared for several years by a brother before going to live in a nursing home. His children are all grown and live in the

Philadelphia area. His daughters want to care for him, but he doesn't want to be a burden to them.

As Devoe tells the story, Shelley called him at the nursing home. He did not have a phone in his room at the time and she had to wait while they tracked him down in the dining room. When he finally came to the phone, she said, "This is Shelley."

"Shelley who?"

"How many Shelleys do you know?"

"Just one. But you can't be her."

"But it is me!"

After initial contact with Devoe, Shelley started contacting the Central High School gang. This crew who had not spoken to each other in thirty years were hearing about Devoe. They called each other, and the network was reborn. Shelley flew to Memphis to spend time with him. She organized donations from 20 of the gang to buy Devoe a speaker phone, laptop computer and voice-recognition software and dial-up access to the Internet. Devoe started getting phone call after phone call from his high school buddies.

Art also flew to Memphis to spend time with Devoe. The over-six-foot-tall guy who in high school had shoulder length curly black hair now works with at-risk kids in San Francisco. He took Devoe out into Memphis, out to eat, to see the sights, just like old times.

Starting in July, Devoe began going to the Memphis Center for Independent Living on Madison Avenue to learn to live by himself. Mike Heinrich at the Center trained Devoe to use the voice recognition software. Devoe's immediate world opened up—now he can e-mail his friends and his children.

He explains that after he was injured, he wanted to withdraw from the world. He did not contact any friends because he didn't know how they would react. For many years no one from high school knew what had happened to him.

After Shelley put Devoe on the radar, the encouragement that he received from his friends helped him rethink what he wanted to do with his life. He has applied to law school. With his 12 years of experience being disabled, he wants to be an advocate for the disabled. The bright articulate young man that I remember from 1971 is still a bright, articulate person—and funny, too.

What is my personal connection with Devoe? I am Chris's younger sister. In 1971, when I was in eighth grade, Devoe was a high school senior who occasionally visited my home when he came to see Chris. To be paid attention by a senior when you are in eighth grade is to be lifted from anonymity and obscurity. Devoe's mannerly and kindly ways made him a favorite with me. Here is what he wrote in my 1971 Snowden Greenies yearbook:

"Well, Laurel, that's L-a-u-r-e-l, I'm a genius. Now I'm supposed to write you a whole page while you keep asking me if Clara has an older sister. How am I supposed to think. Keep up your old self and don't do any work and things will be nicer and you'll enjoy life more. Seriously, do what you feel like doing—even if it's the work. Now to the blah part. I like you. I think you're a nice girl—I'm not sure though. Keep smiling and don't be nasty to your sisters and momma. Love and ice cream, Devoe"

Here is the end of the story—or it might be more appropriate to say the beginning. Devoe moved to Denver, Colo., on Dec. 5. In Colorado, he is living in his own apartment that is completely handicapped accessible and receives home health care three times a day paid for by Medicare. Medicare pays less for Devoe's apartment and care in Denver than it did for the nursing home care in Memphis—much less. He can also get a job there and earn money up to a set limit. If he achieves everything he is setting out to achieve, he will not be dependent on Medicare anymore.

Incredibly, Devoe was not able to do this in Memphis. Since each state sets its own guidelines for how Medicare pays for the care of the disabled, there is a wide disparity in what Medicare will pay for in each state. Tennessee regulations favor care in a nursing home and make it difficult for the disabled to be reimbursed for staying in a private home and receiving home health care, even though such home health care is vastly less expensive than nursing home care. Devoe also cannot work in Tennessee and still receive Medicare. At the age of 52, he is not ready to languish the rest of his days in a nursing home with no possibility of working.

But this is not a story about the strong nursing home lobby in Tennessee. Instead, it is about rekindled 34-year-old friendships. Good luck to you, Devoe. Love and ice cream from your friends.

Laurel Drake, a former Midtowner, now lives in East Memphis.

DOCUMENT 66:

Press Release, "Groundbreaking Ceremony to Celebrate Construction of New Visitor Center at Little Rock Central High School National Historic Site," February 14, 2006.

Courtesy U.S. Federal News Service.

On February 19, 2001, Arkansas became the first state to designate a state holiday in honor of an African American woman. To coincide with the fifth celebration of that holiday, members of the Little Rock Nine and dignitaries from around the state attended a public ceremony to officially unveil the design of the new visitors' center, scheduled to open in September 2007.

The National Park Service's Little Rock Central High School National Historic Site issued the following press release:

A groundbreaking ceremony to kick off the Daisy Bates State Holiday and to celebrate the planned construction of the Little Rock Central High School National Historic Site's new visitor center will take place Sunday, February 19, 2006 at 2:00 p.m. at the historic site, which is located at the intersection of South Park Street and Daisy L. Gatson Bates Drive. Join Senators Mark Pryor and Blanche Lincoln, Congressman Vic Snyder, Mayor Jim Dailey, Judge Wiley Branton, Jr., members of the Little Rock Nine, and others to celebrate this event and witness the first public unveiling of the new visitor center's design.

Judge Wiley Branton, Jr. will deliver the keynote address at the ceremony. Judge Branton is the son of the late Wiley A. Branton, Sr., a distinguished civil rights attorney and former Dean of the Howard University School of Law. Branton, Sr. served as the lead counsel for the black plaintiffs in the case that became known as Cooper v. Aaron, and worked with Thurgood Marshall, Daisy Bates, and others in the legal battles to desegregate Central High School. His remarks will include information about his father's and Mrs. Bate's efforts during the crisis. The new visitor center will help accommodate the growing number of people who are interested in learning more about civil rights and the Little Rock desegregation crisis. Visitation at the historic site has increased from 21,084 in 2001 (the year the National Park Service assumed operation of the visitor center) to 44, 293 in 2005. The new facility will have about 3000 sq. ft. of exhibit space, which is almost six times the space than the current visitor center, which is about 500 sq. ft. The facility also will have climate controlled storage space to protect a collection of archives and museum objects related to the desegregation crisis. The new visitor center's opening in 2007 will allow the NPS to convert the current visitor center, which is housed in the historic Mobil Gas Station, into an education center.

The design team for the new visitor center consists of ajc architects, the exhibit design firm, Quatrefoil Associates of Laurel, Maryland and National Park Service staff. Construction is schedule to begin in June 2006 with the grand opening anticipated in September 2007, which will mark the 50th anniversary commemoration of the desegregation of Central High School.

Little Rock Central High School National Historic Site is one of 388 units of the National Park System, and one of only 76 National Historic Sites across the country.

DOCUMENT 67:
Press Release, "Little Rock Mayor Daily Announces New Diversity Initiative," March 6, 2006.

Courtesy of the City of Little Rock.

To continue to address issues of fairness and equity, Mayor Jim Dailey of Little Rock announced the formation of Diversity Councils in the five Little Rock high schools. The effort was coordinated by the city's Racial and Cultural Diversity Commission, formed in 1994 and directed by Carlette Henderson. The commission's mission "is to ensure that all the residents of the City and all persons subject to its jurisdiction enjoy equal freedom to pursue their aspirations without discrimination because of race, ethnicity, color or national origin." The commission has nineteen members who serve three-year terms, including Spirit Trickey, the daughter of Minnijean Brown, one of the Little Rock Nine.

Flanked by members of Little Rock's Racial and Cultural Diversity Commission (RCDC) and area educators, Little Rock Mayor Jim Dailey today announced the creation of Diversity Councils in area high schools.

This program was made possible by a $35,000 grant from the Arkansas Department of Education. The Department's director, Dr. Ken James was also present at the announcement.

"Since 1994, Little Rock's Racial and Cultural Diversity Commission has been creating programs to increase our awareness of—and appreciation for—other backgrounds, cultures, and races," said Mayor Dailey. "The creation of Diversity Councils is the next step in their efforts," he continued.

Diversity Councils will be established at public, private, and parochial high schools in Central Arkansas to sponsor programs and activities to promote diversity, tolerance, and appreciation of different cultures. Student representatives from each participating school will be selected to serve on a Youth Advisory Council to work with the RCDC's Education Committee.

Currently six schools are participating in the effort: Little Rock Central, Mount St. Mary's Academy, Pulaski Academy, Mills, North Little Rock, and North Pulaski. Five more high schools are interested in participating, according to Carlette Henderson, RCDC executive director.

"Since 2004, the RCDC has sponsored the 'Keeping It Real' youth summit, which brings high school students from Central Arkansas public and private schools together for a day of inspiration, fellowship, and unity," said Henderson. "Each year, this event empowers students to realize that they really can change the course of our City, State, Nation, and World for the better. But "Keeping It Real" is only for one day. We know that there are 364 other days in which we still need to equip youth. The Diversity Councils are the tools for this to happen."

DOCUMENT 68:

Interview with Roy G. Brooks, Superintendent of Schools, Little Rock School District, July 31, 2006.

Courtesy Roy G. Brooks.

Roy G. Brooks became the superintendent of schools of the Little Rock School District in 2004 and consented to an interview with the authors in the summer of 2006. He previously served as an area superintendent in the Orange County Public Schools in Orlando, Florida, the twelfth largest district in the nation. He holds a bachelor of science in education, a masters in administration, and an education doctorate.

I came here in July of 2004, and my first impression was that there was a good group of courageous people who had been working on behalf of the schools for a long, long time. Think back to 1955, when the Little Rock School Board met in a closed session to decide that over a two-year period that they would phase in a desegregation program. This is a bold step for seven white people who were under no pressure to do so. They had a plan after *Brown v. Board of Education* and were prepared to take the lead in implementing it. So many districts just sat and waited. Not Little Rock. This plan was an extension of the goodwill of the people in this community. Nine black teenagers didn't just show up at Central High, it took a lot of work behind the scenes between the white and African American community.

That legacy is still alive today. Now, when I got here, I had all of this history to draw upon. From the outside looking in, I realized that we need to go beyond the shadows of 1957. Too much emphasis today is placed on what was, there is not enough emphasis placed on what is. The district as a whole in 1957 was comprised of twenty thousand students, 28 percent of whom were African American. Today, it only has twenty-six thousand students, but 70 percent are African American. For fifteen years in the 1980s and 1990s, there was very little growth, something like 1 percent over this period. The city grew, but the school district did not. The events of 1957 have had a devastating effect on the growth and perception of the school district. So we can't ignore history, but we have to determine what is the best way to move forward. Today, Little Rock is known in America, not for the Clinton Library, not for the cultural activities that we have, but for what happened in 1957. Well, I would argue that it is time to shift our focus from the Little Rock Nine and what happened in 1957 to the Little Rock twenty-six thousand and what will happen today and tomorrow. Not that those courageous teenagers are not important. But by focusing solely on them, we lose sight of what needs to be done to better educate the youth in our community today. I think it is time to move forward. This is how you salute the Little Rock Nine—by making this a world-class school district. My goal is to make the Little Rock School District the highest-achieving urban school district in the nation. And I think we can do it, because we still have a diverse, committed group of people who are still with us in Little Rock.

I credit some of our recent successes to the board that hired me to fix this school district. It was a balanced group of people who had the best interests of the students at heart. And we need stability. I can't quote the exact figure, but in the last twenty years, we've had something like thirteen or fourteen superintendents. I plan to be here a long time and perhaps that is the kind of stability the district needs. With respect to the desegregation of Central High School, it created an environment where we had to work together to succeed. Had there been no fight, we might not have the cross-racial collaboration that we have today.

DOCUMENT 69:
Photograph, Central High School, 2006.

Courtesy Catherine Lewis.

Little Rock Senior High School (renamed Little Rock Central High) was the most beautiful and largest high school in the nation when it was built in 1927 at a cost of $1.5 million. In 1977, the school was listed on the National Register of Historic Places. Five years later it was designated a National Historic Landmark. In 2003 and 2005, *Newsweek* named Central High among the top 250 best high schools in the nation. In 2006, the magazine again recognized the school, this time naming it among the top 20.

Timeline

1619—Twenty Africans are brought aboard a Dutch ship to Virginia and become the first slaves in America.

1793—Congress adopts the Fugitive Slave Law, making it a criminal offense to protect a fugitive slave throughout the nation. The Compromise of 1850 eventually strengthens the law.

1808—Congress outlaws the importation of slaves.

1822—Denmark Vesey, a free black, organizes a slave rebellion in Charleston, South Carolina.

1831—Nat Turner, a slave in Southampton County, Virginia, leads a rebellion involving fifty slaves and free blacks.

1849—*Roberts v. City of Boston* declares separate black and white schools legal. State law later overturns the ruling.

1857—The *Dred Scott v. Sandford* decision denies U.S. citizenship to blacks.

1861—The Civil War begins.

1863—Abraham Lincoln issues the Emancipation Proclamation on January 1, freeing slaves in all states still in Confederate hands. Later, all slaves are freed by ratification of the Thirteenth Amendment.

1865—The Civil War ends, Reconstruction begins, the Bureau of Refugees, Freedmen and Abandoned Lands (the Freedman's Bureau) is established, and the Thirteenth Amendment ends slavery in the United States.

1866—A Republican-led Congress passes the Civil Rights Act to counter the Black Codes that prevent African Americans from making contracts, serving as witnesses in court, or owning private property. President Andrew Johnson vetoes the bill, but Congress overrides him.

1868—The Fourteenth Amendment extends U.S. citizenship to black men and women.

1870—The Fifteenth Amendment gives black men the right to vote. Black and white women would not be given the right to vote until 1920, with the passage of the Nineteenth Amendment.

1873—Section I of the Fourteenth Amendment is essentially negated by the Slaughter-House Cases, which narrow federal power by asserting that the rights of citizens remained under state control.

1875—The first Civil Rights Act is passed, but legal challenges in 1883 further limit the Fourteenth Amendment because private individuals and businesses were determined to be exempt from the discrimination provision.

1877—Reconstruction ends.

1890—The first Jim Crow laws in the nation are passed in Louisiana, mandating "separate but equal" accommodations for whites and blacks on railroads.

1891—Homer Plessy is arrested in Louisiana for riding in a white car on an intrastate trip.

1896—In *Plessy v. Ferguson,* the Supreme Court upholds the constitutionality of Louisiana's separate but equal law, making segregated public facilities legal.

1899—The Supreme Court declares in *Cummings v. Richmond County Board of Education* that individual states control public school education.

1908—In *Berea College v. Kentucky,* civil rights are further restricted when the Supreme Court rules that private educational institutions must abide by the segregation laws of the state.

1909—The National Association for the Advancement of Colored People (NAACP) is founded.

1917—*Buchanan v. Warley* outlaws a municipal ordinance mandating residential segregation, giving the NAACP one of its first legal victories in this area.

1927—*Gong Lum v. Rice* upholds the right of the state to define and enforce racial classifications for educational purposes. That fall,

Little Rock Senior High School opens its doors (it is renamed Central High School in 1953).

1929—In the fall, Paul Laurence Dunbar High School opens for black students in Little Rock, at a cost of $400,000, compared to the $1.5 million spent on Little Rock Central High.

1933—The NAACP begins targeting educational desegregation in graduate and professional schools through legal action. The first such case, involving the University of North Carolina on behalf of Thomas Hocutt, is lost on a technicality.

1934—Charles Hamilton Houston, dean of the Howard University Law School, is appointed the NAACP special legal counsel.

1935—The Maryland Supreme Court orders in *University of Maryland v. Murray* that a black student be admitted to the law school. That same year, Thurgood Marshall joins the NAACP legal staff.

1938—In *Missouri ex rel. Gaines v. Canada,* the Supreme Court orders that Lloyd Gaines, an African American resident, must be admitted to Missouri's law school.

1939—The NAACP Legal Defense and Educational Fund is established under the leadership of Charles Houston.

1942—President Franklin D. Roosevelt signs Executive Order 8802, banning racial discrimination in government departments and defense industries. The order also creates the Fair Employment Practice Committee to oversee compliance.

1944—Gunnar Myrdal publishes *An American Dilemma,* naming race as a major American problem.

1948—The University of Arkansas becomes the first southern university to be integrated.

1949—President Harry S. Truman signs Executive Order 9981, desegregating the armed forces. His successor, Dwight D. Eisenhower, ultimately implements it. The University of Arkansas School of Law is integrated in time for the fall term.

1950—In *Sweatt v. Painter* and *McLaurin v. Oklahoma State Regents,* the Supreme Court declares that the separate but equal standard in state-supported higher education is unattainable.

1951—In January, the board members of the Little Rock Public Library agree to integrate its facilities.

1952—Initial oral arguments in *Brown v. Board of Education* are presented to the Supreme Court.

1954—On May 17, *Brown* declares "separate but equal" facilities for African Americans violate the Constitution, thus overturning the 1896 *Plessy* decision. On May 22, the Little Rock School Board issues a statement indicating that it plans to comply with the Supreme Court's decision.

1955—On May 24, the Little Rock School Board unanimously accepts Superintendent Virgil Blossom's plan of gradual integration that would begin in the fall of 1957 in the city's four high schools. Lower grades would be gradually added over the next six years. Little Rock names Blossom "Man of the Year." On May 31, *Brown II* declares that segregation in public education must be eliminated "with all deliberate speed." Emmett Till is lynched in Mississippi in August.

1956—On January 23, twenty-seven black students are refused entry into Little Rock schools. On August 28, Federal Judge John E. Miller dismisses the NAACP suit, declaring the Little Rock School Board had acted in "utmost good faith." The NAACP appeals the decision. That fall, Little Rock's public buses are quietly desegregated.

The Montgomery bus boycott, begun in December 1955 to alleviate discrimination on city's bus lines, succeeds and catapults Martin Luther King Jr. into the national spotlight.

Alabama passes a state law preventing the NAACP from operating. Soon after, five other states pass laws requiring the NAACP to turn over registration roles and lists of contributors.

On November 6, Arkansas voters approve three anti-integration measures, including a pupil assignment law.

1957—On February 19, the Arkansas Senate approves four segregationist bills, intending to undermine statewide desegregation efforts. In August, ten African American ministers test the validity of those laws.

On March 16, Wayne Upton and Henry V. Rath are elected to the Little Rock School Board, over two rabid segregationists. They both endorse the gradual integration plan.

Eighty of the 517 eligible students living in Central High's district elect to attend Central High. Seventeen are selected after being interviewed by Virgil Blossom. The number is reduced to nine when eight students elect to remain at Horace Mann High School, an all-black institution.

Over the summer, opponents to the desegregation plan organize the Capital Citizens' Council and an auxiliary, the Mother's League of Central High School.

On August 27, the newly formed Mother's League holds its first meeting and seeks a temporary injunction against school integration, which is granted by Pulaski County Chancellor Murray Reed. Within the week, Federal District Judge Ronald Davies nullifies the injunction.

On September 2, Governor Orval Faubus announces on television that he will call out the Arkansas National Guard to prevent the black students from entering Central High School because of "evidence of disorder and threats of disorder."

On September 3, Judge Davies orders desegregation to begin the following day. Nine black students attempt to enter the school but are thwarted by the National Guard.

On September 9, the Council of Church Women issues a statement opposing segregation and deploring the governor's decision to call out armed troops. President Dwight D. Eisenhower signs the Civil Rights Act, which establishes a six-person Civil Rights Commission. Although weak, it is the first such act passed since Reconstruction.

On September 14, Faubus meets with Eisenhower in Newport, Rhode Island.

On September 20, Judge Davies rules that Faubus used the National Guard solely to prevent integration. The Little Rock Police Department replaces the guard at Central High.

On September 23, as one thousand protesters gather near the front of the school, the nine black students enter through a side door. After a mob learns that they are inside, the students are escorted out the same door for their own safety.

On September 24, Little Rock Mayor Woodrow Mann sends President Eisenhower a telegram asking him to send federal troops to maintain order. The president announces he is sending 1,100 members of the 101st Airborne Division under the command of General Edwin A. Walker. Eisenhower also federalizes the Arkansas National Guard.

On September 25, nine black students are escorted back to Central High with U.S. Army protection.

October 2, twenty-five businessmen in Little Rock sign a "statement of objective and rededication of principles" in support of peaceful compliance of court orders to continue desegregation.

On October 12, more than six thousand black and white citizens of Little Rock participate in a prayer for peace. The day before, six hundred segregationists meet at Central Baptist Church, where ministers pray for Faubus and the removal of federal troops.

On October 24, the students enter the school for the first time through the front door without the troops.

On November 18, the federalized National Guard takes over from the 101st Airborne Division. By November 27, the 101st has left the city.

1958—On February 17, Minnijean Brown is expelled for a year, along with three white students. Two months earlier, she had been suspended for pouring chili on one of her white antagonists. Sammie Dean Parker is also suspended in February for pushing an African American student down a staircase and for attacking, along with her mother, Elizabeth Huckaby, the assistant principal for girls.

On March 4, Amis Guthridge, the leader of the Capital Citizens' Council, interviews Sammie Dean Parker on a paid television program.

On March 5, Faubus announces that he will run for a third term as governor.

On March 11, Sammie Dean Parker is readmitted to Central High after promising to abide by the rules.

On March 20, because of the Little Rock crisis, Pine Bluff, Arkansas, cancels integration plans.

On May 6, the *Arkansas Gazette* is given two Pulitzer prizes for its coverage of the desegregation crisis.

On May 14, Eisenhower denies that the use of federal troops is about segregation, claiming that it was a response to the governor's defiance of a federal court order.

On May 21, the Arkansas Baptist Convention elects Congressman Brooks Hays as president, for a second term.

On May 25, Ernest Green, along with 601 classmates, becomes the first black student to graduate from Central High School. Martin Luther King attends the ceremony as a guest of Green's family. Federal troops and city police are on hand but the event occurs without incident.

On June 21, U.S. District Judge Harry Lemley (replacing Ronald L. Davies) grants a delay, allowing the Little Rock School to postpone full desegregation efforts until January 1961. The Eighth U.S. Circuit Court of Appeals reverses the decision on August 18.

On June 28, Faubus opens his campaign for a third term. He is later elected by a wide margin.

On July 7, a bomb explodes on their front lawn, terrorizing Daisy and L. C. Bates.

On August 23, Faubus calls a special session of the legislature to address desegregation.

On August 25, the Little Rock School Board delays school openings until September 8.

On September 12, the Supreme Court orders in *Cooper v. Aaron* that the desegregation effort at Central High must continue on schedule. The school board orders schools to open on September 15; Faubus orders the high schools closed.

On September 16, fifty-eight white women establish the Women's Emergency Committee to Open Our Schools (WEC) and urge Little Rock residents to accept integration and reopen the schools.

On September 27, Faubus gives Little Rock voters a chance to accept full integration or close the city's four high schools. The final vote, 19,470 to 7,561, ultimately results in the closure of the schools, leaving thousands of students without an alternative during "the Lost Year." Between 1957 and 1959, some schools are also closed in Georgia, Alabama, and Virginia.

On September 29, the Little Rock School Board attempts unsuccessfully to lease the closed schools to the Private School Corporation.

On October 22, twelfth graders have their first day of classes in buildings leased or bought by the Private School Corporation. Students in other grades are registered for classes.

On November 4, Faubus is elected to a third term as governor with 83 percent of the vote. Dale Alford, a segregationist who served on the Little Rock School Board, defeats incumbent Congressman Brooks Hays with a write-in campaign.

On November 12, all members of the school board, except Dale Alford, buy Virgil Blossom's contract and then resign. They claim that they did so to protect Blossom from unfair treatment.

On December 6, 1958, Little Rock elects a new school board, with an equal number of members favoring and opposing desegregation.

On December 16, the legislature and Attorney General Bruce Bennett open hearings to investigate communist subversion among integrationists. The Little Rock School Board appoints Terrell E. Powell, former Hall High principal, as the new superintendent.

On December 28, a Gallup Poll reveals that of the "Ten Men in the World Most Admired by Americans" Eisenhower is number one and Faubus is number ten (making him the first governor to make the list).

1959—On January 6, the Little Rock School Board reports that 2,873 high school students have transferred to other public and private schools.

On January 13, Faubus is inaugurated for a third term.

On January 25, the Little Rock branch of the American Association of University Women reports that business in Little Rock has been severely harmed by the crisis.

On February 25, Faubus signs a bill preventing any public employee from joining the NAACP.

On March 3, the Little Rock Chamber of Commerce votes 819 to 245 to reopen the schools using a federally acceptable integration plan.

On March 11, Faubus proposes a constitutional amendment allowing districts to abolish schools in order to avoid integration.

On April 24, the North Central Association of Secondary Schools and Colleges withdraws accreditation of Central, Hall, and Horace Mann High Schools.

On May 3, Arkansas professors object to Legislative Act 10, which requires teachers and professors to list all organizations to which they belong and reveal any contributions they have given in the last five years. Faubus calls it a "moderate, liberal and tolerant law."

On May 5, members of the school board who oppose integration attempt to fire forty-four administrators and teachers, while the moderate members refuse to participate. Three days later, the Women's Emergency Committee (WEC) and Stop This Outrageous Purge (STOP) attempt to recall the segregationist members. By May 25, they succeed, despite efforts by CROSS (Committee to Retain Our Segregated Schools), and manage to create a board of moderates.

On August 12, Little Rock high schools reopen. Carlotta Walls and Jefferson Thomas are the only two original members of the Little Rock Nine to return to Central High.

1962—James Meredith desegregates the University of Mississippi. That same year, President John F. Kennedy signs Executive Order 11063, banning discrimination in federally funded housing.

1965—President Lyndon B. Johnson signs Executive Order 11246, prohibiting discrimination in employment decisions on the basis of race, color, religion, sex, or national origin.

1971—In *Swann v. Board of Education,* the Supreme Court presents formal guidelines for school desegregation, sixteen years after the passage of *Brown II.*

1972—In the fall, all Little Rock public schools are fully integrated.

1973—The University of Alabama elects its first African American homecoming queen.

1981—*Newsweek* magazine names Central High one of the best public schools in America.

1987—For the first time since 1957, the Little Rock Nine return to Central High School and are greeted by Mayor Lottie Shackelford, the second African American to hold that political office.

1989—In July, Daisy Bates is designated "Arkansas's Matriarch of Integration" and is publicly praised by former Governor Faubus.

1996—The National Trust for Historic Preservation names Central High School one of the nation's eleven "Most Endangered Historic Places."

1997—Little Rock marks the fortieth anniversary of the desegregation of Central High, including a speech by President Bill Clinton honoring the Little Rock Nine. The Central High School Museum, in a converted Mobil service station across the street from the school, opens.

1999—On November 9, 1999, the Little Rock Nine and Daisy Bates, who was buried that day, receive the Congressional Gold Medal, one of the nation's highest civilian honors.

2001—On February 19, 2001, Arkansas becomes the first state to designate a state holiday in honor of an African American woman. Daisy Gatson Bates Holiday becomes a statewide celebration held on the third Monday of February.

2002—In September, the Federal District Court ends more than forty years of court-supervised desegregation monitoring of the Little Rock School District, with the exception of student achievement. The decision is later reversed.

2004—Little Rock Mayor Jim Dailey appoints a fiftieth anniversary committee, co-chaired by Virgil Miller (a local banker) and Nancy Rousseau (principal of Central High), to oversee the 2007 celebration.

2005—On August 30, the U.S. Postal Service issues a commemorative stamp, designed by George Hunt, for the Little Rock Nine.

On August 31, a bronze statue of the Little Rock Nine is unveiled on the state capital grounds.

On December 19, Senator Blanche L. Lincoln, Senator Mark Pryor, and Congressman Vic Snyder sponsor a bill to mint a coin commemorating the fiftieth anniversary of the Little Rock Central High School desegregation crisis, which is submitted to President George W. Bush.

2006—In June, construction begins on a new visitors' center, including facilities for exhibitions and educational programs.

2007—The fiftieth anniversary celebration takes place from September 23 to 27.

Key Players in the Little Rock Crisis

Harry Scott Ashmore (1916–1998) was the executive editor of the city's main newspaper, the *Arkansas Gazette,* and author of a series of Pulitzer prize–winning editorials during the 1957 crisis. An accomplished journalist and author, he worked behind the scenes to help resolve the Little Rock crisis.

Daisy Lee Gatson Bates (1914–1999) was elected president of the Arkansas Chapter of the National Association for the Advancement of Colored People (NAACP) in 1952. She and her husband, L. C. Bates, published an African American newspaper, the *Arkansas State Press.* During the crisis, she guided and advised the Little Rock Nine. Today, a street and an elementary school in Little Rock are named for her. On February 19, 2001, Arkansas became the first state to designate a state holiday in honor of an African American woman.

Bruce Bennett (1917–1979) served two terms as Arkansas attorney general (1957 to 1960 and 1963 to 1966). Bennett supported legislation to undermine federal desegregation orders, claiming that communist influence was responsible for the racial unrest in the state. He supported harassment of the National Association for the Advancement of Colored People and other civil rights organizations. Years later, Bennett was implicated in a fraud scandal involving the Arkansas Loan and Thrift.

Virgil T. Blossom (1907–1965), a native of Missouri, was the superintendent of the Little Rock School District during the crisis. Prior to the passage of *Brown v. Board of Education,* he worked with the school board to develop an integration plan for the district. He was removed from his position in November 1958 and continued his career in New York and Texas. He is the author of *It Has Happened Here.*

Wiley A. Branton (1923–1988) served as an attorney for the NAACP during the numerous court battles surrounding the Central High desegregation effort. A native of Pine Bluff, Arkansas, Branton was the third African American graduate of the University of Arkansas Law School. From 1965 to 1967, Branton served as a special assistant to the U.S. attorney general.

Herbert Brownell (1904–1996) served as U.S. attorney general under President Dwight D. Eisenhower from 1953 to 1957. During the Little Rock crisis, he was the president's main legal adviser and was mainly responsible for drafting a proposal that eventually became the Civil Rights Act of 1957.

Ronald Norwood Davies (1904–1996), son of a small-town newspaper editor, was a World War II veteran, educated at Georgetown University. He practiced law in North Dakota and later became a federal judge. President Eisenhower assigned him to the Eastern District of Arkansas on August 26, 1957. In that capacity, he handed down the *Aaron v Cooper* decision, which required the racial integration of Central High School in Little Rock to proceed on schedule.

Dwight D. Eisenhower (1890–1969) was in the first year of his second term as a Republican president of the United States when the Little Rock crisis began. Eisenhower's inability to articulate a clear civil rights policy and his indecision during the events of September 1957 contributed to the crisis.

Orval Eugene Faubus (1910–1994) served six terms as Arkansas governor (1955 to 1967) and led the fight against the desegregation of Central High School in 1957. Originally a social moderate, Faubus was influenced by segregationist politicians throughout the South to take a firm stand against *Brown v. Board of Education*.

Lawrence Brooks Hays (1898–1981) was a Democratic congressman who advocated a philosophy of southern moderation. In the midst of the Central High crisis, Hays arranged a meeting between Eisenhower and Faubus in Newport, Rhode Island, hoping to assist the two men in reaching a compromise. Hays's moderate position cost him his political career in 1958, though he remained active in public life, serving in both the John F. Kennedy and Lyndon Johnson administrations.

Elizabeth Paisley Huckaby (1906–1999) served as vice principal of Little Rock High School from 1954 to 1969 and was charged with helping the nine black students navigate the desegregation crisis. A graduate of the University of Arkansas at Fayetteville, Huckaby taught English in Fort Smith and Little Rock

The Little Rock Nine were the African American teenagers selected to be the first black students to attend Little Rock's Central High School.*

> **Minnijean Brown** (Trickey) was a junior when she entered Central High School. She was expelled from the school in February 1958 for pouring chili on one of her peers. She moved to New York to complete her education at New Lincoln High School in 1959. She later graduated from Southern Illinois University with a degree in journalism. During the 1960s, she and her husband moved to Canada, where she completed additional degrees at Laurentian University and Carleton University. She eventually became a writer, peace activist, and social worker in Ontario. From 1999 to 2001, she served in the Clinton administration as the deputy assistant secretary for Workforce Diversity at the Department of the Interior.
>
> **Elizabeth Ann Eckford**, one of six children of Oscar and Birdie Eckford, was fifteen when she first came to Central High School. After the 1957 crisis, she joined the U.S. Army, completed her general equivalency diploma (GED), and worked for years as a public information specialist in Alabama and Indiana. She graduated from Central State College in Wilberforce, Ohio, with a degree in history. In 1974, she moved back to Little Rock and became a social worker.
>
> **Ernest G. Green** was a student at Dunbar Junior High School and Horace Mann High School before enrolling as a senior at the age of sixteen at Central High School. He was the first black student to graduate from Central in 1958. After completing his bachelor's and master's degrees at Michigan State

University, Green became an assistant secretary of Housing and Urban Affairs under President Jimmy Carter. He later moved to Washington, D.C., where he worked as a managing partner and vice president at Lehman Brothers.

Thelma Jean Mothershed (Wair) attended Dunbar Junior High School and Horace Mann High School. In 1957, she came to Central High for her junior year. She eventually received her diploma from Central by completing correspondence courses and attending summer school in St. Louis. In 1964, she completed her master's degree at Southern Illinois University, Edwardsville. Wair worked as a junior high school economics teacher for twenty-eight years. She is an active volunteer for numerous organizations, including the American Red Cross and the St. Clair County Jail.

Melba Pattillo (Beals) was the daughter of Lois Patillo, one of the first African American students to attend the University of Arkansas. Patillo was fifteen and a high school junior when she came to Central High. She eventually moved to Santa Rosa, California, to complete her education in 1958. She graduated with a bachelor's degree in journalism and sociology from San Francisco State University and a master's degree in broadcasting from Columbia University. She worked as a journalist for NBC, a freelance writer, and a talk show host in San Francisco. Her memoir, *Warriors Don't Cry: A Searing Memoir of the Battle to Desegregate Little Rock's Central High School,* won the 1995 Robert F. Kennedy Memorial Book Award. In 1999, she published *White Is a State of Mind.*

Gloria Ray (Karlmark) was fifteen when she enrolled at Central High. After the schools closed, she moved to Missouri and attended Kansas City Central High School, which had just been integrated. She completed her degree in chemistry and mathematics at Illinois Institute of Technology and a second degree in Stockholm, Sweden. She became a computer science writer and published magazines, including *Computers in Industry,* in more than thirty-five countries. She is currently retired and travels between Amsterdam and Stockholm, where her husband's family lives.

Terrence Roberts attended Dunbar Junior High School and Horace Mann High School before enrolling at Central High in 1957. He only remained there for a year before his family moved to California, where he graduated from Los Angeles High School. In 1967 he received a degree in sociology from California State University and, later, a master's degree in social welfare from the University of California at Los Angeles. In 1976 Roberts received a PhD in psychology from Southern Illinois University. He served as a faculty member and department chair at Antioch University in Los Angeles.

Jefferson A. Thomas was the youngest of seven children. He attended Dunbar Junior High School, where he was both a track star and student leader. He was fifteen when he entered Central High as a sophomore. Along with Carlotta Walls, he graduated in 1960. He attended Wayne State University, served in the U.S. Army during Vietnam, and worked for Mobil Oil and the federal Defense Logistics Center in Los Angeles and as an accountant for the Department of Defense. In 1966, he narrated the film *The Nine from Little Rock,* produced by the United States Information Agency.

Carlotta Walls (LaNier) was the eldest of three daughters of Caretlyou and Juanita Walls and the youngest of the Little Rock Nine, only fourteen when she entered Central High. She attended Stephens Elementary School and Dunbar High School, then returned to Central High in 1959, where she graduated in 1960. Walls completed her bachelor of science degree at Colorado State College (now University of Northern Colorado) after attending Michigan State University. She made her career in real estate in Denver and helped establish the Little Rock Nine Foundation to promote educational opportunities for African American students.

Woodrow Wilson Mann (1916–2002), born in Little Rock, was an insurance broker who became the Democratic mayor of the city in 1955. A progressive on race, Mann oversaw the integration of Little Rock's bus service and police force. He was the politician who telegraphed President Eisenhower on September 4, 1957, urging him to send federal troops to restore order during the crisis.

Thurgood Marshall (1908–1993) served as the NAACP chief counsel and was responsible for the 1954 victory in *Brown v. Board of Education*. During the 1957 Little Rock Crisis, Marshall visited the city to help with litigation. In 1967, he became the first African American member of the U.S. Supreme Court.

Edwin A. Walker (1909–1993), a native of Texas, was the U.S. Army major general who commanded the 101st Airborne Division sent to Little Rock. Though a rabid segregationist himself, Walker carried out his duties. In the late 1950s, while commanding the 24th Infantry Division in Augsburg, Germany, he was accused of forcing his troops to embrace the philosophy of the John Birch Society and was relieved of his command.

---

*Biographical data on the Little Rock Nine was gathered from a press release, "President Clinton to Join Members of Congress in Presenting Congressional Gold Medals to the Members of the Little Rock Nine," November 9, 1999 (Courtesy of the Clinton Library); "The Little Rock Nine," Central High School Collection, B-12, series II, box 1, file 7, item 23, University of Arkansas at Little Rock Special Collections; 40th Anniversary of Central High, www.centralhigh57.org/The_Little_Rock_Nine.html; and the National Park Service brochure, "Little Rock Central High School."

Questions and Assignments

Questions for Consideration

1. Is it possible to view President Eisenhower's and Governor Faubus's responses to the Little Rock crisis in the context of their own political survival? Were their other forces that motivated their decisions?

2. How were desegregation efforts in the American South shaped by American foreign policy in the midst of the Cold War?

3. How did southern white moderates respond to the crisis? What did they risk in supporting integration?

4. How did the Little Rock crisis influence the implementation of *Brown v. Board of Education* throughout the 1950s and beyond?

5. Why and in what ways did segregationists equate civil rights with communism?

6. Do the documents in "Before the Crisis" offer clues as to why the desegregation effort was so controversial in Little Rock?

7. Why was Eisenhower initially so reluctant to take firm stand in the Little Rock crisis?

8. How have civil rights museums and historic sites, such as Central High School, become part of cultural tourism and economic development in the South?

9. Why did Governor Faubus receive so much support in Arkansas and throughout the nation during and after the crisis?

10. What did the Little Rock crisis reveal about the conflict between states' rights and federal power? What other events in American history have hinged upon this conflict?

11. How are the desegregation efforts of the 1950s, 1960s, and 1970s viewed today?

12. What do the commemorative events over the past half-century reveal about how Little Rock has been remembered?

Classroom and Research Activities

The assignments included this section are intended to span a week-long unit focused on the Little Rock crisis. The activities are based on fifty- or seventy-five-minute class sessions, but could be easily modified.

ACTIVITY 1: In Their Own Words

The goal of this activity is to examine individual responses to desegregation by individuals who were not specifically connected to the Little Rock crisis and compare those responses to reactions from individuals directly involved in the crisis.

STEP 1: In the first class session, students will review the following five quotations and answer the following four questions.

Some of the students I'd known since I was ten years old, who were white, were afraid to speak to me in school. It's true there were only about 50 students who were actively harassing us. But some of those other students, it was my feeling, were cooperating in that violence through their silence.

—ELIZABETH ECKFORD, one of the Little Rock Nine

You can't teach mutual respect and liking between black and white at the end of a bayonet.

—WILLIAM LOEB, Manchester Union
Leader (NH), September 25, 1957

Orval Faubus was the hero to the mob; the nine courageous black children he failed to keep out of Central High were heroes to the world.

—HARRY ASHMORE, editor of the *Arkansas Gazette*

We come then to the question presented: Does segregation of children in public schools solely on the basis of race, even though the physical facilities and other "tangible" factors may be equal, deprive the children of the minority group of equal educational opportunities? We believe that it does. . . . We conclude that in the field of public education the doctrine of "separate but equal" has no place. Separate educational facilities are inherently unequal. Therefore, we hold that the plaintiffs and others similarly situated for whom the actions have been brought are, by reason of the segregation complained of, deprived of the equal protection of the laws guaranteed by the Fourteenth Amendment.

—*Brown v. Board of Education*, 344 U.S. 141

I have always felt, and still firmly believe, that if the school authorities in Little Rock had handled the affair quietly, the intense conflict over integration at Central High would never have developed. If the school authorities had said, "This is our own local problem. We'll handle it the best we can based on our local conditions. This does not concern any other school. Just us." If they had said that and the media had followed that lead, there would have been no Central High School Crisis as we now know it.

—ORVAL FAUBUS, 1991

Questions for Consideration:

1. How does the speaker or author frame the discussion over race?
2. What concerns and issues are raised by the quotation?
3. How does the speaker or author feel about state versus federal power?
4. How might the quotation be perceived outside of its local context?

STEP 2: In the second class session, review the following documents in this volume and ask the same four questions from above.

#19: Governor's Proclamation

#31: Telegram from Parents of Little Rock Nine to Dwight D. Eisenhower

#39: Letter from Henry V. Rath to Wayne Upton

#45: L. C. Bates Annual Report

Step 3: Compare the quotes and documents and consider how direct involvement in a historical event shaped reactions and responses. Consider the following question: How do individuals in either group claim authority to comment on the crisis?

Activity 2: Visual Culture Exercise

The goal of this activity is to encourage students to analyze political cartoons with the kind of nuance that they would bring to printed sources.

Step 1: Review the following cartoons by Bill Mauldin that were published during and after the crisis.

Cartoon #1:
"For Whom
the Bell Tolled,"
May 27, 1959

Cartoon #2:
"Man Frightened by Red Scare," September 5, 1946

Cartoon #3: "I Started a Correspondence Course Until Pa Learned That Was Integrated, Too," November 23, 1958.

Step 2: Answer the following questions for each cartoon.

1. What were the local, national, and international responses to the desegregation order when the cartoon was published?

2. Who is the main audience for the cartoon? Who might be a secondary audience?

3. What issues does the cartoon raise?

4. Who might be most influenced by the cartoon?

5. What techniques does the cartoonist use to create a narrative similar to the primary documents included in this volume?

6. What kinds of character types or stereotypes does Mauldin use to make his point?

Step 3: What similarities do you see between these cartoons and documents #6, #12, #20, #36, #44 in this volume?

Activity 3: Four Corners

The purpose of this assignment is to help students understand the motivation of those persons hostile to the implementation of desegregation.

Step 1: Divide the class into four groups and give each group one of the quotations* or the image listed below. Given thirty minutes, the group should review their quotation or image, focusing first on the speaker's point of view. Before the end of class, the group should determine which members will complete the following tasks before the next class session: (1) research the issues related to desegregation that the speaker addresses or (2) analyze the desegregation efforts in the early 1970s (in the state in which the speaker resides) that may have influenced the response.

Quotation #1: "My kids ain't riding no buses all over the county just to make the damned Supreme Court happy."

—Georgia parent's response to *Alexander v. Holmes*, 1970

Quotation #2: "Clearly one sided . . . the court is talking about the South; the North is still going to be free."

—JIMMY CARTER, Governor of Georgia, upon learning about the Supreme Court's decision in *Swann v. Mecklenburg*, 1971

---

*These quotations are drawn from George R. Metcalf's *From Little Rock to Boston: The History of School Desegregation* (Westport, CT: Greenwood Press, 1983), 51, 97, 109, and 130.

Quotation #3: "Busing, certainly, is an artificial and inadequate instrument of change. Nobody really wants it—not you, not me, not the people, nor the school boards—not even the courts. Yet the law demands, and rightly so, that we put an end to segregation in our society. We must demonstrate good faith in doing just that."

—REUBIN ASKEW, Governor of Florida, 1971

Quotation #4: "Suppose I send my daughter to school and she gets thrown through the window and breaks her neck, or she gets molested or stabbed."

—Pontiac, Michigan, mother opposing school integration, 1971

KEEP OUR WHITE SCHOOLS

WHITE!

TONIGHT AND EVERY NIGHT 'TILL SCHOOL OPENS
(Except Sunday)

IMPORTANT MEETING

TO KEEP THE NIGGERS OUT OF WHITE SCHOOLS

AT THE COURT HOUSE

ON THE SQUARE - 7:00 P.M.

FIND OUT WHAT BEN WEST, FRANK CLEMENT AND
BENNY'S NASHVILLE SCHOOL BOARD ARE DOING TO
RUIN NASHVILLE FOREVER.

SAVE YOUR KIDS! PREVENT RACE RIOTS,

MURDER, DYNAMITINGS, AND HANGINGS!

BRING YOUR FRIENDS EVERY EVENING

AT 7:00 P.M. TO COURTHOURSE ON THE SQUARE.

HONOR - PRIDE - FIGHT - SAVE THE WHITES

Flyer, Keep Our White Schools White, Nashville, Tennessee

Step 2: For the first half of the next class session, the groups should reassemble, review their findings, and prepare a defense of their position, taking on the persona of the person whose quote they selected.

Step 3: In the second half of class, the group should present their position as if they were participating in a press conference.

ANNOTATED BIBLIOGRAPHY

Books

Ashmore, Harry S. *Civil Rights and Wrongs: A Memoir of Race and Politics, 1944–1996.* Columbia: University of South Carolina Press, 1997.

> As executive editor the *Arkansas Gazette* and author of a series of Pulitzer prize–winning editorials during 1957, Ashmore was both an active participant in and concerned observer of the crisis. His memoir begins during World War II and shows how the desegregation effort shaped the second half of the twentieth century.

Bartley, Numan V. *Rise of Massive Resistance: Race and Politics in the South during the 1950's.* Baton Rouge: Louisiana State University Press, 1969.

> Bartley's book is one of the earliest works to address the resistance of southern politicians, churches, businesses, and unions to the integration of public schools. It also provides the most concise overview of the crisis. His argument rests on the assertion that New Deal policies and federal court decisions from the Great Depression forward undermined white supremacy and spurred such backlash movements as the Dixiecrats. He also focuses on how segregation affected whites in the South. Bartley's decision to organize the volume state by state makes it a useful reference tool, and his section on Arkansas is one of the strongest. The inclusion of a thoughtful analysis of the Eisenhower administration's response to the South makes this essential reading.

Bates, Daisy. *The Long Shadow of Little Rock: A Memoir.* Fayetteville: University of Arkansas Press, 1986.

> First published in New York in 1962, Bates's must-read memoir of her involvement as the president of the Arkansas Chapter of the NAACP during the Little Rock crisis was reissued in 1986 and became the first reprinted book to win the American Book Award in 1988. It is also an important contribution to the recent scholarship that analyzes the role of black women as leaders during the civil rights movement. Bates vividly recounts the events of Little Rock, from the initial resistance to integration, to the efforts of nine students to enroll in the school, and to Eisenhower's mobilization of the 101st Airborne to protect the students. She captures the climate in the city as people quickly took sides, and most supported segregation. A less familiar story concerns those whites who supported African Americans during the crisis. Her descriptions of the hatred and anger directed at moderate whites in the community—resulting in the murder-suicide involving Chief of Police Eugene Smith and his wife; the firing of Superintendent of Schools Virgil Blossom and Presbyterian minister Dunbar Ogden; the eventual resignation of the Pulitzer prize–winning editor of the *Arkansas Gazette,*

Harry Ashmore; and the financial ruin of advertising and public relations executive Bill Haldley Jr.—are especially chilling.

Beals, Melba Patillo. *Warriors Don't Cry: A Searing Memoir of the Battle to Integrate Little Rock's Central High.* New York: Pocket Books, 1994.

An emotional and poignant memoir of the Little Rock crisis from one of the Little Rock Nine, this book draws upon newspaper articles, notes taken by the author's mother, and Beals's diary. Writing years after the event, Beals explains, "Enough time has elapsed to allow healing to take place, enabling me to tell my story without bitterness." Her perspective offers scholars an opportunity to examine the role of first-person accounts and the problems of historical memory. It also documents a life that is defined by a single historical event.

Blossom, Virgil T. *It Has Happened Here.* New York: Harper, 1959.

Written from the perspective of the superintendent of the Little Rock School District during the desegregation crisis, Blossom has created a useful firsthand account of the crisis from one of the main players. This book is an extended version of a series of articles he published, entitled "The Untold Story of Little Rock," in the *Saturday Evening Post* from May 23 through June 27, 1959.

Brownell, Herbert, and John P. Burke. *Advising Ike: The Memoirs of Attorney General Herbert Brownell.* Lawrence: University of Kansas Press, 1993.

This memoir, written by Eisenhower's first attorney general, is an account of some of the major issues and decisions of the Eisenhower administration during the 1950s by one of the president's closest confidants. Brownell came to the office with extensive experience, as both a lawyer and a politician, having been in private practice for many years and having served as chair of the Republican Party and campaign manager for Thomas Dewey in his unsuccessful presidential attempts. He also served as a back-stage convention manager at Eisenhower's first presidential nomination. Beyond its obvious use to anyone interested in understanding the often-contradictory nature of Eisenhower's policies, it provides a valuable insider's view of the Little Rock crisis. Brownell's reputation for honesty and candor was widely acknowledged; however, on this topic, it should be read with other available sources for a balanced view.

Burk, Robert Fredrick. *The Eisenhower Administration and Black Civil Rights.* Knoxville: University of Tennessee Press, 1984.

Drawing upon a wealth of primary and secondary sources, memoirs, and selected interviews, Burk examines the role of the Eisenhower administration in civil rights policy to conclude that "symbolic legalism" was often substituted for real progress. The topics under consideration include Truman's legacy, Eisenhower's desegregation of Washington, D.C., various administration committees and initiatives on employment and housing, the Little Rock crisis, Eisenhower's relationship with civil rights leaders such as Adam Clayton Powell, and the federal

Civil Rights Commission. Burk's approach is hampered by a lack of discussion of race relations in the first half of the twentieth century. For a more positive view of Eisenhower's position on race, see James C. Duram's *A Moderate among Extremists: Dwight D. Eisenhower and the School Desegregation Crisis* (Chicago: Nelson-Hall, 1981). For perspective on how Eisenhower himself perceived his role in the crisis, see his book *Waging Peace, 1956–1961: The White House Years* (Garden City, NY: Doubleday, 1965).

Counts, Will. *A Life Is More Than a Moment: The Desegregation of Little Rock's Central High.* Text and photographs by Will Counts; with essays by Will Campbell, Ernest Dumas, and Robert S. McCord. Bloomington: Indiana University Press, 1999.

In 1957, Counts had been employed for only a few months as a photojournalist for the *Arkansas Democrat* before the Little Rock crisis erupted. Dressing himself "like someone from the rural South," he used his 35-mm camera to capture the history unfolding before him. This volume juxtaposes photographs from that period with images of Little Rock and Central High School in the 1990s. One particularly striking image includes Elizabeth Eckford (one of the Little Rock Nine) and Hazel Bryan (a white student whose response to desegregation made her "the poster child for the hate generation") standing arm-in-arm together years later in front of the school. This image, and the text suggesting that the two have become friends, allows scholars to examine issues of evidence, memory, and reconciliation. Counts's accompanying text reinterprets the images for an audience who may be unfamiliar with the story.

Daniel, Pete. *Lost Revolutions: The South in the 1950s.* Chapel Hill: University of North Carolina Press, 2000.

Daniel begins his book, in order to understand the 1950s, by examining how and why Americans after World War II moved away from farms and small communities. That historical background gives way to a nuanced discussion of the interrelationship between working-class culture and the rise of the civil rights movement. Daniel makes much of his argument through the life stories of individuals, including Daisy Bates. This book is helpful in putting the issue of race during the 1950s in a broader historical context.

Halberstam, David. *The Fifties.* New York: Villard Books, 1993.

Halberstam's highly readable eight-hundred-page volume is a thorough review of this significant and often turbulent decade. His lucid prose covers everything from Harry Truman's surprise defeat of Thomas Dewey through the Kennedy-Nixon debate, made especially vivid by the more than one hundred interviews he conducted with individuals significant to the era. Covering topics including the rise of McDonalds, Holiday Inns, Levittown, the Kinsey Report, through the U2 spy plane incident, the Suez Crisis, and the Little Rock Central High School conflict, with McCarthyism and the expansion of the Cold War in between, it is essential reading for anyone hoping to understand the era.

Hays, Brooks. *A Southern Moderate Speaks*. Chapel Hill: University of North Carolina Press, 1959.

A graduate of the University of Arkansas, Hays served as assistant attorney general for Arkansas in 1925 and moved to Little Rock. He ran unsuccessfully for governor in 1928 and from 1932 to 1939 served on the Democratic National Committee. After working for the National Recovery Administration and the Farm Security Administration, two New Deal agencies, Hays mounted a successful campaign for Congress in 1942, representing the Arkansas Fifth District for eight successive terms. He was ultimately defeated by a write-in campaign after the Little Rock crisis because of his moderate stand on desegregation. This memoir documents his political career and offers a perspective on a rapidly changing South in the first part of the twentieth century.

Huckaby, Elizabeth. *Crisis at Central High, 1957–58*. Baton Rouge: Louisiana State University Press, 1980.

Huckaby, who was at the time the school's assistant principal for girls, recounts her memories of the Central High School crisis. Formerly an English teacher at Central, her job was mainly to attend to the welfare and conduct of the school's female students. For this volume, she draws from her collection of personal notes, school memoranda, district documents, and newspaper and magazine articles as she recounts the nine black students' attempts to participate in school life at Central. It is an especially effective retelling of the students' experiences as they went through the routine of homeroom, classes, lunch, and life between classes. They were often the object of cruelty and abuse, even physical assault from racist students, and indifference or hostility from faculty. They also experienced kindness and concern from sympathetic students (who were frequently so abused by other hostile students that they withdrew) and a few of the staff. Huckaby was one of the forty-four staff and administrators, including Principal Jess Matthews and Assistant Principal for Boys J. O. Powell, unsuccessfully targeted for dismissal by the segregationist Little Rock School Board in 1958. In February 1981, CBS aired a television program based on the memoir, entitled *Crisis at Central High*, featuring Joanne Woodward as Huckaby.

Jacoway, Elizabeth, and C. Fred Williams, eds. *Understanding the Little Rock Crisis: An Exercise in Remembrance and Reconciliation*. Fayetteville: University of Arkansas Press, 1999.

This volume is a collection of essays from a 1997 conference held on the fortieth anniversary of the desegregation crisis. Jacoway's introduction offers a concise account of the events and the major players, as well as a brief abstract of each of the twelve essays. Scholars Sheldon Hackney, David Goldfield, George C. Wright and Joel Williamson, John A. Kirk, Anthony J. Badger, Roy Reed, James C. Cobb, Kermit L. Hall, and Tony A. Freyer put the event in broad historical context, examining how the passage of time shapes the memory and codification of the event. One shortcoming of the volume is its primary focus on constitutional issues and white leaders, overshadowing the full cast of characters. A savvy reader will begin with the bibliographical essay by Michal J. Dabrishus for a clear overview of the topic.

Murphy, Sara. *Breaking the Silence: Little Rock's Women's Emergency Committee to Open Our Schools, 1958–1963.* Fayetteville: University of Arkansas Press, 1997.

Born in the South and educated at Columbia University, Sara Murphy moved to Little Rock to join the faculty of the University of Arkansas in 1958. After the desegregation crisis, she joined the board of the Women's Emergency Committee to Open Our Schools (WEC), an organization of moderate white women who worked to reopen the public schools after Orval Faubus had them closed in 1958. Late in life, Murphy began writing *Breaking the Silence* about the WEC's activities, and her son completed the manuscript upon her death in 1995. The firsthand account is based on interviews, correspondence, booklets and pamphlets, newspaper clippings, and broadsides that are part of the University of Arkansas at Fayetteville's Special Collections. A shorter piece to consider on the WEC is Laura A. Miller's "Challenging the Segregationist Power Structure in Little Rock: The Women's Emergency Committee to Open Our Schools," in *Throwing off the Cloak of Privilege: White Southern Women Activists in the Civil Rights Era,* edited by Gail S. Murray (Gainesville: University Press of Florida, 2004).

Record, Wilson, and Jane Cassals Record, eds. *Little Rock, U.S.A.: Materials for Analysis.* San Francisco: Chandler Publishing Company, 1960.

The Records' collection, published three years after the crisis, contains a wealth of primary documents, drawn largely from *Southern School News,* a publication out of Nashville, Tennessee, that is one of the most significant historical sources on school desegregation across the South. Though frustrating for its lack of organization, the collection offers dozens of perspectives and provides scholars with valuable access to documents.

Reed, Roy. *Faubus: The Life and Times of an American Prodigal.* Fayetteville: University of Arkansas Press, 1997.

A former foreign correspondent for the *New York Times,* Reed, in this biography, struggles to understand Faubus's motives by placing them in a wider historical context. On his approach, Reed explains, "A biographer ought to be able to say with some conviction that he has found out what makes his subject run." The fact that Reed is never able to say for certain what motivated Faubus, a man defined by contradiction, is the strength of the book. In trying to understand Faubus, Reed does not ignore the havoc he caused in Arkansas. This balance makes it one of the best biographies of a southern political figure in print.

Roy, Beth. *Bitters in the Honey.* Fayetteville: University of Arkansas Press, 1999.

A sociologist and psychotherapist, Roy uses oral histories of the participants in the 1957 Little Rock crisis to understand the persistence of racism and white supremacy in the American South. She explains her approach: "'The challenge I took on in the beginning of this study was to listen to the life histories of white people from Little Rock who, passively or actively, resisted desegregation in Arkansas." She does interview black participants and include their stories, but her main focus in on white supremacy and its role in the Central High crisis and beyond.

Wilkinson, J. Harvie. *From Brown to Bakke: The Supreme Court and School Integration, 1954–1978.* New York: Oxford University Press, 1979.

A former judge on the U.S. Court of Appeals for the Fourth Circuit and faculty member of the University of Virginia Law School, Wilkinson wrote this book in the wake of the 1987 *Bakke* decision, for which he wrote the court's opinion. His main argument is that "race-conscience remedies" must be consistent with the Constitution's guarantee of equal protection. This conservative judge's attempts to make sense of race and public accommodations in the past half-century are both revealing and useful. For another perspective, see George Matcalf's *From Little Rock to Boston: The History of School Desegregation* (Westport, CT: Greenwood Press, 1983).

Woods, Jeff. *Black Struggle, Red Scare: Segregation and Anticommunism in the South, 1948–1968.* Baton Rouge: Louisiana State University Press, 2004.

Along with Numan Bartley's *The Rise of Massive Resistance* (1969) and Neil McMillen's *The Citizens' Council: Organized Resistance to the Second Reconstruction* (Urbana: University of Illinois Press, 1971), Woods's book offers a useful analysis of southern resistance to desegregation and the role of red-baiting. Much of McMillen's book focuses on Senator James Eastland, who, as chair of the Senate Internal Security Subcommittee, was a major anticommunist in the post–World War II South.

Young, William H., and, Nancy K. Young. *The 1950's.* Westport, CT: Greenwood Press, 2004.

An excellent companion volume to David Halberstam's *The Fifties,* this volume opens with a highly useful timeline. At 349 pages, it naturally does not cover the era as completely or as seriously as Halberstam, but it organizes the decade thematically, providing a useful lens through which to view the era. Part 1, "Life and Youth during the 1950's," offers a solid overview of the economy, technological changes, civil rights, and women's changing roles, as well as the Eisenhower administration. It is especially effective in describing what it was like to be young during the decade, including teen fashions, leisure, music, and courtship. Part I2, "Popular Culture in the 1950's," is separated by topics such as advertising, architecture, food and drink, entertainment, and the arts. It has only a brief section on civil rights, but overall it offers an informative view of the decade.

Web-Based Resources

Arkansas History Commission at http://www.ark-ives.com.

> Operated by the Arkansas History Commission, the official state archives (founded in 1905), and the Arkansas Department of Parks and Tourism, the Web site's mission is to collect, preserve, and disseminate materials related to Arkansas history. For researchers, the site includes selected bibliographies on topics such as African American newspapers; databases that link to newspapers, county records, and photographs; and research tip sheets on topics such as "Little Rock Central High School Crisis Time Line and Source Material." Researchers interested in primary documents (including photographs) can order those materials directly from this site.

Dwight D. Eisenhower Presidential Library at http://www.eisenhower.archives.gov.

> This Web site is operated by the National Archives and Records Administration and includes vast resources related to Eisenhower's two terms as president. The Eisenhower Library groundbreaking was held on October 13, 1959, and the archives have been collecting materials ever since. There are numerous primary documents, bibliographies, and finding aids available online at http://www.eisenhower.archives.gov/research/finding_aids.html.

Little Rock Central High School National Historic Site at http://www.nps.gov/chsc/.

> The National Park Service currently manages the historic site, in a renovated Mobil station next door to Little Rock's Central High School. The park's purpose is "to preserve, protect, and interpret for the benefit, education, and inspiration of present and future generations, Central High School in Little Rock, Arkansas, and to interpret its role in the integration of public schools and the development of the Civil Rights movement in the United States." The site offers information about planning a visit as well as teacher and student resources.

Little Rock Central High 40th Anniversary at http://www.centralhigh57.org/.

> This Web site was organized around the fortieth anniversary commemoration of the desegregation crisis. It includes background on the events of the 1950s, details about the participants, and news from the 1990s. The most useful component features articles from *The Tiger,* Central High's yearbook. It has not been updated since 1997.

Little Rock 1957: Pages from History at http://www.ardemgaz.com/prev/central/.

> This useful Web site includes half a century of newspaper accounts during and after the crisis from the *Arkansas Democrat* and *Arkansas Gazette*. It is a rich and diverse collection of primary sources. The first group of documents is organized chronologically, the second part by topic or theme. Arkansas Online, an electronic version of the *Arkansas-Democrat Gazette,* maintains the site.

Organization of American Historians: Desegregation on the Web: A List of Internet Resources at http://www.oah.org/pubs/magazine/deseg/webresources.html.

The Organization of American Historians has selected reliable Web-based resources related to desegregation and compiled a useful list with links, including several related to Little Rock. It also offers brief annotations to guide researchers. Founded in 1907, OAH describes itself as "the largest learned society devoted to the study of American history."

INDEX

Note: Page numbers followed by *c* indicate a political cartoon, *d* indicates a document, and *p* indicates a photograph.

Ware, Harold, 81

War Manpower Commission Act, 105d

Warren, Earl, *xv, xviii*

Warriors Don't Cry: A Searing Memoir of the Battle to Desegregate Little Rock's Central High School (Patillo), *xxiv,* 122d, 204

Washington, D.C., desegregation in, 157–59d

Washington Post, 43

WEC. *See* Women's Emergency Committee to Open Our Schools (WEC)

West African Pilot, xxvi

West, Ben, 50–51d

Whatley, Joe, 163d

white flight, 156, 158d, 160d, 169d

White Is a State of Mind (Patillo), 204

whites: economic, social, political control by, 6; justification of vigilante violence by, 1–3d; press response to *Brown II, xviii*

white students: Clinton's commendation of, 121d; education of during Lost Year, 98, 101–4d, 119d; exclusion of

from fortieth anniversary commemoration, 118–19d; Huckabee's commendation of, 129d; report on transfers of, 197; view of desegregation, 51–52d, 71d, 79d, 102d

white supremacy, *xv*

Whittaker, Charles E., 89–98d

Williams, C. Fred, *xxix*

Williams, Hugh, 64d

Wilson, William, Jr., 173, 175d

Wilson, Winston B., 43

Wolfe, Ron, 134d

Women's Emergency Committee to Open Our Schools (WEC): attempt to recall segregationist members of school board, 197; formation of, *xxv,* 101; plea to open schools, 196; purpose and policy of, 101; report on effects of crisis, *xxvii,* 101–4d, 113

Yelemisov, Galim, 160d

Youth Advisory Council, 185d

Zeuch, William E., 37d

ABOUT THE AUTHORS

Catherine M. Lewis is an associate professor of history at Kennesaw State University and a curator the special projects coordinator for the Atlanta History Center. She completed a BA in English and History with honors at Emory University and an MA and PhD in American Studies at the University of Iowa. She has curated more than twenty exhibitions throughout the nation and has published six books, including *The Changing Face of Public History: The Chicago Historical Society and the Transformation of an American History Museum* (Northern Illinois University Press, 2005) and *Don't Ask What I Shot: How Eisenhower's Love of Golf Helped Shape 1950s America* (McGraw-Hill, 2007).

J. Richard Lewis is president of JRL Educational Services, Inc. He completed his BA in English at Mercer University, his MA in English at Florida State University, and his PhD in curriculum and instruction at the University of Maryland. He spent his career as an educator and administrator in Florida, Maryland, and Virginia. He has served as a visiting faculty member at Western Maryland College and Johns Hopkins University. He retired as the director of Success for All and as a researcher at Johns Hopkins University in 2001. He has served as a desegregation consultant for the Miami Desegregation Assistance Center, the Urban Education Center and Milwaukee Public Schools, the Cincinnati Desegregation Assistance Center at the University of Cincinnati, Memphis State University, and others.